MW01294347

Mystery

(GENRE WRITER SERIES)

MYSTERY

HOW TO WRITE TRADITIONAL & COZY WHODUNITS

PAUL TOMLINSON

Copyright © 2017 by Paul Tomlinson

All rights reserved. This book may not be reproduced or transmitted, in whole or in part, or used in any manner whatsoever, without the express permission of the copyright owner, except for the use of brief quotations in the context of a book review.

The content of this book is provided for educational purposes. Every effort has been made to ensure the accuracy of the information presented. However, the information is sold without warranty, either express or implied, and the author shall not be liable for any loss or damage caused – directly or indirectly – by its use.

For country of manufacture, please see final page.

ISBN: 978-1-977898-37-1

First published October 2017
Publisher: Paul Tomlinson

www.paultomlinson.org/how-to

Cover image and design © 2017 by Paul Tomlinson

Contents

Introduction

I should make it clear from the beginning which types of story are covered in this book – and which aren't. A 'whodunit' or traditional murder mystery is the kind of story Agatha Christie wrote – her Hercule Poirot and Miss Marple stories. There were many successful writers in the genre, especially during the 'golden years' between the two world wars, but Christie is the writer whose books are still bestsellers today. She will be our model. These stories were sometimes referred to as 'English country house' or 'cozy' mysteries. In more recent years, 'cozy' has been used to describe contemporary mystery novels that feature some of the same characteristics as the traditional murder mystery – notably the amateur sleuth and an absence of blood, violence, sex, and profanity. To avoid confusion, I'm going to refer to those as 'modern cozy mysteries.' This book is about how to create both the traditional and modern type of cozy murder mystery.

You will not find information here about creating the 'hardboiled' private eye novel made famous by Raymond Chandler and Dashiell Hammett. Nor will you find coverage of police procedurals like Ed McBain's 87th Precinct series, or forensic investigation thrillers such as those by Kathy Reichs and Patricia Cornwell. Those are all so different from the traditional or cozy mystery as to need a book of their own.

The plot structures I discuss in detail are designed for full-length novels or screenplays. They might also work for a novella with a bit of adaptation, but they certainly cannot be used for short stories.

The first time I set down to write a murder mystery novel it all went horribly wrong. I'd read mysteries and watched mystery movies, and I had made a list of all the ingredients that needed to be included. I created a cast of slightly eccentric characters; I had a nice Gothic setting; I had a dramatic scene for the discovery of a body, and my little group of suspects all had guilty secrets and there was a tangled web of relationships between them. I had a pair of characters to act as sleuth and sleuth's assistant and practised writing banter between them to establish their relationship. I was also aware of the clichés of the murder mystery genre, so knew what I had to avoid or refer to only ironically. Armed with my copy of H. R. F. Keating's excellent *Writing Crime Fiction,* I set forth. And wrote 20,000 words that ended up deader than my chapter three corpse.

I had discovered, as I am sure many writers do, that knowing *what* goes into a genre novel isn't enough. You also need to know how all of those various elements work together to create a fully-functioning story. I set my murder mystery aside and moved on to other things. But it was always there in the back of my head that I needed to learn how to write a proper murder mystery. I thought that there had to be some secret – a trick that only successful mystery writers knew, and if I could just uncover that secret...

Is there a secret formula? Did I find it, and will I share it with you in the pages of this book? I *am* going to share with you everything I learned about writing a murder mystery novel. It isn't a formula as such – you can't put all of the ingredients in one end and turn a handle and have a successful novel come out the pipe at the other end – but it is a process and a set of tools that will enable you to build a functioning murder mystery novel. You'll need to put in some hard work, and you'll need some inspiration and a bit of luck, but if you stick with it you should end up with a novel. The first one may not be publishable – and the first draft certainly won't be – but when you have written one, you should find that the next one is easier, more fun to write, and a better book. Either that or you'll discover that the murder mystery genre isn't really your cup of cyanide and you need to try something different.

Writing is always a learning experience. It's a bit like learning to drive a stick-shift – there's all those buttons and levers and pedals, and you think you'll never get the hang of it all, and then one day – after hours and hours of practice – something clicks inside you, and you find you can do it after all.

Then you discover that you actually *enjoy* driving. Or you hit a tree and decide that taking the bus isn't so bad after all. But even if you do become a proficient driver, you still have to practice, to improve your skills and keep them sharp, and there are always new things to learn – like how to program the damn satnav...

I made a major breakthrough in my own learning about genre plotting when I picked up a copy of John G. Cawelti's book *Adventure, Mystery, and Romance: Formula Stories as Art and Popular Culture.* As the subtitle suggests, it is an academic text – it was published by the University of Chicago Press. It was the first academic book I'd read on what genre fiction is and how it works – and *why* the various conventional elements of a genre work together to give the reader the reading experience they seek. This was an important discovery for me because it helped me understand that changing or missing out some conventional elements doesn't make your genre story better because it is fresh and original, it makes it weaker because you aren't giving the reader what they are looking for. Cawelti's book, and other academic texts on genre, showed me how all of the elements typical of a murder mystery story worked *together* to create a functioning whole.

Writers in a genre who publish 'how to' books will tell you what to do based on their years of experience reading and writing within the genre. Academic writers offer a new perspective, looking *objectively* at typical genre stories and deconstructing them to see how they work. Most academics who write about a particular genre are also fans of it, and so have read widely in the genre and are able to analyse their own experience and set down what – to them as a reader – is a successful example of that type of story. Genres and texts within genres are also studied from different theoretical perspectives: much of what I draw on here is from a *structuralist* viewpoint because I'm interested in taking things apart to see how they work, with a view to constructing something similar. If you encountered literary theory or narratology in college, this is probably familiar to you; if you didn't, it doesn't matter – I mention it only to show where I have taken ideas from.

Other academic writers explore the dominant themes and ideologies reflected by the genre, and this gives us another way of knowing what readers are looking for in their preferred genre. Genre readers typically like books that reinforce their own beliefs in terms of what constitutes correct or moral behaviour – if you write a novel that challenges that, either deliberately or accidentally, then the reader may find your book dissatisfying without necessarily being able to pinpoint why.

Having read a number of texts about specific genres and books about genre in general, I began to see things that I could use practically in my own writing. I could use the objective viewpoint to examine what I was trying to achieve, and use techniques I'd seen discussed to accomplish my goals.

In a previous (working) life I wrote in-house technical manuals for the implementation and use of library management software systems, and I trained people in how to use those systems. My approach was to lock myself away in an office with the software and the suppliers' technical manuals and teach myself how to use it. As I went along I would write step-by-step guidelines for each task, with accompanying screenshots, gradually putting together a user guide that fitted the workflow of the library where I was then working. Then I would give my guide to someone and ask them to test it out and give me feedback on which parts of it worked for them and which didn't. Then I'd revise the guide before making it available to the people I needed to train. This is the same sort of approach I take whenever I have to learn something new – I sit and I write myself a user guide. I test it out and add to it until I feel I have all I need to start using the software or whatever. I did it when I learned how to create and format ebooks for publishing on Amazon, and I did it when I taught myself how to write a murder mystery novel. This book is a revised and expanded version of my own 'how to' guide. At the end of the book is a section where I show how I used it to create my first murder mystery novel *The Sword in the Stone-Dead*. I wrote that book partly as a proof of concept. The second one, *Murder by Magic*, is where I really started to have fun with the genre.

In laying out how the archetypal plots are constructed in the murder mystery, I use an adaptation of Frank Daniel's eight sequence model that was developed to teach screenwriters at UCLA. You may be familiar with this from Paul Gulino's book *Screenwriting: The Sequence Approach*. If you've never come across it before, and want to explore it in more detail, I wrote about it in my *Plot Basics* book. When it comes to character and character archetypes, my own thoughts are based in part on Carl Jung's work on personality (which forms the basis for the Myers-Briggs personality type test) and in part on a simplified version of the Enneagram. In this book, I refer mainly to the 'Thinker' and 'Carer' archetypes for the creating of detectives and amateur sleuths – these exist in various personality- and character-type models under different names. I also talk a little bit about the theory of 'emotional intelligence' when I discuss the difference between the traditional 'Great Detective' – such as Sherlock Holmes or Poirot – and the sleuth in the modern cozy. You probably don't need to know anything more about these things than I give here, but I'll include some references as we go in case you want to learn more.

If you've read this far in the introduction, you will have seen that my research into the murder mystery genre included resources from the academic and business worlds, as well as more traditional materials. There is a lot more in-depth detail in these pages than you will typically find in a 'how to write' guide. I didn't want to regurgitate stuff you can find in dozens of other places – what would be the point? But I did want to share with you some of the more interesting things I have discovered so far on my own writer's journey. You might find some of the material here a bit dense and as much fun to read as a college textbook – I have tried to make it as readable as I can, but sometimes I have a lot of material to cover and I thought 'dense' was preferable to superficial. The best approach might be to read the whole book through once to get an overview, skimming the detail occasionally, and then dip into each section of the books as you begin to develop your own story.

Mystery stories have existed since ancient times – there are examples in the Bible, and there are puzzle and riddle stories that pre-date those. This is a book providing practical advice, so I don't want to fill pages here with a history of the genre. It *is* important if you are going to write in a particular genre to have a good knowledge of its history – if only so that you don't duplicate what has been done before – so I have included two brief appendices: an overview of the development of the genre and a selection of highlights from the 'golden age' of the murder mystery. There are also some suggested readings for those who want to dive more deeply into the history of the genre.

Before we move on, I will add one final caveat: The process I present in these pages is not *the* way to write a murder mystery or whodunit, it is *a* way and I have found that it works for me. You may find another writer who has an approach that works better for you – if you do, leave a review on that person's book or write about it on your blog or social media, as that will help other writers discover it too. If you disagree intensely with something I say here, that's good too – at least I have helped you clarify and articulate your own ideas. In the end, every writer is on a journey to discover what works best for them – and that journey lasts the whole of our writing lives. Hopefully, my guidebook will help you a little way along this part of your journey and highlight a few things you might have missed otherwise.

Genre Conventions

People choose to read genre fiction because they enjoy certain things that are common to all novels in that genre, while at the same time seeking a fresh new story. The trick for the writer is identifying those things that need to remain constant and those areas where originality is required – how can we create something that is 'the same only different?'

In the *Genre Writer* series I am going to use a standard set of genre conventions and use those to show what readers of a particular genre expect to find in their novels:

- *Setting* – Where and when is the story set. This includes the 'social milieu.'
- *Iconography* – What objects do we 'see' that are genre-specific, and how are these objects used? What meaning do they have?
- *Themes* – What values are defended or opposed? What issues or concepts are explored?
- *Tone* – What is the emotional tone of the story?
- *Characters* – What roles do we typically see? What types of people do we see in those roles?
- *Plots* – What is the typical sequence of events that a reader or audience expects to find in this type of story?

Let's take each of these in turn and see what readers expect from a murder mystery story.

Setting – The Scene of the Crime

The classical detective mystery is set in a 'closed' world – that is, the place in which the story take place is in some way isolated and contains a limited number of people who will serve as the suspects. We must create a setting such that there is no possibility of an 'outsider' being the murderer.

W. H. Auden ('The Guilty Vicarage,' 1948) said that the setting ought to be as Eden-like as possible so that the intrusion of the corpse is all the more shocking and unwelcome. John G. Cawelti (*Adventure, Mystery and Romance,* 1976) wrote that the contrast between a comfortable, orderly setting and the disorder of the crime scene symbolically heightened the difference between order and chaos, rationality and guilt.

The setting also establishes a specific social milieu – typically, in this genre, a middle-class one. A place of safety and material comfort – somewhere 'cozy.' The English country house, the idyllic village, the old university campus, the hotel, the ocean liner, or the steam train – these are typical settings in the detective mystery. A map of the village or a plan of the country house is often included, emphasising its closed nature. During the story, we expect to see scenes set in the dining room, the library, and – ultimately – the drawing room, where the detective draws everyone together and explains whodunit.

The murder mystery genre has been established for so long that certain recurring backgrounds or settings have been noted. The following list is based on the 'milieus' included in *The Oxford Companion to Crime and Mystery Writing:*

Academic
Advertising
Archaeological
Arts & Antiques
Aviation
Banking & Financial
Cathedral Close
Circus & Carnival
Clerical
Club, Gentlemen's
Country House
English Village
Gardening
Holidays
Horse Racing
Hotel
Island
Journalism & Newspaper
Library
Medical
Military
Musical
Nautical
Publishing & Bookshop
Railway
Rural
Sports, incl. cricket, golf, tennis, football
Theatrical, incl. television, radio, and film
Travel

Critics have noted that these milieus are often stratified in some way and mysteries accept and indirectly approve of whatever unfairness is inherent in such a hierarchical system. This is almost inevitable in a genre where a startling event – the discovery of a body – disturbs the status quo and the hero sets out to restore equilibrium top the setting. The milieu must be one in which truth can be sought and revealed, no matter who the guilty person turns out to be. In theory, this rules out basing a detective mystery in any sort of despotic regime or dictatorship, whether national or local – though Ellery Queen's *The King is Dead* (1951) may be the exception that proves this rule.

S. S. Van Dine, in his 'Twenty Rules,' (see *Rules of the Game* below) said that there should be "no long descriptive passages" and "no 'atmospheric' preoccupations." In the detective mystery, plot is everything and the writer is expected to be economical in the provision of background detail. One reason for this is related to the idea of 'fair play,' in that anything that is presented to the reader is expected to be *relevant* to the story – either as a clue or as a red herring. There should be "no literary dallying with side issues," as Van Dine puts it.

The downside of this approach is that classical detective stories are often criticised for their absence of 'poetic' or 'literary' writing in terms of creating a sense of place.

Marie F. Rodell (*Mystery Fiction,* 1943) advises that a setting should only be used where some detail of the setting "influences the manner of the murder or the course of detection." To set a story in a specific location and then to use none of the unique features of that place is a missed opportunity. She also tells us: "Setting and the character of a society will determine in part the nature of the crime, the motive which prompts it, and the way it is carried out."

The location usually determines who is present, the mix of character types: in Agatha Christie's stories, this is usually someplace where upper-middle-class people of different backgrounds and occupations come together, with a handful of working-class characters on the periphery. It also determines the 'closed circle' of suspects. Having brought them together, it provides a situation where (a) no one can leave until the mystery is solved, and (b) no external person can enter, meaning that the murderer must be one of those already present.

Another function of the location is to make the murder stand out in stark relief: the corpse is out of place in such a location. As Carolyn Wells wrote, in *The Technique of the Mystery Story* (1913), "The facts of the murder are in themselves sufficiently unattractive to make it unnecessary to add to the distastefulness of the story by unpleasant surroundings ... Unless absolutely necessary to have it otherwise, let the house or scene of the crime be attractive or interesting, and let even the subordinate characters be of refined and intelligent type." Barbara Norville (*Writing the Modern Mystery*, 1992) notes that it is common – perhaps almost a cliché – in the detective mystery is to have a description of a room that seems entirely normal except for the last detail noted: the corpse.

Wells also warns the writer to choose a location and social customs with which he or she is familiar: the detective mystery story depends on logic and plausibility, and so errors in fact relating to a setting are to be avoided.

While we have said that lengthy passages of scenic description do not belong in the detective mystery, there is one place where they have their use, which is in the hiding of clues: the significant fact is then 'lost' amongst the other details provided. We will talk more about clues later.

Setting also includes the *historical period* during which the story is set. 'Golden age' detective stories were set in the present day when the present day was the period between the First and Second World Wars. Whodunits have been written against the backdrop of past historical periods – Ancient Greece or Rome, or the reign of Elizabeth I, for example – and during the modern era of the late 20th and early 21st centuries. Setting a story during any period other than the here and now presents the writer with all of the obligations of the historical novelist in terms of ensuring that period details are correct. Detective mysteries have also been successfully staged in science fictional settings – the future, the enclosed space station or spacecraft, the alien world, or the 'alternate' world where history has been subtly altered.

Also on the subject of time period, we should consider the *season* during which the story is set. Snow often features, as does mud, because this allows for the presence or absence of footprints. Whatever season you choose, ensure that all details are consistent with that time of year – *except* where an unseasonal detail is actually a clue. A blazing fire in summer may be significant, as might the presence of a flower that is not normally in bloom at that time of year; so too the wearing of garments that are not appropriate to the weather.

As with historical accuracy, geographical knowledge is also important – if you are writing about somewhere other than your own country, or even county, be aware of local seasonal conditions.

In the modern cozy mystery, the setting or 'milieu' is often a key element and we'll discuss that in more detail in the next chapter.

A final note related to setting is that there is no place in the classical or cozy mystery for organised crime or criminal gangs: the murder is committed by one individual (or a 'murderous couple' at most) who had a *personal* reason for killing the victim. This type of story focuses on the relationships between people.

Iconography

What do we expect to 'see' in a classical detective mystery? There are any number of visual objects that we associate with the genre – including setting, already mentioned, and characters, which we will explore below. Many of the objects are used in the cover images of mystery novels – usually, but not always, depicting or representing something in the story.

There are murder weapons – the dagger, the gun (usually a revolver), the poison bottle, the rope or hangman's noose, scissors, cut-throat razor, or the 'blunt instrument,' usually represented by a candlestick. Then there is the corpse – lying on the carpet, sometimes just a chalk or tape outline, and sometimes just the feet of the victim (we don't want to put off potential readers by showing the bloody bit!) If a corpse is considered a bit too much, there might be a more symbolic representation of violence – broken spectacles, a bullet-hole in a window, a broken string of pearls. A skull or a raven might also do the trick. And if you must, you can have a glossy splash of blood accompanying any of these.

A magnifying glass, or the detective's pipe, is probably too much of a cliché – though you might include them in a still-life composition that also includes one or more clues: a finger-print, a footprint, a train ticket, a broken and stopped watch or clock, a map, a timetable... Other objects might emphasise the idea of a puzzle or game: jigsaw pieces, chess pieces, or playing cards. Or perhaps something that calls to mind a childhood game or nursery rhyme: many mystery novel titles are taken from such rhymes. Then there are handcuffs, shadows or silhouettes, a key in a lock for a 'locked room' mystery, or a gloved hand: the murderer wears black leather, but the butler wears white cotton and may be presenting the murder weapon on a silver tray.

The country house or idyllic village might be shown on the cover. Or a period vehicle – steam train, ocean liner, or motor car – if it features in the story. Women will be shown in 1920s or 30s fashions, and men will be in tuxedos or country tweeds. Art Deco is the style to aim for, though it is also acceptable to hark back to the Victorian era of foggy cobbled streets lit by gas lamps.

I have mentioned all of these in relation to book covers, because they are an obvious visual element of the murder mystery novel. The same or similar objects will be found in the text as well. Much of what I said above applies to the iconography of the modern cozy mystery as well, though these are usually set in the present day. In the chapter on the modern cozy, we explore the kind of backgrounds against which the stories are set: these provide additional iconic visuals including pets (especially cats), food, and crafts or hobbies.

Themes

The themes found in detective mysteries come in two forms – the values the writer *chooses* to promote, and those which he or she *subconsciously* defends.

The most obvious theme in this genre is that of justice versus injustice. This is not justice in terms of what is *legal* versus what is *illegal*, but rather what is *morally* right. Sometimes a classical detective must act in a way which he believes is *just*, even if his action is – technically – outside the law.

Other values are explored via the *motivations* of the suspects and the murderer. The suspects each have their own 'guilty secret' and so engage in some form of suspicious behaviour in an attempt to hide this from the detective and from others. Usually, these 'sins' are of a lesser significance than murder, and the suspect – in relative terms – is shown to be innocent. The murderer's motivation – greed, jealousy, fear, vengeance, or whatever – may also be demonstrated by other characters, but he is guilty of an unforgivable sin because he decides that murdering another person is an appropriate way to deal with his problem. We will explore motivation in more detail later.

The murder mystery always advocates a return to the *status quo*, to a pre-existing social stability. Crime intrudes on an 'ideal,' setting, bringing the threat of chaos – then the detective resolves the problem, and balance is restored. These stories are based on the assumption that the existing order is correct and must be protected and preserved.

Golden age mystery stories have been criticised for ignoring the realities of life in the 1920s and 30s – the depression, the Wall Street crash, and the poverty which affected millions of people does not feature. Agatha Christie and Dorothy L. Sayers, to name only two, defended and even glorified the British class system in their stories. Working class people only ever appeared in the roles of servants, cooks, and cleaners – with the police occupying a sort of no-man's land between middle and working class, but generally regarded as being 'common.' Main characters were virtually always white and middle class. Ethnic minorities appeared only in the working classes, and there was what Julian Symons called a 'casual anti-Semitism' in Sayers' work and that of other writers. Foreigners generally were regarded as 'suspicious' and 'not like us.'

Sexism went unchallenged – logic and reasoning were assumed to be the preserve of males, intuition of females.

Emotion – a 'feminine' trait – was scorned by the Great Detective, from Sherlock Holmes onwards. Homosexuality was only ever hinted at, with gay males treated as either camp stereotypes or perverts. Homosexuality was a criminal offence in England until 1967. Lesbianism was sometimes suggested but regarded as a harmless curiosity rather than a sickness or an offence.

These negative values in the stories were a reflection of attitudes of the time – it would not be appropriate for a writer to espouse them today, but at the same time – in the interests of historical accuracy – it would be a mistake to deny these pervasive attitudes in a story set during the 1920s or 30s.

Britain between the First and Second World Wars – the period of the Empire's last gasp – was a curious mix of nostalgia for the 'good old days' of the Victorian era, and of an 'anything goes' embrace of 'Jazz Age' music, fashion, and *joi de vivre*. This is reflected in the popularity of both 'serious' and 'What fun!' mystery stories – see *Tone* below.

The treatment of the *victim* in the murder mystery involves a curious moral grey area. Murder is chosen as the crime because it is a terrible, irreversible thing demanding that action be taken to bring the killer to justice. But the victim is not someone whose loss is grieved to any great extent. In practical terms – as far as writer and reader are concerned – the victim exists to provide a corpse and a mystery to solve. In order to assuage our guilt at this casual callousness, we are usually led to believe that the victim was a nasty person who actually deserved to die – or at least was undeserving of continued life – or they are presented as cyphers: ghost-like people who didn't really have any sort of life to lose. The existence of the necessary corpse requires a little sleight of hand on the part of the writer, and a suspension of disbelief on the part of the reader. And a stiff upper lip on the part of the other characters.

Tone

The detective mystery can be either serious or humorous. All detective stories are comedies rather than tragedies – a problem is posed, action is taken, and there is a *desired* outcome in that the solution to the mystery is found. Even in the serious stories, there is often some element of comic relief, gallows humour, or playfulness.

Mystery stories are quite clearly artificial constructs – their game-like structure requires a particular kind of suspension of disbelief. There is no requirement for them to be naturalistic or true to life in setting, character, or event – so even when they are serious, they are seldom realistic.

When they are humorous, mystery stories tend to be either farce or fun. In farce, the comedy comes from ridiculous situations that the characters take seriously. The novels of Michael Innes and Edmund Crispin are examples of this form. In 'what fun' mysteries, bright young things tend to run around exclaiming that investigating a murder is exciting and entertaining – they deny the seriousness of the situation: to them, it is literally a game.

H. Douglas Thomson (*Masters of Mystery,* 1931) described A. A. Milne's *The Red House Mystery* as an example of the "Lord, what fun!" type of mystery – "where detection is the amateur's recipe against rainy day ennui, and the murder is acclaimed as a happy stroke of Providence." This type of story owes as much to P. G. Wodehouse as it does to Edgar Allan Poe. Georgette Heyer's novels belong in this category, as do Dorothy L. Sayers' early novels, and the Tommy and Tuppence Beresford stories of Agatha Christie. Its inherent artificiality means that the pure murder mystery cannot be put to more serious use in either a 'straight' novel or as satire. The outward form can be adopted for a mainstream novel, as in Umberto Eco's *The Name of the Rose,* but at that point, it becomes something else entirely.

Characters

The detective mystery requires that a number of characters are present to play particular roles:

- the murderer, sometimes a murderous couple or pair working together;
- a victim – a second or multiple victims are optional;
- a detective, amateur or professional, to conduct the investigation;
- the detective's partner or 'Watson' is optional;
- suspects – usually at least five or six in a novel;
- witnesses and other walk-on parts are optional, as is the presence of
- the police.

We will look at creating each of these in later chapters – where we will also look at the types of character that typically fill these different roles.

Plots

There are a few plot types that are regularly used in the detective mystery genre. First, there are two variations of the straightforward murder investigation: one where the murder occurs at the beginning of the story, and one where it does not occur until the midpoint. A third variation is the 'most likely suspect' story, or 'innocent accused,' where someone the reader feels sympathetic towards is accused of murder, and the detective must help prove their innocence. There is the locked room or 'impossible crime' story, which is concerned with *how* the crime was committed. And finally the 'inverted' mystery story, which begins with the crime and how it was committed – usually also revealing the identity of the murderer – and then concerns either the detective's attempts to solve the crime and prove the murderer guilty; or it begins with a criminal setting out to commit a crime, and follows him or her as they try to commit the murder and/or escape detection.

Towards the end of the book, we will break down these different types and provide full structures for the main types, showing what sequence of events the reader expects to find in them.

The Rules of the Game

The classical mystery story is unusual in that a number of 'rules' have been laid down for writers by other practitioners. No less than three separate lists of do's and don'ts have been created: S. S. Van Dine wrote 'Twenty Rules for Writing Detective Stories' in 1928, and Ronald A. Knox wrote what is now known as a 'Detective Story Decalogue' in the same year. Members of Britain's Detection Club also had their own list. It has been argued that most of these 'rules' are merely preferences or prejudices, but that being said, I think there are three unbreakable rules – and one optional rule that I strongly advocate.

The detective mystery *must* have the following attributes:

(i)   A character who acts as a 'detective' – they do not have to have the title of detective, but they do need to conduct an investigation into the mystery in the manner of a detective.

(ii) A solution arrived at as a result of detection – the uncovering of clues and the deduction of the meaning of those clues. It should not be solved as a result of luck, coincidence, or by tricking the unknown criminal into confessing (though it is acceptable to trick a known criminal into confessing after they have been identified as a result of deductive reasoning).

(iii) No supernatural elements – if there is anything that appears to be supernatural, it should – by the end of the story – be explained rationally.

And I believe that it should have the following:

(iv) Fair play – which means that the reader should have access to all of the information available to the detective, including all of the clues he discovers during his investigation and any specialist knowledge he looks up or sends away for.

The reason I say that this last one is optional is because many writers, including some of the best-known, regularly 'break' this rule and keep things from the reader. It is often said that part of the appeal of the detective mystery is that it is a puzzle that the reader tries to solve before the detective reveals the answer. In order for the reader to be able to do this, the author must 'play fair' and offer the reader all that is necessary to solve the puzzle.

While it may be true that some readers do want to try and solve the puzzle themselves, this is not true for all readers. Other readers gain their enjoyment of this genre from seeing an expert – the detective – in action. And others enjoy the re-assurance that problems can be solved, that when chaos enters our world, upsetting its balance, equilibrium can be restored by someone suitably qualified.

So rule (iv) is optional – but I still think you should obey it.

The Modern Cozy Mystery

'Cozy mystery' is a term first coined in 1958 for traditional mystery stories, including those of Agatha Christie and S. S. Van Dine. More recently it has found popularity as a sub-genre of modern mystery fiction. To distinguish between the two, I will refer to (i) golden age or traditional mysteries and (ii) modern cozy mysteries. The two have many similarities but there are also important differences between them, particularly regarding their detective or sleuth characters.

The Oxford Companion to Crime and Mystery Writing (1999) does not treat the modern cozy as a separate sub-genre, and *The Cambridge Companion to Crime Fiction* (2003) makes no reference to them, so we must look elsewhere for a definition. Erin Martin, aka 'Danna,' on her website www.cozy-mystery.com sets out two important features about this sub-genre in her 'Definition of a Cozy Mystery':

(i) *Cozy mysteries are considered 'gentle' books – no graphic violence, no profanity, and no explicit sex. Most often, the crime takes place 'off stage' and death is usually very quick. Prolonged torture is not a staple in cozy mysteries! The victim is usually a character who had terrible vices or who treated others very badly ... and 'deserves to die'...*

(ii) *Sex (if there is any) is always behind closed doors. It is implied – at most!*

A later addendum acknowledges *"I should have added 'most of the time' as a clause,"* because some titles classified as cozy mysteries do contain profanity, violence and sexual references. The addendum was added after a reader of the website complained about books being included that broke the no sex, no profanity, no physical violence rule. I know from reader reviews of my own books that this is definitely an issue for some people. In the cozy mystery, murders generally occur off-stage and crime scenes are relatively bloodless: killings involving poison or a fall down the stairs are preferred over shooting or stabbing.

Erin Martin's article refers to Jessica Fletcher in the television series *Murder, She Wrote*, which is one of the maid models of the modern cozy mystery and contains virtually all of the key features:

- The plot is a 'whodunit' with the victim effectively serving as a MacGuffin – an excuse for an investigation to take place. The victim is usually someone who nobody likes and who few people will miss.
- The main character is usually a female amateur sleuth who is intelligent and intuitive and has an occupation (or hobby) that brings her into contact with a broad range of people.
- The location is usually a 'closed' setting of some type – a small village, such as Miss Marple's St. Mary Mead or Jessica Fletcher's Cabot Cove, or one related to her occupation or hobby activity which functions as a small community.
- There is usually some kind of 'nosey neighbour' character on hand to provide gossip and point a finger.
- The main character is often friends with, or related to, a professional detective, sheriff, or policeman who can provide access to official information that an amateur would not normally have access to. And who can be on-hand to make the formal arrest at the end of the story. Though, in the Miss Marple tradition, the main character's suspicions are not initially taken seriously by the authorities.
- There are often other recurring characters that feature in a series.
- Plots usually involve several twists and possibly red herrings.
- The final solution is achieved through the use of intelligence and deduction rather than physical action or forensic techniques.

- The pace of the story is usually quite brisk and there is often a light or humorous tone.

Cozy mysteries tend to be set in small towns or villages, or other enclosed communities, rather than in the big city. Many use eccentric local characters, often used for comic effect. The person investigating the crime is usually an amateur and is more likely to be female than male. The stories are, broadly speaking, descended from Agatha Christie's Miss Marple and Tommy and Tuppence stories, rather than from Poirot or Sherlock Holmes.

While sex is (for the most part) absent, romance is more likely to be present in the cozy than it is in the traditional 'great detective' mystery. Particularly if it tends towards the verbal sparring of the romantic comedy.

The modern cozy does have things in common with the golden age mystery. *Means, motive,* and *opportunity* remain key elements in the investigation. We also still have a closed circle of suspects, all related in some way to the victim, and all providing an *alibi* for the amateur sleuth to test. The solution should rely on logic and not feature any magical or spiritual element. And any clues discovered by the detective should not be kept from the reader – that is still regarded as cheating. The motive for murder is also one of those that Poirot lists: greed, revenge, or fear.

The structure of the plot will broadly follow that of the classical mystery. The main differences come in the creation of the characters and milieu of the story. Let's consider the setting first.

Setting or Milieu

We've already said that, like the traditional murder mystery, the modern cozy typically has a 'closed' setting, so that you have a limited number of witnesses and suspects. A small-town setting, or some other enclosed community, such as a workplace or a hobby group, is ideal because it limits the number of people onstage, and provides an environment where the amateur investigator is likely to know everyone, and where people are going to feel comfortable talking to her.

Creating or using a distinctive milieu can be one of the things that attracts readers to your novel. The headline of an August 2015 article in *The Guardian* newspaper tells us something about the modern cozy mystery: *Murder most cosy - why mystery novels involving quilts and cats are big business*. Many cozy stories, particularly those within series, have a common theme, related to the interests of the amateur detective or the location. The amateur sleuth might be a gardener or florist, a librarian or writer, a dog-sitter, or a bookstore owner. On the Amazon website, *cozy* is a sub-genre of *mystery* and is itself broken down into three subcategories: animals, crafts and hobbies, and culinary.

In the 'animals' category, cats are the firm favourite with dogs and other animals some way behind. Examples include Rita Mae Brown, who has written twenty-six novels featuring the feline detective Mrs. Murphy and her human assistant Mary Minor 'Harry' Haristeen, beginning with *Wish You Were Here?* (1990). Brown's stories are probably unique in being 'co-authored' by her cat Sneaky Pie Brown. Lilian Jackson Braun (1913-2011) wrote twenty-nine novels and three collections of short stories about James Qwilleran and his Siamese cats Koko and Yum Yum, the first being *The Cat Who Could Read Backwards* (1966).

In 'crafts and hobbies' we find the Mary Marks' *Quilting Mystery* or 'Knot' series, beginning with *Forget Me Knot* (2014) in which sarcastic heroine Martha Rose and her friends Lucy and Birdie investigate the death of a fellow-quilter and the theft of her prize-winning quilt. Sewing, knitting and witchcraft also feature in this category. Gardening has also featured in mystery stories from Miss Marple onwards.

And in the in the 'culinary' sub-group we have several series centring on the world of cookery and baking, or on specific types of food from doughnuts to pies to cookies and candies. These include the Hannah Swensen series by Joanna Fluke: movies based on this series were produced by the Hallmark Channel under the series title *Murder, She Baked*.

For more examples check out the 'Cozy Mystery' entry on Wikipedia and the coverage at www.cozy-mystery.com

The background against which the mystery is set is an important part of this sub-genre. If the amateur sleuth is a cake-decorator or a dog-groomer, details about the hobby or occupation can be used to add colour and originality. Some writers even include recipes for food or for home-made beauty products. This activity also serves as the thing that draws the characters together (including the sleuth, the victim and the murderer) and acts as a sort of crucible, containing the action and ensuring a limited set of suspects to be investigated.

Not every cozy mystery fits neatly into one of Amazon's sub-categories. Under the broader cozy heading you will find examples such as the works of Scottish author M. C. Beaton (Marion Chesney), who created both the Hamish Macbeth series, featuring a police constable in a small Scottish town, turned into a TV series by the BBC in 1995; and the Agatha Raisin series, beginning with *Agatha Raisin and the Quiche of Death,* which were filmed for Sky television in 2014 and 2016.

Elizabeth Spann Craig is the author of the Southern Quilting mysteries, the Memphis Barbeque mysteries, and the Myrtle Clover series. She also blogs about writing the modern cozy mystery, and has written a series of articles beginning at the following link:

http://elizabethspanncraig.com/3334/writing-the-cozy-mystery-the-sleuth/

Characters

Cozy mystery writers continue the tradition begun with Agatha Christie's Miss Marple, having an amateur sleuth who is not taken seriously by official investigators, but who somehow gains access to official sources of information. In modern stories, as we've said, the amateur often has a friend, relative or husband who is connected with the official investigation. But the investigation will almost always rely on good old-fashioned puzzle-solving type detective skills, rather than forensic science.

If you look at lists of the most popular cozy mysteries, you will see that readers like series. With this in mind, it is a good idea to make sure that you create an amateur sleuth who has 'series potential.' She (and it is usually *she*) must be somewhere or doing something, that means she can come into contact with multiple potential victims and multiple potential murderers. Readers allow you a fair amount of leeway here: it's almost a joke that *Murder, She Wrote*'s Jessica Fletcher encounters murder wherever she goes and that the population of Cabot's Cove must have suffered a steady decline over the years!

Elizabeth Spann Craig suggests that, especially with the first book in a series, you should have a good reason for your main character becoming involved in a murder investigation. She, or someone close to her, could be suspected of the murder, for example. Or she may be the one who discovers the body. Or the victim may be a friend or relative or may have some other kind of connection with the amateur detective.

Your main character must also be someone who is in a position to be able to speak to all of the witnesses and potential suspects. An amateur has no official status, and so cannot insist that people make themselves available for interview. This is one reason why this type of story is often set in a small community – physical, social or occupational – where the main character knows all of the witnesses and suspects personally. Your amateur sleuth should also be someone who people are likely to feel comfortable talking to, even if they are reluctant to be interviewed. This is one area where the amateur detective often has an advantage over the official detective: people are more likely to share gossip with someone they know and trust.

I mentioned above that the characters in the location chosen for a cozy are likely to include some eccentrics, and I think it helps if your main character has some quirks of her own. The aged spinster Miss Marple is the archetypal least-likely-to-be-the-detective character. You should try and give your main character an idiosyncrasy or flaw that makes them both memorable and endearing. The idea of the interfering busy-body has been overused, but it gives you an idea of the sort of thing to aim for. If it also causes the police and the murderer to underestimate your amateur sleuth, you're on the right track. Giving the sleuth an unusual hobby or pet has enabled some authors to individualise their characters. Though you probably want to make your main character more than just 'the one who makes sock-puppets' or 'the one with the Schnauzer.'

The one thing your main character cannot be is stupid. They may be – or *seem* to be – naïve or inexperienced in some areas, but if they fail to see things that are obvious to the reader, or they make decisions that the reader thinks are just foolish, you're unlikely to build an audience. The same is true when it comes to putting themselves in dangerous situations.

Some writers have said that your amateur detective needs to have a college education, but I think that's a bit prescriptive: you want your amateur to be someone who has experience of some kind to draw on and to have a good idea of how people think and behave. Someone like a retired teacher or midwife is ideal, but anyone whose work relies on an understanding of human psychology would be equally effective: a used car salesperson, a bar or coffee-shop waitress, a sports coach... In a later chapter, we will look at the investigative methods of the modern cozy sleuth in more detail.

While some modern cozy sleuths have a cat or some other pet as their sidekick, others may have a human 'Watson.' The reasons for including this sort of character are the same here as they are for the Great Detective. Having a lead character with only herself to talk to can make it tough to write (and to read): people like dialogue. It can help move a story along if the main character has someone to bounce ideas off. And, as Elizabeth Spann Craig points out, you can use the sidekick to provide additional conflict in the story. The relationship between the two can also be a source of humour.

Tone

The modern cozy mystery tends to have a light, even humorous, tone and moves along at a fairly brisk pace. These are qualities it inherits more from the private detective thriller than the traditional mystery. I've also mentioned that elements of the romantic comedy – such as the witty banter – can also be found. This sense of fun is reflected in the titles of many novels in this genre which feature puns or other humorous references.

The Crime – Murder Most Foul

Does the crime in a mystery have to be murder? In a novel, almost certainly. As S. S. Van Dine put it: "There simply must be a corpse in a detective novel, and the deader the corpse the better ... Three hundred pages is far too much bother for a crime other than murder." As Marie F. Rodell wrote, "Murder is the most irrevocable and final of crimes: it cannot be undone. Unlike theft, treason, and rape, it springs from an infinite variety of motives and is committed by an infinite variety of human beings."

In any story there must be something at stake, otherwise why should the reader care about the outcome? In the detective mystery, what is at stake is *justice*: Will the criminal get away with murder? This is a higher stake than: Will the criminal get away with burglary? It gives the reader a sense that something important is in the balance. Also, for the murderer himself, the stakes are high – the punishment for murder is more severe than that for theft, especially during a period of English history when murderers would be executed if convicted. The murderer will try all the harder to outwit the detective with such a fate awaiting him.

Rodell identifies three variations: the murder which does not seek to disguise the fact of murder; the murder which seeks to disguise the fact that there has been a death at all; and the murder which seeks to disguise itself as suicide or an accident.

When the murderer aims to conceal the fact of a death, he must dispose of the body. He may choose to hide the body so that there is doubt that murder has, in fact, occurred so that the prosecution would have no case. Or he may conceal the body for a length of time so that he can make good his escape, perfect his alibi, or change his identity. The corpse may be hidden so as to make it impossible to discover when the crime actually took place, or to obscure the identity of the corpse.

In a murder mystery, we do need a corpse, but the search for the body may form part of the investigation.

A quick factual note here: some writers wrongly believe that the Latin phrase *corpus delicti* refers to the body of the murder victim; it actually refers the 'body of the offence' which is the combination of facts and circumstances which constitute the breaking of a law. When it is used in relation to an investigator's inability to bring a criminal to justice, it refers to an absence of evidence of the facts, rather than simply the absence of a body. The body itself may be one part of the evidence – and an important one – but murder can still be proved even if a corpse isn't found.

Concealing the *time* of the murder is another way of deepening the mystery. If the crime is not discovered for a very long time, it is more difficult for the detective to build up an exact picture of what happened leading up to and following the murder. If discovery of the corpse is delayed only a short time, this may be to enable the murderer to provide himself with an alibi for the apparent time of death. Keeping the body warm – in a bath, turning up the central heating, or direct sun – can delay the onset of rigor mortis, making it more difficult to pinpoint the true time of death.

Bloody Murder?

In both the traditional and the cozy murder mystery, the killing is done off-stage and in largely bloodless circumstances: a poisoning; a single thrust of a dagger; a neat bullet-hole in the temple. In this kind of mystery, the corpse exists almost solely to provide the puzzle for the detective to solve. In the crime thriller or hardboiled detective genres, the murder is often much more gruesome, in an attempt to arouse an emotional response in the reader, whether it be horror, indignation, or sympathy for the victim, but not in our present genre.

The appropriate level of gore should be determined by the story and its characters: the form which the murder takes should be relevant to the character of either murderer or victim, it should not be bizarre and/or revolting for the sake of it.

The Discovery of the Corpse

How is the body described to the reader by the narrator of the story? Barbara Norville gives three possibilities:

Dispassionately. A description noting the position of the body, the time and cause of death, any struggle that ensued, the victim's gender, clothes, etc. By eliminating emotion, the narrator allows the reader to provide their own response.

Humanely. The narrator sees the body as a once-living human being and has respect for what that person was and compassion for what he or she no longer is. The narrator may be angered by the brutality and saddened by the waste. This attitude is the most sympathetic, and also the most uncomfortable to deal with.

Callously. The narrator is not at all fazed by death, and even makes sarcastic comments about the corpse.

We might add a third, appropriate to the 'What fun!' mystery – *Flippantly.*

Shakespeare knew a thing or two about the corpses of murder victims, as Thomas De Quincey says in *On Murder, Considered as One of the Fine Arts* (1827) "there never was better; witness his description of the murdered Duncan, Banquo, etc.; and above all witness his incomparable miniature, in Henry VI, of the murdered Gloucester."

The Corpse Lay Face-Down...

In *Murder Ink* (1978), an uncredited sidebar explores why the body is often discovered face-down in mysteries: it prolongs the mystery of the identity of the corpse for just a little longer. The victim is wearing Lady Teasdale's coat, so everyone assumes it is she until the body is turned over and it is revealed to be the kitchen maid, Gladys. The question now becomes, was she murdered because she was *mistaken* for Lady Teasdale, or did the murderer intend to kill Gladys all along? This adds an extra layer of mystery that the detective must resolve.

The Victim

"The victim is always important," said Poirot. "The victim, you see, is so often the cause of the crime." – Agatha Christie, *Hallowe'en Party*

"...I know that everything is all right when it says, The body was that of an elderly gentleman, well-dressed but upside down. Always, you notice, an 'elderly gentleman' ... you see, if it said that the body was that of a woman – that's a tragedy. The body was that of a child! – that's a horror. But the body was that of an elderly gentleman – oh, pshaw! that's all right. Anyway he's had his life..." – Stephen Leacock, 'Murder at $2.50 a Crime'

"... something absolutely fascinating happened to the character: He got murdered." – William G. Tapply, *The Elements of Mystery Fiction*.

The victim, as Marie F. Rodell has said, functions on two levels – as a person who existed *before* the murder and as am object of study as a result of the murder. *Why* the victim was killed – the *motive* a person might have had for wishing him dead – we will explore as part of the characters of the murderer and of the suspects. And *how* he was killed is handled under *means* and *opportunity*. For the moment, we will concentrate on *who* the victim was.

Who the victim is may be known from the outset, but as Rodell says, you can conceal or disguise the identity of the corpse. This adds to the mystery, as the detective must now investigate and try to identify both the murderer and the victim.

If the killer chooses to obscure the identity of the victim, there must be a reason for it – perhaps because if the victim's identity was known, the identity of the murderer could be easily deduced.

Hiding the identity could involve something as simple as removing the usual clothing of the victim and replacing it with something that they would not normally wear. Or placing them in a place where they would not normally venture. Or something more complicated, such as the removal of teeth or fingerprints – or even fingers – may be employed to prevent identification. The corpse might be mutilated in some other way to remove or disguise some other identifying mark such as a scar, tattoo or birthmark. Or the head may be removed.

In *Evil Under the Sun,* Poirot says: "Because the victim was the kind of person he or she was, therefore was he or she murdered!" In *Mrs. McGinty's Dead* he says much the same thing: "Usually it is in the personality of the murdered person that the crux of the situation lies."

But, Earl F. Bargainnier says (*The Gentle Art of Murder,* 1980), despite what Poirot says, Christie's victims are in fact "uninteresting, unsympathetic, or essentially unknown." The apparent conflict between Poirot's statements and the actual victims can be accounted for, Bargainnier says, by the conventions of the genre: "... the reader must not be unduly disturbed by the victim's death."

Carolyn Wells argues the same point: "... the victim must be of the greatest possible importance generally, yet not specifically in the sympathy of the reader. Indeed, the victim, if beautiful or worthy, must be almost or entirely a stranger to the reader. But if the victim be wicked or unattractive, it matters not how great the reader's acquaintance with him."

In some mysteries, we meet the victim before the murder and see them in action in events which lead up to their death. In other stories, they are only ever seen as a corpse, and we learn of their actions only through the remembrances of others. As Barbara Norville says, it is up to you to "decide on how much emphasis you want to place on the victim-as-person and how much emphasis on the other characters' responses to the person-as-victim." She presents an argument in favour of allowing the victim to appear on stage before the murder is committed, saying that the reader will become interested in the character while they are alive, and so more involved in the story when that character is killed.

Delaying the actual murder until halfway through the novel allows the author to explore the relationships between the various characters – victim, murderer and suspects – and keeps the reader wondering which character is to be killer and which victim. It is even possible to have the character who has been set up to seem most likely to be the murderer to turn out to be the victim. Or vice versa. Delaying the murder allows the writer to create a dramatic scene (or scenes) which build up to the murder, followed by the dramatic scene of the murder (or discovery of the murder)

In the classic murder mystery, victims turn out not to have been nice people in their everyday lives, and there are very good reasons for this, Bargainnier explains: "If the victim is so objectionable that everyone has a motive, not only does this intensify the mystery, but it also frees the reader from any sense of guilt in accepting the death calmly." He notes that what actually makes a character objectionable can range from having 'minor irritating habits' to committing 'immoral or illegal acts.' Whatever their sins, they have to be shown to have gone beyond the socially accepted bounds for behaviour.

Who deserves to die? Bargainnier lists the traits of some of the victims in Agatha Christie novels. Women include a demanding hypochondriac, 'vamps,' a malicious games mistress, and a couple of victims who are "wilful, even tyrannical, as a result of wealth." Male victims are usually cruel and criminal or sexually immoral (often unfaithful husbands) and include blackmailers and murderers. In *Lord Edgware Dies* the eponymous victim, according to Poirot, probably "practices many curious vices."

"A favourite victim with the writers of Detective Fiction is an elderly man, perhaps a banker, or some other wealthy citizen of importance to the community," says Carolyn Wells. "This is a reasonable choice, for the character has the regard and interest of his fellow townsmen, without too great sympathy on the part of the reader." Bargainnier says that, in Christie's novels, elderly women are equally at risk, describing the most common victim as being "the elderly 'blocking character' of either sex ... this person is an 'expendable obstacle.' Standing in the way of youth, either through denial of money or hindering of romance..."

To ensure lack of sympathy for Mrs. Boynton in *Appointment with Death,* Christie describes her as "that hulk of shapeless flesh with her evil gloating eyes" and "a stupid, malignant, posturing old woman." She is called tyrannical, and compared to a snake and a spider.

Carolyn Wells advises the author to choose a victim "... in whom we have no personal interest, but whose importance we recognise." She also says that "... a charming young woman may be chosen for this role, but in this case the reader must not be allowed to know and love her before the tragedy," a view that is echoed by Bargainnier: "If a victim is admirable in any way, he or she must be basically a stranger to the reader." He notes that the victim usually disappears offstage as soon as its purpose has been fulfilled. And the easiest way to prevent the reader becoming attached to a victim is to have that person dead as the story opens or soon after.

The Victim's Guilty Secrets

Often, writes William G. Tapply, "... a murder victim has secrets that provide the murderer with a motive. The connection between the victim's secret and the murderer's motive is the solution to the puzzle." To arrive at this solution, the detective has to slowly piece together details of the victim's life and their relationships with other characters. And if the victim is dead in chapter one, the only source of information the detective has is what the remaining characters have to say about the victim. These accounts may be unreliable or contradictory.

In creating your main murder victim, there are two questions you need to answer:

(i) Do you wish to show the victim alive and interacting with other characters before they are killed? If the answer is yes, then you're likely to want to use the 'murder at the midpoint' type of plot: it saves you having to mess around with multiple flashbacks. If the answer is no, then you're likely to want to have your murder happen either before the story opens – having it open with the discovery of the body; or to have the murder happen within the first couple of chapters.

(ii) Do you want to open with a body? If so, your reader will never see the victim, except through the recollections of other characters. The victim can be either a good person, or a terrible one, but we won't learn too much about them either way: they're really just there to provide a reason for the investigation. They serve a plot point.

Or would you prefer to have the murder committed later in the story, around the midpoint? In this case, you will probably want to create a truly unpleasant victim, so that the reader does not feel sympathy for or empathy with, them. Seeing the victim interact with other characters, the reader can make up their own mind about the victim and any potential motive for murder.

The Second Murder Victim

"I should say it's about time for the next murder ... in books there's always a second murder about now. Someone who knows something is bumped off before they can tell what they know." Agatha Christie, *Crooked House*

According to Bargainnier, where her short stories have only one murder, around sixty-percent of Christie's novels have two or more murders. Usually, there are only one or two additional murders. Typically, the first murder is intentional and cold-blooded; the subsequent ones being the result of fear on the part of the murderer. The most likely victim is the character who knows something about the original murder – or is believed by the murderer to know something. Sometimes a character is withholding evidence with the intention of blackmailing the murderer.

These subsequent victims are also usually either unsympathetic or unknown. They are often greedy or stupid. If the reader has little emotional investment in the main victim, they will have even less in the second, who serves only to disrupt or complicate the investigation.

In rare circumstances, it is the second victim who is the 'main' victim, with the first victim having been killed by mistake, or because they discovered the murderer's plans, or simply because the murderer is seeking to make his true motive more difficult to detect.

The Suspects

One of the conventions of the classic murder mystery is that everyone – including the murderer – should be suspected at least once; and that there should be a closed circle of suspects, each of whom will potentially have the means, motive and/or opportunity to kill the victim. One of the rules of 'fair play' is that the murderer will be found within this small group, rather than from the world outside.

How do you create a closed circle of suspects? The cliché is to have a country house surrounded by untrodden snow, or an island cut off by the tide, or some other physical limitation – a ship at sea or a train stranded in a snow-drift. Or you can simply say 'Only someone who knew that Professor Purple was going to be in this place at this time could have killed him.' As long as you can give some semi-plausible reason, the reader will accept it, as it is part of the 'game.' Agatha Christie could have one of her investigators say, 'It must be one of the guests, I don't think it could have been any of the domestic staff,' and the job was done.

How many suspects should you have? The minimum for a novel is probably three, and the maximum about ten. You might have two or three that are quickly eliminated – lacking means, motive and opportunity – and then have three to six real suspects who need further investigation. And the reader should feel that any one of them could potentially be the murderer. Too many suspects and you risk the middle of your story, the investigation, being an endless parade of people being interviewed by the detective, going over the same sequence of events. Too few, and the mystery won't be sufficiently baffling.

As mentioned previously, for plot reasons, suspects tend to be presented on a fairly superficial level, with no deep psychological probing. Typically, they behave according to only one personality trait, or perhaps two contradictory ones. For this reason, it is best to make them as different from each other as possible, so that the reader can easily keep track of them. This probably accounts for the fact that the characters in this type of story are often eccentric – it helps the reader in telling them apart.

The suspects often appear as 'types' rather than as real people: in Agatha Christie's novels, there is a fairly common cast of characters including what she describes in her notebooks as a 'frog-eyed major.' Alongside him there is often a demanding invalid spinster or widow, usually accompanied by a younger and poorer niece whose search for romance is blocked by the need to care for her aunt; a couple who are married – usually unhappily, with him being tempted by another woman; a femme fatale; a ne'er-do-well young man; a butch horsey woman; a doctor or academic, often in some way discredited; a naïve young woman, and a dashing young man.

As well as being on hand to be suspected, each suspect should play a genuine role in the story. They each perform one of two functions – or occasionally both: they provide information that helps the detective in his investigation, or they misdirect him, either deliberately or accidentally.

Some suspects do have means, motive *and* opportunity, but are not the murderer – they are red herrings, diverting the attention of the detective, and the reader, away from the real murderer.

Suspects may also complicate the story in other ways. They may attempt to solve the mystery themselves, and in doing so obstruct the progress of the detective. Or they may fear for another character's safety and so withhold or distort information, even lie or provide a false alibi. This is particularly true in the case of lovers and family members (see below).

Guilty Secrets

Suspects need to act suspiciously. If everyone has nothing to hide and speaks openly and honestly to the detective, they make his job easy, and the mystery is quickly solved. That's not what we want.

Suspects tend to have some kind of secret – some illegal or immoral act, not connected to the murder, of which they are guilty – and this leads them to either lie to the detective or avoid telling him the whole truth. Or they may be aware of another character's secret and wish to protect them.

Poirot, in *Hercule Poirot's Christmas*, says that the detective's task is "to separate the harmless lies from the vital ones." He needs to figure out what information is true and relevant and what is not.

Earl F. Bargainnier lists the suspects in *Death of the Nile* as including a "jewel thief, a terrorist, a kleptomaniac, an alcoholic, a blackmailer, a communist nobleman, a jilted lover following her now married boyfriend, his millionairess wife, and assorted lesser characters." Partly this is Agatha Christie providing a cast of characters who are sufficiently different from each other so that the reader can keep track of them. Partly it is the use of a repertory of 'stock characters' that allows her to people her novel as economically as possible. And using stock characters, even stereotypes, and then subverting the reader's expectations of that type is one of the ways the author deceives us and keeps the mystery alive.

Lovers

"There must be no love interest. The business in hand is to bring a criminal to the bar of justice, not to bring a lovelorn couple to the hymeneal altar." Number 3 of S. S. Van Dine's 'Twenty Rules for Writing Detective Stories'

"It may be that love makes the world go round, but not in the world of detective stories; it makes it go very much askew ... the philandering of young women, however charming, with

young gentlemen, however lantern-jawed, is a tiresome diver-sion from the theme." – W. Somerset Maugham, 'The Decline and Fall of the Detective Story' (1952)

The detective mystery is perhaps unique, at least at novel length, in having no subplot. A romantic subplot is found in many thrillers and adventure stories, and romance stories will often have an action or mystery subplot. But in the tradi-tional murder mystery there is only the investigation, with no room for a romantic interlude for the detective.

But it is wrong to say that there is no place at all for romance in this genre. Among the suspects, there is almost always at least one pair of lovers. They typically represent the innocence that the detective is attempting to restore to the world. And as such, as Marie F. Rodell tells us, when it comes to murder suspects, "… the reader will not seriously consider either or both of the partners in a sympathetic romance unless a potential and acceptable rival is on hand to furnish a happy ending." She goes on to say that casting suspicion on either of both of the young lovers is a way of creating suspense and increasing the reader's desire to see the real murderer identi-fied.

While the lovers may be placed in jeopardy for the purpose of suspense, it is rare for either of them to become a victim – either primary or secondary – of the murderer.

Families

It was Aristotle who first pointed out that a man killing a stranger is much less dramatic than a man killing his own brother. Because most readers have experience of family rela-tionships, they are more easily able to empathise with them in a story. A murder within a family setting, with family mem-bers as suspects, heightens the tension.

Earl F. Bargainnier notes that large families feature in eleven of Agatha Christie's novels. Family groups provide a number of advantages to the writer. They gather for ritual occasions such as birthdays and holiday celebrations and by definition, they are a closed circle. Different relationships exist between family members, some loving and some openly hostile, and some involving hidden and long-standing grievances. Families tend to be hierarchical, with a father or a strong matriarchal figure being the head of the family. Sons and daughters, like the members of a royal family, have an implied order of succession based on birth order and – at least traditionally – by gender. These children may have husbands or wives or fiancées, and there may also be nephews and nieces, cousins, friends, and perhaps a spinster aunt. Family relations can become more complicated – and antagonistic – if the head of the family has been married more than once. Most families also have a black sheep or someone who is romantically involved with a rogue or ne'er-do-well.

Where there is a family, there is almost always a will and the motive of personal gain in the event of the head of the family dying.

Character Clichés

Readers of mystery novels are aware of the conventions and clichés of the genre – a fact that the writer can take advantage of, by subverting these expectations.

The 'least likely suspect' is usually expected to turn out to be the murderer. Or the murderer will be the one person with the cast-iron, unbreakable alibi. Or it will be the person whose innocence is established very early on – often this person is the 'too obvious' suspect, or the person disliked by everyone else, who is eliminated as a suspect until new evidence comes to light later.

Another tradition is that if there is a pleasant young couple who are involved romantically, neither of them can be the murderer. This cliché too can be subverted, by having an innocent lover paired up with the 'wrong' person, and having a suitable replacement lover on hand to provide the required happy ending. This is because the ending of a mystery story needs to establish a new equilibrium, showing that everything has been restored to order. And one easy way of doing that is to have the happy couple go off hand in hand, secure in the knowledge that evil has been thwarted.

Marie F. Rodell writes that if you have a mystery where the main suspects are "...a pretty and sweet young girl of nineteen, a boy in love with her, a sinister Japanese houseboy, a man with motive, means and opportunity, plain to all, and a sweet gentle spinster aunt of the girl's, without apparent motive, means, or opportunity, the aunt is the only suspect to the astute reader." The young lovers cannot be considered suspects, the sinister Japanese youth is too obvious a suspect, and the man with means, motive and opportunity is a classic case of 'most-likely suspect.'

That is not to say that the author cannot exploit his happy young couple to get the maximum suspense out of their situation. The 'innocent accused' is one of the plot variations we will explore more fully when we look at plot.

The Murderer

"... every murderer ... claims the right to be omnipotent ... The problem for the writer is to conceal his demonic pride from the other characters and from the reader..." – W. H. Auden, 'The Guilty Vicarage.'

The murderer needs to be intelligent, ingenious and resourceful. He or she will have to match wits with the detective, and we want the battle to be an entertaining contest. Poe referred to him as "an unprincipled man of genius." But the murderer must also blend into the crowd, seeming to be just another person caught up in events. He must appear, as Carolyn Wells says, to be what he is not; or not appear to be what he is. He is cold and self-centered, but must not appear this way to others.

The murder is premeditated – carefully planned and executed. The murderer is a 'cold-blooded' killer, not acting angrily on the spur of the moment. He tries not leave physical clues behind – unless they are 'red herrings' to lead the detective off on the wrong trail. His coolness means the murderer does not panic, even when the detective appears to be making progress in his investigation. He is careful not to act in any way that might reveal his guilt. He lies convincingly and is able to misdirect attention whenever it seems he might be suspected.

The murderer is the character who drives the action of the story: it is he whose actions set events in motion, creating a situation which the other characters – including the detective – must respond to. The murderer is perhaps the most complex character in the story, but this complexity is not revealed until the climax when the 'other side' of his character is finally revealed.

The murderer should be in plain view from the beginning, and yet be someone the reader never really suspects. Only the author will know that he is the murderer until the climax of the story. One of the things that makes detective stories fun is that the murderer could be anyone – as far as the suspects are concerned, he is 'one of us.' They look at each other suspiciously, wondering who the killer is.

Because we don't actually see the murderer as the murderer until the end of the story, he isn't the kind of villain we can boo or hate every time he comes on stage. The only sight of him we have is the murder itself and its consequences. The circumstances of the murder – where it takes place, the weapon, the level of violence involved – tell us something about the killer. The feelings of fear and outrage experienced by the other characters help to show what a terrible thing he has done. Although we do not yet know who he is, we hate him for what he has done, and what he might do next.

Eventually, the murderer must be unmasked. He thought his plan was foolproof, but somehow the detective has seen through it. The murderer himself is a flawed person, and it is probably this flaw that leads to his undoing. We have said that the murderer is arrogant, ego-driven, and this often leads to his undoing. He may become over-confident. Or the detective may force him into an error – an action out of his assumed character – by forcing him to respond instantly, rather than taking his usual time to meticulously plan. As he begins to lose control of the situation, the murderer may become angry and/or afraid, panic may set in, and his carefully created false façade may begin to slip.

As with all of the other suspects, the detective will need to explore whether the person who is the murderer had means, motive, and opportunity. Usually, the murderer will have a cast-iron alibi, proving that he could not have been at the scene when the murder took place – or is believed to have taken place.

The Qualities & Character of the Murderer

The murderer leads a double life: he is able to conceal himself among the other suspects because he appears to be one of them. He usually belongs to the same social class as the victim and the other suspects. He is accepted within their group, and he is safe there as long as he behaves like one of them. If his feelings of fear or guilt – or his egotism – cause him to deviate from accepted social behaviours, then he is at risk of exposure. For this reason, the murderer often appears to be a more like-able – or at least acceptable – person than his victim.

Hiding the murderer's true nature has a dramatic benefit also, as James N. Frey (*How to Write a Damn Good Mystery*) describes: "We have a greater fear of evil people who are pre-tending to be good. The impact of the revelation in the end will be greater if the author has cleverly concealed the evil one's murderous nature from the reader."

Carolyn Wells: "The ideal criminal is a sane, respectable and well-educated man … these escape the reader's suspicion by seeming to belong among the reputable characters of the story."

The murderer acts out of self-interest. He puts his own wants above the rights and needs of others – to the point where he is willing and able to take the life of another person to fulfil his own wishes. His actions are immoral – we might even label them as 'evil' – but he will not *appear* to be evil; he will keep this quality hidden – for the obvious reason that he does not want to be caught.

Bargainnier argues that the murderers in Agatha Christie's detective mysteries are both morally immature and ego-cen-tric. They believe that it is acceptable to solve their own per-sonal problems at the expense of the life of another human being. And that it is acceptable to put other people at risk by making them suspects: in trying to conceal his own guilt, he is quite happy for innocent people to take the blame for his selfish actions. The murderer's pride, his desire to outwit the detective, are a result of his immaturity and egotism. And it is this quality which can lead to his downfall.

The murderer is a deeply flawed or wounded character – some incident in his past makes him believe that his actions are justified: his reasons for committing murder are accept-able in his personal value system, whether he is motivated by jealousy, revenge, ambition, greed, fear – or some combination of these. The murderer must believe that murder is unavoidable: it is the only solution he can see to his problem. He does not see the difference between desire and need. He or she will not differentiate between mistaken self-interest and true self-preservation. But even though he is a damaged person, in the detective mystery the reader should have no liking or pity for the murderer, according to Carolyn Wells, a view backed up by Barbara Norville, who says that he should not be presented as a "wretched victim or circumstances." He is not insane. On the contrary, he is entirely in control of, and responsible for, his own actions. What he does is carefully planned – premeditated, cold-blooded – and carefully carried out. He must be regarded as beyond help – beyond redemption – so that the only way to deal with him is to remove him from society. Permanently.

The murderer will be caught – not because he does something stupid, but because of the fatal flaw in his character. He is either too smart for his own good, or too complacent. It could be a clue overlooked, or an action hastily devised as part of the cover-up that seems to put the character out of character. As the net closes in, panic, fear or anger could cause the murderer to make a serious misstep. Arrogance – and an inability to distinguish between need and desire are among the most prominent of fatal flaws. Murderers who are motivated by a need for revenge, who seek to 'get even' with someone who they believe has wronged them, may be subject to feelings of paranoia: they may feel that everyone is out to get them, fuelling their need to 'prove' themselves by taking control and proving themselves all-powerful. Murder is, as W. H. Auden wrote, a way of attempting to prove one's own omnipotence.

Introducing the Murderer

As we have already noted, the murderer must be in plain view from the very beginning, along with the other suspects. He should never be revealed to be someone who has been off-stage throughout the story or someone the reader has never heard of.

You can introduce the murderer in the first scene as a shad-owy, unidentified figure carrying out the murder. Or we may only see the aftermath of his actions. Either way, when he first appears in daylight, as one of the closed circle of suspects, he should be introduced casually, walking into a scene as if he naturally belongs there. If the murderer seems to be just one among several suspects, part of the group to which all belong, then it will seem natural when the spotlight of suspicion falls on him – he will not seem any more or less likely a suspect than the others. Unless he seeks to be so...

The Least-Likely Suspect

Almost half of Christie's novels and a number of her short stories use this device, and she has been criticised for overus-ing it. The least likely suspect is the person who appears most innocent or who has been most helpful to the detective during the investigation. They have behaved least suspiciously, have the least obvious motive, or seem the least physically capable of carrying out the murder. Sometimes they are even regarded as a potential victim or may seem to have been injured by the murderer.

Earl F. Bargainnier listed the four main ways this can be used:

Supposed Victim as Murderer – Here a person is murdered, but circumstances are such that the reader, and other wit-nesses, believe that the victim was killed in error: it was a case of mistaken identity, and the murderer was really the intended victim. And if the murderer was the intended victim, then they can't possibly be a killer themselves, or so the reader believes. Sometimes the murderer even calls on the detective to protect him or her from a would-be murderer. Here the murderer is so sure of his own superiority that he approaches the detective directly and draws him into the story, believing himself more than a match for the sleuth.

Watson as Murderer – Here someone assisting the detective in his investigation turns out to be the murderer. Agatha

Christie had such a character also be the narrator in one notorious story, but this is a trick that can really only be pulled on the reader once, and so the Watson-murderer is not normally the narrator in such stories.

The Double-Bluff – The murderer is the principal suspect, but then is apparently proved innocent, until the end when he is finally demonstrated to be the murderer after all. The murderer, again believing himself smarter than everyone else, including the detective, may arrange things so that he is bound to be accused, or he may even confess. Either way, he has arranged an alibi such that the detective himself 'proves' the murderer's 'innocence.' Usually, the murderer has an accomplice in such cases. See also 'most-likely suspect' below.

Fake Murder Attempts – The murderer engineers fake attempts on his or her own life in order to divert suspicion. If an attempt is made on someone's life early in the story, then the murderer, the reader assumes, must be someone other than this victim who has suffered the near-miss. This became almost a cliché in Agatha Christie's works, such that her readers were automatically suspicious of any character who was almost but not quite killed.

The least-likely suspect may be someone who is suspected early on then cleared, with suspicion then falling on other characters until the end, or they may never actually fall under suspicion during the course of the detective's investigations, seeming to be beyond suspicion.

The Most-Likely Suspect

This device, according to Bargainnier, is used less often in Agatha Christie's novels, and is used more often in her short stories: the smaller number of suspects in a short story means that the mystery often centres on *how* the murder was committed rather than who did it.

Here the murderer is the person with the strongest motive for wanting the victim dead – he is the one with the most to gain from the death of the victim, and so is the first person everyone suspects.

In such stories, the reader must believe that the murderer is too obvious a suspect so that he can't possibly be the killer. There may be too much evidence pointing to his guilt, arousing the suspicions of the detective: surely no murderer would leave so many clues pointing to himself? Or perhaps the murderer has planted incriminating 'evidence' of his guilt in such a way that it is obvious to detective and reader than it has been planted.

The Murderous Pair

The murderous pair, always a man and a woman, is employed in nineteen of Agatha Christie's novels and six short stories, according to Earl F. Bargainnier. These couples are usually motivated either by a desire to obtain wealth or to eliminate an obstacle to their love – an unwanted husband or wife. The murderous pair have advantages that a lone murderer does not: they can supply alibis for each other and they can act together or separately as needed. In some stories, one of the pair adopts a disguise so as to pretend to be the victim and so confuse witnesses into mistaking the time of the victim's death: the victim is seen alive after the real time of death or witnessed lying dead before the time of death, and so providing the murderer with an alibi.

Sometimes the woman is the man's accomplice, sometimes – like Lady Macbeth – she is the driving force, and sometimes she herself is the actual murderer.

Agatha Christie seemed to enjoy pairing together the most unlikely people: those from different social classes; people of wildly different ages, or degrees of physical attractiveness. She paired people who appeared to despise one another, or who seemed not to know one another. Only when the detective uncovers the connection between the two is he able to unravel the mystery.

Misdirection

The murderous pair, the most-likely and least-likely suspect devices are all means of misdirection, a way for the writer to deceive the reader. Bargainnier lists several other types of misdirection employed by Agatha Christie that are worth considering for your own stories:

He Can't Have Done It – One or more characters – but never the author, who must not mislead the reader – say that the murderer cannot possibly have killed the victim. This is especially effective if the speaker appears to have authorial approval, and if an 'explanation' of why they couldn't possibly have done it is also provided.

Glowing References – Related to the above, here an 'authorially approved' character evaluates the character and/or actions of the murderer is such a way that he appears anything but murderous.

The Murderer in Love – The love of the main romantic couple in a story is usually seen as something innocent and honest, and worth protecting from the suspicion thrown on the couple by the actions of the murderer. Romance is a part of the status quo that the investigator seeks to restore. If the murderer – usually a man – is in a romance with an innocent woman, he is typically seen as above suspicion.

The Murderer is Allowed to Lie – Whereas innocent people are expected to tell the truth, the murderer has no qualms about lying and seeking to throw suspicion on other people. Many times, the murderer is actually describing himself when he speaks about the actions or feelings of another character.

Clues to the Identity of the Murderer

Although the identity of the murderer must remain hidden, clues reveal something about him. *When* and *where* the victim was killed will give some indication of how the murderer operated. *How* the victim was killed will add to the profile: the kind of weapon used. If it is a garrotte, then the killer was coldly efficient and silent, and relatively strong. A more emotional victim picks up a bronze statue and bashes in the victim's head. Poison – at least in Agatha Christie's view – is more likely to be used by women than men. Clues are covered in more depth on the chapter on The Investigation.

The Final Revelation of the Murderer's Identity and Motivation

"The identity of the criminal, disclosed at the last, must be the greatest surprise of the story," writes Carolyn Wells. Information about the murderer has been held back and is only revealed at the end, when the reader then sees this character in a new light. In the murder mystery, he is the only character who seems to change, as he is revealed to have a hidden complexity: a deep emotional need to solve some problem by taking the life of another person. We see that he is more than he appeared to be.

Why the murderer killed the victim is of more importance to the reader than the identity of the murderer. According to the conventions of the genre, there must be a rational explanation – the murder wasn't a random act or the act of a deranged mind. The detective's explanation of the *reason* for the murder is a vital part of the final act of the story. What prompted this person to commit murder? We will also look at motivation in more detail in the chapter on The Investigation.

The Murderer's Fate

It is a convention of the detective mystery genre that truth is triumphant and that justice is seen to be served. Typically, this means that the murderer must be captured and punished. The murderer, in taking the life of another, has broken a moral code, and by causing those around him to fall under suspicion he has broken a social code: the only acceptable fate for him is banishment from society.

The murderer may be taken away, under arrest, to be subjected to trial by jury and, when found guilty – at least in a 1930s murder mystery – to be hanged. Alternatively, at the climax of the story, he or she may suffer an emotional collapse and be declared insane, and taken away to an appropriate institution. But often the murderer is allowed an opportunity to take the 'gentleman's way out' – he is permitted to take his own life. This has the advantage of having a definitive ending to his actions – there is no prolonged wait for a trial and execution. It also helps avoid any complications if the detective's methods might prove to be less than legal if challenged during a trial, or if his evidence is perhaps a little too circumstantial or unlikely.

The Watson

"Sherlock Holmes ... could not tell his own exploits, so he must have a commonplace comrade as a foil – an educated man of action who could both join in the exploits and narrate them. A drab, quiet name for this unostentatious man. Watson would do." – Sir Arthur Conan Doyle

"I am lost without my Boswell." – Sherlock Holmes

"If I irritated him by a certain methodical slowness in my mentality, that irritation served only to make his own flame-like intuitions and impressions flash up the more vividly and swiftly. Such was my humble role in our alliance." – Dr. John H. Watson

"You know, Hastings, in many ways I regard you as my mascot." – Hercule Poirot

Although he is almost always referred to as 'the Watson,' the great detective's assistant was actually created by Poe, not Conan Doyle: but Watson had a name, and the narrator in 'The Murders in the Rue Morgue' didn't.

The Watson character is optional. Not all detectives have them – Miss Marple and Father Brown didn't. Poirot had Captain Hastings. Nero Wolfe had Archie Goodwin. Philo Vance had S. S. Van Dine. Dr Thorndyke had Christopher Jervis. Dr Gideon Fell had Tad Rampole. These characters don't necessarily appear in every story, sometimes they're replaced by another character who acts as the detective's stooge, and sometimes there is both a Watson and an official police inspector in supporting roles.

The murder mystery has some point-of-view restrictions that other genres do not: we don't share the thoughts of the characters, especially the suspects, because to do so would risk giving the game away: we'd know who was telling the truth, and who had something to hide – the murderer would expose himself, or be exposed by the fact that he was the only one whose thoughts we never share, and the suspects would reveal themselves as red herrings. In theory, there is no reason why we could not share the thoughts of the detective – he could narrate his own story, without the need for a Watson. But as storytellers, we often want the detective to keep his own secrets until we reach the moment when an announcement of 'whodunit' will be most dramatic. And you can avoid having your detective pointing out to the reader which clues are significant. Having a Watson also means that our detective doesn't spend all his time talking to himself.

Another theory has it that the Watson is a 'stand-in' for the reader: "He is supposed to say all the things we would if we were in his place. His insights are our insights, so the theory goes, and his confusion is our confusion," writes Frederick Arnold in his essay 'Watsons' (*Murder Ink*). Arnold doesn't believe this, and argues that Watsons exist to be misled by the trail of red herrings, and to misinterpret the clues he finds, until the point where the great detective explains it all to him: "… if there's a wrong conclusion to jump to, he swings into it with the enthusiasm of Tarzan on the vine."

Watsons also exist to give the detective an excuse for explaining things to the reader – there would be no use for his explanation if the Watson knew as much as he did: we've all seen those terrible science fiction movies where the one scientist says to another "As you know, professor…" and proceeds to explain things that the audience needs to know.

It's a mistake to think that Watson's are meant to be dim-witted* – a myth that comes in part from Nigel Bruce's portrayal of Watson opposite Basil Rathbone's Sherlock Holmes. Bruce's bumbling portrayal of Watson is a joy to watch but doesn't do the 'real' Watson full justice.

Bargainnier, perhaps a little unkindly, writes: "Poirot, the man of thought, is balanced by Hastings, the man of action without thought." Hastings complains that Poirot doesn't confide in him – there are two reasons for this. One, it suits the author's purpose not to reveal Poirot's thoughts until the dramatic moment of the announcement of 'whodunit.' And two, Poirot can't share secrets with Hastings, because Hastings is unable to keep a secret, he is – as Bargainnier says – 'utterly transparent' and 'cannot dissemble.' The second reason, of course, being the author's explanation to hide the fact of the first.

Most of the great detectives refuse to share their thinking with their respective Watsons – another excuse they give for this is that they want the Watson to develop their own skills of observation and deduction. And the final excuse being that the detective doesn't want to explain his theory until he has all of the evidence to prove it.

H. R. F. Keating (*Writing Crime Fiction*) has said that a Watson "... needs to be just a little less intelligent than you conceive your readers to be. But only a little." He, along with the reader, is presented with all of the clues, but he fails to see the significance of some things which the reader will spot. Conan Doyle wrote of his own creation, "Watson never for one instant as chorus and chronicler transcends his own limitations. Never once does a flash of wit or wisdom come from him. All is remorselessly eliminated so that he may be Watson." If the reader cannot match wits with the great detective, he likes to think that he can at least do better than dear old Watson. But according to Bargainnier: "This self-satisfaction is, in reality, a clever delusion arranged by the author, for the reader may be as bewildered as the Watson."

Carolyn Wells refers to the Watson as 'the secondary detective': "He serves as a foil for the higher detective's glories. He makes mistakes for the other to correct. He starts false trails to lead the reader astray and to give the superior detective opportunity to scoff at him and to set him right ... this character is a detective who variously hinders or assists..."

One of the things that the detective needs to do during the story is to formulate and disprove hypotheses. Having a Watson character there to present his own theories about what might have happened is one way to allow the detective to discount one or more wrong hypotheses.

Whatever his other characteristics, the Watson is a reliable witness of events: he will repeat what he sees and hears – the relevant and irrelevant. He never lies, but by sharing his own interpretations of events, or by sharing lies which have been told to him, he may unwittingly mislead the reader. And a murderer may sometimes exploit this.

Watsons are often the butt of humour – Sherlock Holmes occasionally makes a comment at his friend's expense; Poirot often does – but are themselves devoid of humour. Even Sir Arthur Conan Doyle observed this: "... Watson ... in the course of seven volumes never knows one gleam of humour or makes a single joke."

Sherlock Holmes narrated his own adventures on only two occasions – Holmes notes that Watson would have made a better job of telling the stories, and Conan Doyle said: "'The Lion's Mane' ... is hampered by being told by Holmes himself, a method which I employed only twice, as it certainly cramps the narrative."

Assuming that you are going to create a Watson for your story, what qualities does he need to have?

First of all, he should *not* be an example of the Thinker personality archetype: you only need one of those in a story! Your Watson should embody the empathy (from the Carer archetype) that the great detective lacks, but also have something of the Warrior in him, if he is to be a man of action. Detective and Watson should both complement and conflict with each other: they should be an 'odd couple' whose friendship ought not to work, but does. Each character should have something to learn from the other.

Honesty and loyalty are almost certain to be required, and a commitment to seeing justice served. And your Watson should probably, as H. R. F. Keating suggests, be not quite as smart as you expect your readers to be; or at least demonstrate some element of weakness that allows the reader to both identify with, and feel superior to, the character. I would suggest making your Watson a novice or 'secondary detective,' someone learning and practising observation and deduction, rather than a bumbling idiot. Whether or not your Watson has a sense of humour is up to you, and you must also decide whether your detective will make jokes at his expense.

You should also make sure your Watson has a reason for being there, other than just to serve as narrator and stooge: Watson being a doctor meant he could contribute something at the scene of the crime, and he was introduced because Holmes needed a roommate. Archie Goodwin served as the man in the field for his house-bound employer. Give your characters a reason for teaming up, and for staying together.

Your Watson should not be so colourful as to outshine your detective – though some have argued that Archie is the main character in the Nero Wolfe stories – but that doesn't mean he has to be a grey man with no personality. By creating contrast with the personality of the detective, you should be able to create a successful partnership that will work through an ongoing series of stories.

And if you're interested in turning the tables in the Holmes-Watson partnership, have a look at the film *Without a Clue* with Michael Caine as Holmes and Ben Kingsley as Watson – great fun!

Minor Characters

Major characters in the mystery get the minimum of characterisation, so minor characters need to get next to nothing. If you invest words in a description of a character and give him a backstory, the reader will expect him to play a significant role. Putting him there as a red herring is a bit of a cheat and is frowned upon.

That is not to say that you can't have one of your characters disguise themselves as a walk-on character at some point in the story, but even then – especially then – you do not want to draw attention to them with elaborate coverage.

The Police

In real life, if a murder occurs the police are called in to investigate. In the detective mystery, we often want someone other than the police to investigate, and so must account for the absence of the usual detective machinery. Sometimes the story detective is a real inspector, acting in an 'off-duty' capacity until the full might of the police can be assembled. Or our detective may have the blessing of a real inspector – as in the case of Poirot and Inspector Japp. Or the amateur might be called in to assist a baffled police force. Or he might investigate a 'cold case' which the police have abandoned, or a case the police believe to be an accident or suicide rather than murder.

The official police force may resent the amateur's 'meddling' in their business, and then we have the antagonistic relationship between Sherlock Holmes and Inspector Lestrade.

Often the official police are relegated to the role of supplying information to the amateur or unofficial detective. Occasionally the official police are portrayed as comically stupid or egotistical. More often they are stolid and unimaginative. But as upholders of the law – part of the status quo of the detective mystery world – they are always honourable, and never brutal or corrupt.

Servants and the Working Class

"... murder is an awkward thing – it upsets the servants and puts the general routine out..." – Lady Angkatell, *Murder After Hours* by Agatha Christie.

In Agatha Christie's fiction – which is typical of the genre in this respect – England consists of the wealthy upper-middle class and the lower orders. The characters of the novel, including the suspects, belong to the first group. The working class, as Bargainnier notes, are either servants or they are 'types' – "...pompous clerks, officious nurses, put-upon secretaries, scruffy radicals, giggly or adenoidal shopgirls, cantankerous gardeners, bored or surly waitresses, and so on."

The servants in a Christie novel tend to resent the upset caused by a murder in the house: "A thing like that – happening to us," says Mrs Medway, the cook in *Murder After Hours*. "I don't feel that I'm going to have a light hand with my pastry." She also warns the parlour maid that it is "... common to be mixed up with the police..."

On the whole, servants demonstrate distrust, fear and even contempt for the police, but tend to be more accepting of an 'unofficial' investigator. If they can be persuaded to talk, the parlour maid can be a valuable source of above and below stairs gossip. But it is necessary to be cautious when using domestic staff to reveal information: Tom Stoppard parodies this at the beginning of his play *The Real Inspector Hound*.

Having covered everyone else, there remains only one more character to explore: the detective. We will look first at the 'Great Detective' of which Sherlock Holmes and Hercule Poirot are the best-known examples. Then we will spend some time with the spinster sleuth, with Miss Marple as our model. And finally, we'll explore what the modern cozy mystery sleuth has in common with the first two types, and how she differs from them.

The Great Detective

"The detective story in the grand manner demands a Great Detective." – Anthony Boucher

One of the best bits about writing a classic mystery story is creating your own detective – coming up with a character that is original, captivating, brilliant, and just a little bit odd: from his beginnings in Edgar Allan Poe's Auguste Dupin, the classic detective has been something of an eccentric. When you think of the great classic detectives, who are the characters that you remember? Sherlock Holmes, of course. Hercule Poirot and Miss Marple. These, along with Nero Wolfe, are the ones we know from movie and television adaptations. Who else was there? S. S. Van Dine's Philo Vance; R. Austin Freeman's Doctor Thorndyke; G. K. Chesterton's Father Brown, and then there was Dr. Gideon Fell, created by John Dickson Carr, who modelled his character in part on G. K. Chesterton. Beyond that, there was a whole slew of grey-suited Inspectors who barely anyone remembers as characters, and who needn't concern us here. There was also Margery Allingham's Albert Campion who, to me, seems lacking in personality; and Dorothy L. Sayer's Lord Peter Wimsey, who is too much of a stereotyped English toff to be much use to us as an example.

Anthony Boucher refers to the Great Detective, and the capital letters are deliberate. He means someone in the Sherlock Holmes or Hercule Poirot style – a larger-than-life investigator whose life revolves around his work. This the detective bequeathed to us by Edgar Allan Poe, and we shall examine him in detail below. As well as Poirot, Agatha Christie created a second memorable investigator, Miss Jane Marple. Miss Marple was an example of the amateur 'spinster sleuth,' created in part as a reaction against the over-the-top eccentric Great Detective: she is so ordinary that she may go almost unnoticed. We must explore how she differs in character and in approach to investigation to our Great Detective. Miss Marple then serves as a prototype for our third and final type of sleuth, the hero of the modern cozy mystery. This character is usually a strong and vibrant amateur sleuth, typically female, but no longer a maiden aunt. She combines some elements of the Great Detective and the Spinster Sleuth but also draws on some characteristics of the heroine in the romance genre.

To discover what makes a successful Great Detective we can examine the classic examples listed above to see what features they have in common, and what factors make them unique and memorable. I will pick out a few quotations that give a taste of these characters, but I would recommend reading the first novels and short stories that feature each of these characters in order to see how each detective was introduced to the world by their creator.

To give some structure to our study of the great detective, I'm going to split it into three parts: the *character* of the detective; that is, the personality archetype most commonly associated with the classic detective; and then the *skills and experience* this person must possess in order to operate successfully as an investigator; and finally some notes on the *physical appearance* of detectives.

Character Archetype: The Thinker

The detective in the classic mystery story is an example of the Thinker character archetype. The detective is one of the few Thinker-heroes we find in popular fiction and movies – the scientist and certain types of medical investigators are probably the only others. The classic detective conforms fairly closely to the archetype, demonstrating most of the positive qualities, and some of the negative ones.

Before looking at the detective in detail, let's quickly recap the main features of the Thinker archetype. Most systems of personality or character archetypes include a 'thinker,' and it is one of the six character archetypes I prefer to use.

The Thinker Archetype

Motivation: To seek the truth; to pursue knowledge.

Behaviours: Responds to life with the head rather than the heart; able to think about solutions to problems, but tends to overthink options and consequences, so is less able to take action to put them to practical effect; shuns emotion, seeing it as a weakness.

Values: Truth is the absolute goal, with logic and reason valued as the tools for reaching it. Moral and ethical values, and a respect for justice, are valued insofar as they are accepted as corollaries of truth.

Weaknesses: Sees everything in terms of cause and effect, so is challenged by random events and chaotic circumstances, seeking to impose order in all things; tends to overthink things, lacking the ability to make a pragmatic choice in the face of lack of data; withdraws into an internal world, rather than engaging with the real world. Valuing absolute truth at all times, his words can sometimes seem callous, lacking the tact needed in everyday relationships with other human beings.

Needs: As the Thinkers lacks both the Warrior and Carer aspects of character, he needs to develop (a) an ability to take action based on what he has learned; and (b) empathy – an acceptance and understanding of his own emotions and of the feelings of others. A practical and empathic application of knowledge and experience will enable him to develop genuine wisdom.

The classic detective is an almost pure example of this archetype. As a Thinker, the detective has an approach to life that centres almost entirely on the cerebral, depending on the powers of the mind, and for the most part, his existence is internal. He shuns emotion – the Carer aspects of himself – but does, to some extent, embrace aspects of his Warrior-self: he is able to put what he has learned to practical use – to take action in order to bring about a solution to a problem, and in doing so he can take on the role of leader. And his egotism can occasionally develop into a Warrior-like battle of wills with a rival or opponent. While he pursues knowledge and truth, he does not typically see them as a source of power, except perhaps in his attempts to impose order on a chaotic world.

In the classic mystery story, there is no character development on the part of the detective-hero – he does not grow to overcome his weaknesses, nor does he come to meet his needs as a human being. There is often a Watson character who serves as a contrast to the hero, and who possesses the quality of empathy that the detective lacks.

A lack of empathy means that the detective's social skills are often under-developed, and he is often an outsider, feeling no sense of belonging to any particular group. He is aware of the importance of society on an intellectual level, that its rules are necessary in order for large groups of people to be able to co-exist in a limited space, and he understands the interdependence of its systems, but he feels no emotional attachment to it. The detective regards this absence of emotional connection as an important asset, as we'll see below. And being an 'outsider' is often demonstrated in non-conformist or eccentric behaviour, particularly in terms of lifestyle and living space.

Let's look at some of the key aspects of the Thinker, and see how they are manifested in the classic detective.

A Lack of Emotion

"Detection is, or ought to be, an exact science and should be treated in the same cold and unemotional manner." So says Sherlock Holmes in *The Sign of Four*. In the same novel, Watson accuses him of being 'an automaton – a calculating machine' and says: "There is something positively inhuman in you at times." To which Holmes says: "The emotional qualities are antagonistic to clear reasoning."

The Thinker mistrusts emotional feeling, believing it be the antithesis of objective observation and reasoning. To become emotionally involved is to introduce the possibility of bias, and of wishful thinking. And so The Thinker remains cold and aloof.

"It is not I who am sentimental! That is an English failing! It is in England that they weep over young sweethearts and dying mothers and devoted children. Me, I am logical!" – Hercule Poirot, *Overdose of Death*

The Detective's Ego

"My name is Hercule Poirot," he said quietly, "and I am probably the greatest detective in the world." – Agatha Christie, *The Mystery of the Blue Train*

In *The Sign of Four,* Sherlock Holmes describes himself as 'the only unofficial consulting detective': "I am the last and highest court of appeal in detection. When Gregson, or Lestrade, or Athelney Jones are out of their depths – which, by the way, is their normal state – the matter is laid before me. I examine the data, as an expert, and pronounce a specialist's opinion." And in *A Study in Scarlet*, he says: "I know well that I have it in me to make my name famous. No man lives or has ever lived who has brought the same amount of study and of natural talent to the detection of crime which I have done."

Hercule Poirot says he is not burdened with an Englishman's false modesty: "The talents that I possess - I would salute them in another. As it happens, in my own particular line, there is no one to touch me. *C'est dommage!* As it is, I admit freely and without the hypocrisy that I am a great man. I have the order, the method and the psychology in an unusual degree. I am, in fact, Hercule Poirot ('The Mystery of the Bagdad Chest')

The Thinker archetype feels safety in, and is protected by, his intellectual capabilities. His intelligence is a form of strength that he relies on. This can mean that he may feel challenged by the intellectual abilities of others, and so may be reluctant to acknowledge them. He may feel a need to prove himself intellectually superior to those around him, and so may belittle their abilities. Or he may seek to baffle them or challenge them to prove his greater worth.

Eccentricity

Earl F. Bargainnier has said that there are three main ways to create a bond between the detective hero and the reader, "… so that if the reader does not 'identify,' he will at least admire and wish to follow the detective's processes of discovery." The first method is to make the detective an amateur, or at least an unofficial investigator. It is easier for the reader to see himself alongside such a character, than with a professional police officer. The second method is through use of a 'Watson' – a loyal partner or assistant.

"The third and most important method of creating reader response to a detective is to incorporate into his personality features which make his intellectual and moral superiority less formidable," writes Bargainnier. The detective needs to have "… eccentricities, idiosyncrasies, mannerisms or other distinctive peculiarities which offset his immense intellect." These may be related to the way he speaks, his appearance, or habits. Poirot is a monstrous egotist, but by allowing us to laugh at his excesses, to 'bring him down a notch,' his creator enables us to enjoy him. These lesser qualities should be enough to entertain, but not so extreme that they turn the reader off.

"Hercule Poirot shrugged his shoulders. He was at his most foreign today. He was out to be despised but patronised." – Five Little Pigs

The detective's faults and eccentricities help him to appeal to the reader. They can also help him, as in the quote above, by causing others to underestimate his abilities.

Physical appearance is one aspect of character that can reflect the detective's eccentricity – we will explore that shortly. Edgar Allan Poe didn't give us much of a description of Auguste Dupin, instead relying on two things which have been much used by subsequent writers: an unusual place of residence and eccentric behaviours. Having met Dupin, the unnamed narrator of 'The Murders in the Rue Morgue,'

"...was permitted to be at the expense of renting, and furnishing in a style which suited the rather fantastic gloom of our common temper, a time-eaten and grotesque mansion, long deserted through superstitions into which we did not inquire, and tottering to its fall in a retired and desolate portion of the Faubourg St. Germain." And it is within this decaying building that the two bachelors live their eccentric lives:

Had the routine of our life at this place been known to the world, we should have been regarded as madmen – although, perhaps, as madmen of a harmless nature. Our seclusion was perfect. We admitted no visitors. Indeed the locality of our retirement had been carefully kept a secret from my own former associates; and it had been many years since Dupin had ceased to know or be known in Paris. We existed within ourselves alone.

It was a freak of fancy in my friend (for what else shall I call it?) to be enamoured of the night for her own sake; and into this bizarrerie, as into all his others, I quietly fell; giving myself up to his wild whims with a perfect abandon. The sable divinity would not herself dwell with us always; but we could counterfeit her presence. At the first dawn of the morning we closed all the massy shutters of our old building; lighted a couple of tapers which, strongly perfumed, threw out only the ghastliest and feeblest of rays. By the aid of these we then busied our souls in dreams – reading, writing, or conversing, until warned by the clock of the advent of the true Darkness. Then we sallied forth into the streets, arm in arm, continuing the topics of the day, or roaming far and wide until a late hour, seeking, amid the wild lights and shadows of the populous city, that infinity of mental excitement which quiet observation can afford.

Arthur Conan Doyle created a similarly bohemian residence for his principal characters at 221b Baker Street, adding a level of detail that has allowed recognisable reconstructions of the sitting room to be created in museums in several countries, as well as in television and film adaptations:

*An anomaly which often struck me in the character of my
friend Sherlock Holmes was that, although in his methods of
thought he was the neatest and most methodical of mankind,
and although also he affected a certain quiet primness of dress,
he was none the less in his personal habits one of the most
untidy men that ever drove a fellow-lodger to distraction. Not
that I am in the least conventional in that respect myself. The
rough-and-tumble work in Afghanistan, coming on the top of
a natural Bohemianism of disposition, has made me rather
more lax than befits a medical man. But with me there is a
limit, and when I find a man who keeps his cigars in the coal-
scuttle, his tobacco in the toe end of a Persian slipper, and his
unanswered correspondence transfixed by a jack-knife into the
very centre of his wooden mantelpiece, then I begin to give myself virtuous airs. I have always held, too, that pistol practice
should be distinctly an open-air pastime; and when Holmes,
in one of his queer humours, would sit in an arm-chair with
his hair-trigger and a hundred Boxer cartridges, and proceed
to adorn the opposite wall with a patriotic V. R. done in bullet-
pocks, I felt strongly that neither the atmosphere nor the
appearance of our room was improved by it.*

*Our chambers were always full of chemicals and of criminal
relics which had a way of wandering into unlikely positions,
and of turning up in the butter-dish or in even less desirable
places. But his papers were my great crux. He had a horror of
destroying documents, especially those which were connected
with his past cases, and yet it was only once in every year or
two that he would muster energy to docket and arrange them...*
('The Musgrave Ritual')

Hercule Poirot could not live in such surroundings: "For neatness of any kind he had an absolute passion. To see an orna-
ment set crookedly, or a speck of dust, or a slight disarray in
one's attire, was torture to the little man until he could ease
his feelings by remedying the matter." (*Murder on the Links*)
Accordingly, Poirot makes his home in Whitehaven Mansions
– "... having chosen this particular building entirely on

account of its strictly geometrical appearance and proportions." (*The ABC Murders*)

Poirot, of course, had other eccentricities beyond his need for neatness. Bargainnier writes that Agatha Christie used the typical English person's stereotype of a 'comic foreigner' who struggles to speak English correctly.

But, of course, Poirot's 'foreignness' is something that he occasionally hides behind, in order that people might underestimate him:

"It is true that I can speak the exact, the idiomatic English. But, my friend, to speak the broken English is an enormous asset. It leads people to despise you. They say - a foreigner - he can't even speak English properly. It is not my policy to terrify people - instead I invite their gentle ridicule. Also I boast! An Englishman he says often, 'A fellow who thinks as much of himself as that cannot be worth much.' That is the English point of view. It is not at all true. And so, you see, I put people off their guard. Besides, he added, it has become a habit." (*Three-Act Tragedy*)

Poirot demonstrates his mastery of English in the 'drawing room scene,' where he draws together the suspects and gives his final explanation of the solution to the mystery: "A new note crept into his voice. He was no longer a ridiculous little man with an absurd moustache and dyed hair, he was a hunter very close to his quarry." (*Mrs McGinty's Dead*)

Skills and Experience
"A detective novel must have a detective in it; and a detective is not a detective unless he detects." – S. S. Van Dine.

Writing about the creation of Sherlock Holmes, Conan Doyle acknowledged that his detective had been 'suggested' in part "... by Edgar Allen Poe's detective, which, after all, ran on the lines of all other detectives who have appeared in literature." In the opening chapter of *The Sign of Four*, Sherlock Holmes reveals three of the qualities necessary for the 'ideal detective' to have: the powers of observation and deduction, coupled with the knowledge that comes with experience. Sir Sydney

Smith, a real-life professor of forensic medicine, in his book *Mostly Murder* (1959), identifies a fourth: "... the power of constructive imagination, always strictly controlled by the intellect, an essential quality when there are no more facts to be observed and no further inferences to be drawn. Holmes himself used this power successfully in *The Sign of Four* when he was baffled in his search for the missing launch. 'I then put myself in the place of Small [the criminal] and looked at it as a man of his capacity would ... I wondered what I should do myself if I were in his shoes.'"

Let's look at each of these four in more detail.

Observation

"...observation has become with me, of late, a species of necessity." – Auguste Dupin, 'The Murders in the Rue Morgue.'

"You see, but you do not observe." – Sherlock Holmes, 'A Scandal in Bohemia.'

"The world is full of obvious things which nobody by any chance ever observes." – Sherlock Holmes, *The Hound of the Baskervilles*

Poe was the first to compare the tale of ratiocination with a game, though he preferred draughts to chess for his analogy, and wrote that "...the analyst throws himself into the spirit of his opponent, identifies himself therewith, and not unfrequently sees thus, at a glance, the sole methods (sometimes indeed absurdly simple ones) by which he may seduce into error or hurry into miscalculation." He must move beyond mere knowledge of the rules of the game: "He makes, in silence, a host of observations and inferences. So, perhaps, do his companions; and the difference in the extent of the information obtained, lies not so much in the validity of the inference as in the quality of the observation. The necessary knowledge is that of what to observe. Our player confines himself not at all; nor, because the game is the object, does he reject deductions from things external to the game. He examines the countenance of his partner, comparing it carefully with that of each of his opponents." ('The Murders in the Rue Morgue')

Dupin scrutinized everything – not excepting the bodies of the victims. We then went into the other rooms, and into the yard ... The examination occupied us until dark, when we took our departure. ('The Murders in the Rue Morgue')

After which the detective engages in an action which is explained neither to the reader nor the narrator: "On our way home my companion stepped in for a moment at the office of one of the daily papers." Following the search, the narrator admits that he observed nothing which he had not already gleaned from the newspaper reports. Dupin astonishes him by stating that he saw something 'peculiar' which has enabled him to solve the mystery of the murders. He has, he says, put in motion events which will enable him to prove his theory correct.

Dupin says that the narrator, in reading the witness accounts, has failed to see the evidence they present. "You have observed nothing distinctive. Yet there was something to be observed." To Dupin, the meaning of the evidence is clear, and enabled him to form his theory even before he visited the scene. There follows a detailed exploration of the evidence, including the details of the 'locked room' and its surroundings, and of the injuries on the bodies of the women.

Dupin's plans then come to fruition, and his hypothesis is proved true.

Deduction – Deductive and Inductive Reasoning

"How in the world did you deduce that?" – Watson, *The Sign of Four*

"... when you have eliminated the impossible, whatever remains, however improbable, must be the truth." – Sherlock Holmes, *The Sign of Four*

"I never guess. It is a shocking habit – destructive to the logical faculty. What seems strange to you is only so because you do

not follow my train of thought or observe the small facts upon which large inferences may depend." – Sherlock Holmes, *The Sign of Four*

"The true work, it is done from within. The little grey cells - remember always the little grey cells, mon ami!" – Hercule Poirot, *Murder on the Links*

Poe called his three detective stories tales of *ratiocination*, referring to the act of analytical reasoning, which includes the act of inferring by deduction or induction. More on each of these shortly. The narrator of 'The Murders in the Rue Morgue' has this to say about his friend, Dupin:

At such times I could not help remarking and admiring (although from his rich ideality I had been prepared to expect it) a peculiar analytic ability in Dupin. He seemed, too, to take an eager delight in its exercise – if not exactly in its display – and did not hesitate to confess the pleasure thus derived. He boasted to me, with a low chuckling laugh, that most men, in respect to himself, wore windows in their bosoms, and was wont to follow up such assertions by direct and very startling proofs of his intimate knowledge of my own. His manner at these moments was frigid and abstract; his eyes were vacant in expression; while his voice, usually a rich tenor, rose into a treble which would have sounded petulant but for the deliber- ateness and entire distinctness of the enunciation.

Early in *The Sign of Four*, Sherlock Holmes describes his method as 'analytical reasoning from effects to causes,' and expands on this later in the story:

"In solving a problem of this sort, the grand thing is to be able to reason backward. That is a very useful accomplishment, and a very easy one, but people do not prac- tise it much. In the everyday affairs of life it is more useful to reason forward, and so the other comes to be neglected. There are fifty who can reason synthetically for one who can reason analytically ...

"Most people, if you describe a train of events to them, will tell you what the result would be. They can put those events together in their minds, and argue from them that something

will come to pass. There are few people, however, who, if you told them a result, would be able to evolve from their own inner consciousness what the steps were which led up to that result. This power is what I mean when I talk of reasoning backward or analytically."

If you try and approach 'deduction' in terms of formal theories of logic or valid reasoning, you quickly become bogged down in syllogisms and various laws which take you further and further away from what fictional detectives do. Deduction as practised by Sherlock Holmes is actually based on the *scientific method*, which the *Oxford English Dictionary* defines as: "a method or procedure that has characterized natural science since the 17th century, consisting in systematic observation, measurement, and experiment, and the formulation, testing, and modification of hypotheses."

This method begins with an observation of reality, and a theory or hypothesis is then put forward to explain the phenomena that have been observed. The theory is then tested by using it to predict an outcome: experiments are then carried out to see if the prediction is true. If the prediction is proved true, the theory is accepted as a possible explanation of the observed phenomena. The 'proof' must be repeatable to be accepted. If the prediction is proved false, the theory must be replaced or rethought. Scientific inquiry is expected to be as objective as possible in order to minimize bias. The aim is to provide a theory that supports the observable facts, not to seek facts which support a pet theory. Though a theory can be used as a way of exploring what and where to look for observable phenomena.

In science, any theory is only ever the 'best possible explanation we have at the present time,' and is always subject to be disproved or in need of further development, as more facts are uncovered. As such, a scientific theory is never accepted as an absolute truth. It is the best possible explanation of a set of known data. The theory seeks to account for the reality that has been observed, ideally providing the simplest and most likely – the most 'economical' or 'elegant' – explanation.

American philosopher Charles Sanders Peirce, who developed the concept of abductive reasoning, offered the following form:

The surprising fact, C, is observed;
But if A were true, C would be a matter of course,
Hence, there is reason to suspect that A is true.

Where A is an explanation of the cause of C or even a scientific 'law.'

As Sherlock Holmes explains, he must work backwards from what he has observed – the evidence or effect – and seek to develop a theory regarding what brought about this outcome, the cause.

We can see the stages in Holmes' method as being:

   i.   Observation – gathering evidence and information
   ii. Application of specialist knowledge and experience
   iii. Deduction – exploring the possible meaning(s) of the evidence
   iv. Theorising – using constructive imagination to create a number of hypotheses that explain the evidence
   v.   Testing the hypotheses – discounting those that are proved false; adapting those that show promise as new facts emerge; eliminating the theories in turn – the 'impossible' – so that only the truth – 'however improbable' – remains.
   vi. Solution

In practice, Holmes appears to move from (i) directly to (vi), as if by magic – and it is only when he explains the steps he took to reach the solution that (ii) to (v) become apparent.

"One forms provisional theories and then waits for time or fuller knowledge to explode them." – Sherlock Holmes, 'The Sussex Vampire'

Another kind of deduction practised by fictional detectives is based on a form of case-based inductive reasoning. Inductive reasoning uses specific premises to supply strong evidence for the truth of the conclusion; the conclusion is supposed to be *probable*, based upon the evidence given, rather than an absolute proof.

For example:

- There are 20 balls in a bag, some are black and some white.
- Four balls are drawn from the bag, three black and one white.
- Therefore, it is probable that initially, the bag contained 15 black balls and 5 white.

Inductive reasoning also allows for reasoning by analogy, as often practised by Miss Marple when she compares a character in an investigation with a character she knows from her own village:

- P and Q are similar in respect to properties a, b, and c.
- Object P has been observed to have further property x.
- Therefore, Q probably also has property x.

Analogical reasoning is frequently used in common sense. A more refined version of it is *case-based* reasoning, which is the process of solving new problems based on the solutions of similar past problems. A car mechanic, a doctor, and a detective will all use this method to some extent.

In the journal *Artificial Intelligence Communications* (1994), Agnar Aamodt and Enric Plaza wrote that case-based reasoning involves the following four steps:

- *Retrieve:* Given a problem, retrieve from memory cases relevant to solving it.
- *Reuse:* Map the solution from the previous case to the new problem. This may involve adapting the solution as needed to fit the new situation.
- *Revise:* Having mapped the previous solution to the target situation, test the new solution in the real world (or a simulation) and, if necessary, revise.

- *Retain:* After the solution has been successfully adapted to the target problem, store the resulting experience as a new case in memory.

In *A Study in Scarlet*, Sherlock Holmes speaks of applying a case-based approach: "Here in London we have lots of government detectives and lots of private ones. When these fellows are at fault, they come to me, and I manage to put them on the right scent. They lay all the evidence before me, and I am generally able, by the help of my knowledge of the history of crime, to set them straight. There is a strong family resemblance about misdeeds, and if you have all the details of a thousand at your finger ends, it is odd if you can't unravel the thousand and first."

Knowledge – Forensic versus Psychological

Fictional detectives tend to fall into one of two categories – those who seek physical evidence in their investigations, and those who seek psychological evidence. Sherlock Holmes and Doctor Thorndyke, for example, deal mostly with physical evidence; Hercule Poirot and Father Brown with psychological.

Holmes has written monographs on specific topics in relation to his work, including 'Upon the Distinction between the Ashes of the Various Tobaccos,' which enumerates "a hundred and forty forms of cigar, cigarette, and pipe tobacco, with coloured plates illustrating the difference in the ash." Then there is his "... monograph on the tracing of footsteps, with some remarks upon the uses of plaster of Paris as a preservative of impresses." And finally, "...a curious little work upon the influence of a trade upon the form of the hand, with lithotypes of the hands of slaters, sailors, cork-cutters, compositors, weavers, and diamond-polishers. That is a matter of great practical interest to the scientific detective – especially in cases of unclaimed bodies, or in discovering the antecedents of criminals." All are mentioned in *The Sign of Four*.

In the same story, Holmes examines a pocket watch and is able to deduce a number of things about its previous owner. In *The Hound of the Baskervilles* he performs a similar feat with a walking stick; in 'The Blue Carbuncle' it is a hat, in 'The Yellow Face' a pipe. Footprints are mentioned in 26 of the 60 Sherlock Holmes stories.

Again in *The Hound of the Baskervilles*, Holmes says: "There are seventy-five perfumes, which it is very necessary that a criminal expert should be able to distinguish from each other, and cases have more than once within my own experience depended on their prompt recognition."

The Little Grey Cells of the Brain – Psychological Detection

In the Hercule Poirot novel *Murder on the Links*, the narrator says: "'Order' and 'Method' were his gods. He had a certain disdain for tangible evidence, such as footprints and cigarette ash, and would maintain that taken by themselves, they would never enable a detective to solve a problem." And in *The Big Four:* "He had always scoffed at the popular idea of the human bloodhound who assumed wonderful disguises to track criminals, and who paused at every footprint to measure it." When Poirot adopts a disguise in the same novel, it is left for the reader to decide whether this statement is irony, a clue, or misdirection.

Poirot described his own approach to detection in *Murder on the Links:*

"There is such a thing as the individual touch." Poirot suddenly assumed his lecturing manner, and addressed us collectively. "I am speaking to you now of the psychology of crime. Monsieur Giraud knows quite well that each criminal has his particular method, and that the police, when called in to investigate, say, a case of burglary, can often make a shrewd guess at the offender, simply by the peculiar methods he has employed ... Man is an unoriginal animal. Unoriginal within the law in his daily respectable life, equally unoriginal outside the law. If a man commits a crime, any other crime he commits will resemble it closely. The English murderer who disposed of his wives in succession by drowning them in their baths was a case in point. Had he varied his methods, he might have escaped detection to this day. But he obeyed the common dictates of human nature, arguing that what had once succeeded

would succeed again, and he paid the penalty of his lack of originality."

"And the point of all this?" sneered Giraud.

"That, when you have two crimes precisely similar in design and execution, you find the same brain behind them both. I am looking for that brain, Monsieur Giraud, and I shall find it. Here we have a true clue – a psychological clue. You may know all about cigarettes and match ends, Monsieur Giraud, but I, Hercule Poirot, know the mind of man."

Constructive Imagination – Theorising

"It is a capital mistake to theorise before one has data. Insensibly one begins to twist the facts to suit theories, instead of theories to suit facts." – Sherlock Holmes, 'A Scandal in Bohemia'

"I wondered what I should do myself if I were in his shoes." – Sherlock Holmes, *The Sign of Four*

Poe, in his prologue for 'The Murders in the Rue Morgue,' also credited the analytical mind with imagination, and argued that such a faculty should be differentiated from mere fancy: "The analytical power should not be confounded with simple ingenuity; for while the analyst is necessarily ingenious, the ingenious man is often remarkably incapable of analysis. The constructive or combining power, by which ingenuity is usually manifested ... has been so frequently seen in those whose intellect bordered otherwise upon idiocy, as to have attracted general observation among writers on morals. Between ingenuity and the analytic ability there exists a difference far greater, indeed, than that between the fancy and the imagination, but of a character very strictly analogous. It will be found, in fact, that the ingenious are always fanciful, and the truly imaginative never otherwise than analytic."

Observation and Deduction in Action 1 – The Great Detective's 'Mind-Reading Trick'

Also in the prologue to 'The Murders in the Rue Morgue,' Poe writes that as a strong man enjoys putting his muscles into action, so the analytical mind derives pleasure from such mental challenges as 'enigmas, conundrums, and hieroglyphics,' and that his solutions – the disentangling of such mysteries or puzzles – can seem, to the ordinary mind, to be "...preternatural. His results, brought about by the very soul and essence of method, have, in truth, the whole air of intuition."

Sherlock Holmes, in *A Study in Scarlet*, is less than complimentary about Poe's detective: "Dupin was a very inferior fellow. That trick of his of breaking in on his friends' thoughts with an apropos remark after a quarter of an hour's silence is really very showy and superficial." But while Holmes claimed not to be impressed, Conan Doyle obviously was: he had Holmes demonstrate the 'mind-reading trick' in both 'The Adventure of the Dancing Men' – "So Watson, you do not propose to invest in South African Securities." – and 'The Adventure of the Cardboard Box' (later cut and repeated in 'The Adventure of the Resident Patient') – "You are right, Watson. It does seem a most preposterous way of settling a dispute."

A journal article written by Holmes on the 'Science of Deduction and Analysis' (mentioned in *A Study in Scarlet*) speaks of "...a momentary expression, a twitch of a muscle or a glance of an eye, to fathom a man's inmost thoughts. Deceit, according to him, was an impossibility in the case of one trained to observation and analysis. His conclusions were as infallible as so many propositions of Euclid. So startling would his results appear to the uninitiated that until they learned the processes by which he had arrived at them they might well consider him as a necromancer."

Observation and Deduction in Action 2 – Sherlock Holmes' Party Piece

In *A Study in Scarlet*, when he comes upon the magazine article written by Holmes, Watson initially dismisses it as 'ineffable twaddle':

... it attempted to show how much an observant man might learn by an accurate and systematic examination of all that came in his way ... Like all other arts, the Science of Deduction and Analysis is one which can only be acquired by long and

patient study, nor is life long enough to allow any mortal to attain the highest possible perfection in it. Before turning to those moral and mental aspects of the matter which present the greatest difficulties, let the inquirer begin by mastering more elementary problems. Let him, on meeting a fellow-mortal, learn at a glance to distinguish the history of the man, and the trade or profession to which he belongs. Puerile as such an exercise may seem, it sharpens the faculties of observation, and teaches one where to look and what to look for. By a man's finger-nails, by his coat-sleeve, by his boots, by his trouser-knees, by the callosities of his forefinger and thumb, by his expression, by his shirt-cuffs–by each of these things a man's calling is plainly revealed. That all united should fail to enlighten the competent inquirer in any case is almost inconceivable.

Holmes defends his article: "I have a turn both for observation and for deduction. The theories which I have expressed there, and which appear to you to be so chimerical, are really extremely practical – so practical that I depend upon them for my bread and cheese." In order to prove that this is more than twaddle, Holmes explains to Watson how he had been able to deduce, at their first meeting, that Watson had been a medical officer in Afghanistan.

Arthur Conan Doyle based this ability of Holmes' on incidents he had observed during his medical training at the University of Edinburgh, where the surgeon Doctor Joseph Bell was a teacher: "Bell was a very remarkable man in body and mind," Conan Doyle wrote. "He was thin, wiry, dark with a high-nosed, acute face, penetrating grey eyes, angular shoulders, and a jerky way of walking. His voice was high and discordant. He was a very skilful surgeon, but his strong point was diagnosis, not only of disease, but of occupation and character." And also: "... he often learned more of the patient by a few quick glances than I had done by my questions. Occasionally the results were very dramatic..."

Later in the same piece, recalling the creation of Sherlock Holmes, Conan Doyle said: "Gaboriau had rather attracted me by the neat dovetailing of his plots, and Poe's masterful detective, M. Dupin, had from boyhood been one of my heroes. But could I bring an addition of my own? I thought of my old teacher Joe Bell, of his eagle face, of his curious ways, of his eerie trick of spotting details. If he were a detective he would surely reduce this fascinating but unorganized business to something nearer to an exact science. I would try if I could get this effect. It was surely possible in real life, so why should I not make it plausible in fiction? It is all very well to say that a man is clever, but the reader wants to see examples of it – such examples as Bell gave us every day in the wards."

Conan Doyle employed this technique in many of the Holmes stories, usually early on as an introduction, a way of demonstrating the detective's abilities: "He shows his powers by ... clever little deductions, which often have nothing to do with the matter in hand, but impress the reader with a general sense of power." Examples include:

'The Red-Headed League' – *"Beyond the obvious facts that he has at some time done manual labour, that he takes snuff, that he a is a Freemason, that he has been in China, and that he has done a considerable amount of writing lately, I can deduce nothing else."*

'The Norwood Builder' – *"You mentioned your name as if I should recognize it, but I assure you, that beyond the obvious facts that you are a bachelor, a solicitor, a Freemason, and an asthmatic. I know nothing whatever about you."*

In 'The Greek Interpreter' Holmes and his brother Mycroft analyse two men coming towards them, casually trading deductions.

Physical Appearance – What Does a Great Detective Look Like?

The short answer to this is: He can look any way you want him to look. But let's look at how some of the greatest great detectives have been 'shown' to their readers.

The fact that almost everyone in the world seems to know what Sherlock Holmes looks like is a result of the skills of artist Sidney Paget as much as those of Holmes' creator Sir Arthur Conan Doyle. Paget drew Holmes with a deerstalker hat and Inverness cape, neither of which is mentioned in the stories. Paget also made Holmes more handsome than Conan Doyle imagined him: "I saw him as very tall ... He had, as I imagined him, a thin razor-like face, with a great hawk's-bill of a nose, and two small eyes, set close together on either side of it." And elsewhere Conan Doyle said he saw Holmes as a "... hawk-faced man, approaching more to the Red Indian type..."

The First Appearance of Sherlock Holmes

Holmes does not appear until late in the first chapter of *A Study in Scarlet* – initially, we are introduced by reputation: Watson's acquaintance 'young Stamford' says:

"He is a little queer in his ideas – an enthusiast in some branches of science ... I have no idea what he intends to go in for. I believe he is well up in anatomy, and he is a first-class chemist; but, as far as I know, he has never taken out any systematic medical classes. His studies are very desultory and eccentric, but he has amassed a lot of out-of-the-way knowledge which would astonish his professors."

And:

"Holmes is a little too scientific for my tastes – it approaches to cold-bloodedness. I could imagine his giving a friend a little pinch of the latest vegetable alkaloid, not out of malevolence, you understand, but simply out of a spirit of inquiry in order to have an accurate idea of the effects. To do him justice, I think that he would take it himself with the same readiness. He appears to have a passion for definite and exact knowledge."

And his thirst for knowledge – "... may be pushed to excess. When it comes to beating the subjects in the dissecting-rooms with a stick, it is certainly taking rather a bizarre shape..." – "...to verify how far bruises may be produced after death."

When we do finally meet Holmes, he greets Watson and says: "You have been in Afghanistan, I perceive." And proceeds with enthusiasm to show him a chemical discovery he has just made which will enable him to confirm the presence of bloodstains. We then see Holmes "sticking a small piece of plaster over the prick on his finger. 'I have to be careful,' he continued, turning to me with a smile, 'for I dabble with poisons a good deal.' He held out his hand as he spoke, and I noticed that it was all mottled over with similar pieces of plaster, and discoloured with strong acids."

It is his enthusiasm and these small details we are given before we ever gain a physical description of him.

Holmes and Watson discuss sharing rooms: "I have my eye on a suite in Baker Street ... which would suit us down to the ground. You don't mind the smell of strong tobacco, I hope?" Holmes asks. And then: "I generally have chemicals about, and occasionally do experiments. Would that annoy you?" And: "Let me see – what are my other shortcomings? I get in the dumps at times, and don't open my mouth for days on end. You must not think I am sulky when I do that. Just let me alone, and I'll soon be right." And finally, he adds that he also plays the violin.

The physical description of Holmes comes in chapter 2:

In height he was rather over six feet, and so excessively lean that he seemed to be considerably taller. His eyes were sharp and piercing, save during those intervals of torpor to which I have alluded; and his thin, hawk-like nose gave his whole expression an air of alertness and decision. His chin, too, had the prominence and squareness which mark the man of determination. His hands were invariably blotted with ink and stained with chemicals, yet he was possessed of extraordinary delicacy of touch, as I frequently had occasion to observe when I watched him manipulating his fragile philosophical instruments.

Intrigued by his new roommate, Watson takes inventory of Holmes' knowledge and skills, concluding that of literature, philosophy and astronomy he knows nothing; his awareness of politics is feeble; botanical knowledge is variable; geology 'practical, but limited,' in that he can recognise different types of soils at a glance and name their local places of origin. He has a profound knowledge of chemistry, and an accurate but 'unsystematic' understanding of human anatomy. He plays the violin well, and is 'an expert singlestick player, boxer and swordsman.' He has a 'good practical knowledge of British law,' and an immense knowledge of 'sensational literature': "He appears to know every detail of every horror perpetrated in the century."

From this, Watson is unable to discern Holmes' calling in life. Making Holmes, at his first appearance, an enigmatic figure serves to increase the reader's interest in him: we read on because we want to find out more about this unusual man.

The Appearance of Hercule Poirot

Poirot is probably second only to Sherlock Holmes in his popularity around the world and is the only fictional character to have had his obituary published on the front page of the *New York Times*. He featured in thirty-three novels and fifty-two short stories, first appearing in *The Mysterious Affair at Styles* in 1920.

An admirer of the Sherlock Holmes stories, Agatha Christie decided she would create a detective of her own, and wanted to make him 'not like Sherlock Holmes' – "I should never be able to emulate him," she wrote in her autobiography – and besides, she wanted to create something of her own. "Who could I have? A schoolboy? Rather difficult. A scientist? What did I know of scientists? Then I remembered our Belgian refugees."

She made Poirot a war refugee, a retired Belgian police inspector, and "...a tidy little man, always arranging things, liking things in pairs, liking things square instead of round." Christie thought it would be ironic to name this little man after the Greek hero Hercules, shortening it to Hercule to make it sound better with the surname she picked, Poirot. Here is Poirot's first appearance, in chapter two of *The Mysterious Affair at Styles*:

Poirot was an extraordinary-looking little man. He was hardly more than five feet four inches, but carried himself with great dignity. His head was exactly the shape of an egg, and he always perched it a little on one side. His moustache was very stiff and military. The neatness of his attire was almost incredible. I believe a speck of dust would have caused him more pain than a bullet wound. Yet this quaint dandified little man ... had been in his time one of the most celebrated members of the Belgian police. As a detective, his flair had been extraordinary, and he had achieved triumphs by unravelling some of the most baffling cases of the day.

Later in that first novel, we see that Poirot's eyes are "as green as a cat's" and in *Murder on the Links* that they "shone green when he was excited." While in *The ABC Murders* it is revealed that Poirot dyes his hair black. In *Murder in Mesopotamia* the narrator describes Poirot as "an odd plump little man ... he looked like a hairdresser in a comic play."

The Role of the Great Detective

Having explored the golden age detective's personality type and necessary abilities, is there much else we need to consider? Their role in society is worth a few words. By this I mean their job and/or position, and also their standing in relation to the closed group of suspects – the 'mini-society' – they will investigate.

In discussions about the creation of detectives, you are often told that you have a choice between making your sleuth a professional or an amateur. And sometimes you're offered a choice of suitable jobs that offer opportunities for detection – a newspaper reporter, a lawyer, a doctor or medical examiner, or whatever. Your detective's actual occupation, the way he makes a living, is pretty much irrelevant – except perhaps in that the Thinker archetype is drawn to certain types of employment. But even then, of course, they may be placed in employment that is at odds with their personality type, in order to create dramatic conflict or at the very least to highlight their personality by the irony of their position.

The truth is that your detective can be anybody. As quoted earlier, Agatha Christie considered making her detective a scientist or even a schoolboy. She made Poirot a retired Belgian policeman turned consulting detective, but Miss Marple was created to be very different from the expected detective type. Others have created blind detectives and housebound agoraphobics. Physical ability is unimportant, as the great detective's skills are all in their heads.

Within the confines of personality type and required skills, have fun creating the physical appearance of your character, and their day-to-day role. Make them a little theatrical, larger-than-life. Eccentric, but not irritatingly grotesque.

A question is sometimes asked about how the 'consulting detective' makes a living, as they rarely seem to be paid for their services. Sometimes there is mention of a modest inherited income, or occasionally of a generous gift from a client, perhaps a member of a European royal household, or a grateful government. But in all honesty, it is of no great importance – a few hints are enough. Classical detective mysteries, as we have said, present an illusion of reality – enough details, but no more.

More important is the detective's role in relation to the cast of suspects. Two things must be borne in mind:

(i) The detective must be seen as a genius who can fix the problem. As we have seen, Sir Arthur Conan Doyle often began his stories by having Holmes demonstrate an amazing bit of deduction, unrelated to the case. Other detectives are introduced by their Watson's as being masters of detection. Their reputation is established as being a person who can lift the shadow of suspicion from the assembled suspects. Nicholas Blake has said: "The detective is ... the Fairy Godmother of the twentieth-century folk-myth, his magic abilities only modified to the requirements of a would-be scientific and rational generation."

(ii) The detective must be seen as objective – an outsider, who cannot be regarded as a suspect themselves, and who does not have any relationship to any of the characters such that their investigation could be suspected of being biased.

This combination of *capability* and *objectivity* serves to give the detective credibility in the eyes of the suspects, who then give the detective the authority to carry out the investigation.

There is an unspoken, perhaps grudging, approval – and a tacit agreement to accept the outcome of the investigation.

A Summary of the Evidence

In summary: to create a classical mystery detective, you should:

(a) give them a personality based on the *Thinker* archetype, with
(b) the following skills and abilities
- observation
- deduction
- knowledge
- constructive imagination, and

(c) make them an *outsider* who is seen by the suspects as being both *objective* and able to conduct an unbiased investigation, and *capable* in being able to demonstrate the skills in (b).

The Spinster Sleuth

"There is no detective in England equal to a spinster lady of uncertain age with plenty of time on her hands." – Agatha Christie, *Murder at the Vicarage*

"I think it is possible that Miss Marple arose from the pleasure I had taken in portraying Dr Sheppard's sister in The Murder of Roger Ackroyd. *She had been my favourite character in the book – an acidulated spinster, full of curiosity, knowing everything, hearing everything: the complete detective service in the home."* – Agatha Christie, *An Autobiography*

'Acidulated' – I had to look it up. It means soured and/or made slightly acidic. It's also the process used to sour milk to make cheese. As Agatha Christie noted, Miss Jane Marple – who first appeared in the short story 'The Tuesday Night Club' in 1927 – grew out of the character of Caroline Sheppard, a sharp-tongued, gossipy spinster with an eye for spotting a murderer, who featured in the 1926 novel *The Murder of Roger Ackroyd*. Christie often refers to her old ladies as 'fluffy old pussies' – which is usually translated to 'tabbies' in the American editions, for some reason...

Neither of Christie's characters was the first 'sour old maid' in detective fiction. E. T. A. Hoffman's short story 'Das Fräulein von Scuderi' ('Mademoiselle Scudéri'), published in 1819, is set during the reign of Louis XIV and tells of an elderly poet who assists the police in their search for a murderer. Amelia Butterworth assisted Anna Katharine Green's Ebenezer Gryce in *That Affair Next Door* (1897), *Lost Man's Lane* (1988) and *The Circular Study* (1900).

The first solo fictional female detective is believed to be 'Mrs. Gladden' in Andrew Forrester's collection of seven stories *The Lady Detective* which was first published in 1864.

Also published in 1864 was William Stephens Hayward's collection *Revelations of a Lady Detective* featuring the widowed Mrs. Paschal. Have a look at The *Penguin Book of Victorian Women in Crime*, edited by Michael Sim for a good selection of early examples of this type of story. In 1908 Mary Roberts Rinehart, introduced Rachel Innes, a wealthy fifty-something spinster in *The Circular Staircase:* the story was adapted into a successful stage play called *The Bat*. 1917 saw the first appearance of Jennette Lee's Millicent Newberry in *The Green Jacket:* she joins Tom Corbin's detective agency and goes undercover to investigate the disappearance of emeralds.

But the late 1920s and early 1930s seemed to be the period during which the spinster amateur detective took hold of the imagination. In 1927, Dorothy L. Sayers introduced Miss Kitty Climpson, who ran a secretarial agency and provided occasional assistance to Lord Peter Wimsey beginning with *Unnatural Death* (vt. *The Dawson Pedigree*) Wimsey says that she is able to ask "questions which a young man would not put without a blush." 1928 saw Patricia Wentworth's Miss Maud Silver appear in *Grey Mask* – she featured in thirty-two novels in total. And in 1931 Stuart Palmer brought us Miss Hildegarde Withers in *The Penguin Pool Murder*: it was filmed in 1932 and several more films followed.

Lesser-known examples include Courtland Fitzsimmons' Ethel Thomas; D. B. Olsen's Rachel Murdock; Charlotte Murray Russell's Jane Amanda Edwards; R. C. Woodthorpe's Matilda Perks; Louise Revell's Julia Tyler; Austin Lee's Flora Hogg; Heron Carvic's Miss Emily Seeton (the 'Battling Brolly,' whose adventures were continued by Hamilton Crane); Margaret Scherf's Grace Severance; Gwen Moffat's Melinda Pink; Joyce Porter's the Honorable Constance Morrison-Burke; Mary Roberts Rinehart's Miss Pinkerton; and Josephine Tey's Miss Lucy Pym. More modern takes on this type of character include Antonia Fraser's Jemima Shore, and M. C. Beaton's Agatha Raisin.

Even in the 1920s, the spinster or old maid was a cliché, a stereotype. She was inexperienced and unworldly, and had not normally travelled much beyond the world she was born into. During the day, she pottered around her garden, baked

cakes and made jam. In the evening, she sat by the fire knitting. Usually, she had a cat – often several of them. She was
nosey – having no immediate family, personal relationships
or occupation of her own, she had time on her hands and liked
to observe other people. And then gossip about them to her
other old lady friends. Though she seemed harmless, she often
had a nasty streak – a bitterness arising from the fact that
she felt the world treated her unfairly by not allowing her to
achieve the fulfilment of being a wife and a mother. As a
result, she didn't approve of other people enjoying themselves.
Other people tended to regard her as a failure – someone who
had not achieved what women were meant to achieve. They
made allowances for her and indulged her bitchiness and
spiteful criticisms. They felt sorry for her, responding in a way
that was condescending and ultimately dismissive: she was
irrelevant and didn't matter.

The writers who created spinster detectives took this
stereotype and subverted it – for dramatic purposes rather
than political ones. Because she was seen as non-threatening,
she could be used ironically to challenge the superiority and
authority of the official detective, the man. The spinster
detective used people's expectations of her against them. Her
'dotty old woman' persona was a disguise, hiding a sharply
intelligent mind. As an outside observer, she often provides
an objective viewpoint, and her advanced age means that she
typically has years of experience observing the behaviour of
others – often within her local microcosm – to draw on and is
far from the unworldly old lady she appears to be. Because
they were not threatened by her – as they might be of the
official detective – people felt comfortable revealing their
secrets to her. Women in particular could share 'gossip' with
her that they would never have shared with a man. This
allowed for investigations that operated on a much more
domestic level. Her non-threatening nature and ordinariness
mean that she is usually underestimated or not taken seriously – by police, suspects, witnesses and murderer. Her
deductions are usually based on observation and an understanding of human nature, rather than the interpretation of

clues or forensic evidence – though she may occasionally learn of some important fact from the official investigators.

We discussed Miss Marple's way of reasoning by analogy in the previous chapter. In the next chapter, I will cover the methods used by the modern cozy mystery sleuth, who is a different type of character to the spinster sleuth, but whose methods could also be used if you are creating a spinster sleuth today.

A weakness in this type of character is that they are often more of a background character, sitting in on the investigations which are headed by other (male) characters and offering insights which eventually allow the official detective to claim the credit for solving the mystery. In the end, she may seem little more than the woman behind the throne – like a wife or mother who sacrifices her own ambitions in order that her man may succeed in his. The danger in this portrayal is that the spinster is not a 'complete' woman, and she isn't a fully-fledged detective either. There are stronger and better female detectives created since the 'golden age' to look to for models – but if you want to create a spinster detective for a modern audience, you will need to look beyond the stereotype and create someone who much better reflects the reality of such an older woman's life.

The Modern Cozy Sleuth

"There have . . . been a few women detectives, but on the whole, they have not been very successful. In order to justify their choice of sex, they are obliged to be so irritatingly intuitive as to destroy that quiet enjoyment of the logical which we look for in our detective reading." – Dorothy L. Sayers, *Omnibus of Crime* (1928)

The modern cozy mystery has much in common with the 1930s whodunit, but it has also been influenced by developments in popular fiction that have occurred since the 1930s. The modern cozy heroine – and the sleuth is almost always female – has some elements taken from the spinster sleuth and perhaps some from the Great Detective, but she also draws on the female private eye who grew out of the hardboiled detective tradition. In addition, I would argue that she also has much in common with the type of female character who appears in the genre romance and the romantic comedy.

The Hardboiled Female Detective

The hardboiled detective genre cannot be adequately covered in a few paragraphs, so I will mention it only briefly here. In a paper titled 'The New Female Detective' in *Yale Journal of Law and Feminism*, Professor Carolyn G. Heilbrum writes about the type of character who appeared during the 1970s and rapidly grew in popularity: "... the contemporary female detective scorns the dictates of custom, history, and the earlier restrictions of womanhood..." and such characters "...forge for themselves the chance to enter the world of 'men's work.'" Heilbrum also notes that "... crime fiction is uniquely attractive because it demonstrates how women may achieve autonomy at least as that available to men: they willingly engage, though differently, with the same kinds of risks and dangers as men ... Combining American self-employment with English sensitivity and moral passion, these new fictional women detectives move in a world they partially create, of which they are the first inhabitants."

Modern cozy heroines are perhaps the second set of inhabitants of this world, existing in an environment that was forged by those pioneers. As Heilbrum says, "... feminism and the female detective danced hand in hand into the last third of the twentieth century." The examples she lists are P. D. James' Kate Miskin; Laurie R. King's Kate Martinelli; Margaret Maron's Deborah Knott; Janet Neel's Francesca Wilson; Sara Paretsky's V. I. Warshawski; and, Marissa Piesman's Nina Fischman. Of these characters Heilbrum says:

Above all, these new women detectives prize their independence, offering no hostages to romance. Their living space remains their own, suited only to their needs. They know that the passion of love transmutes too easily to the passion of hate, and they are not prepared to sacrifice their own need for moral action to others' principles. They do not put men first in their lives, but they are rich in friends, sometimes men, and in lovers, sometimes women. Marriage cannot lure them, at least, not more than once, and then briefly. Childless, they often mentor girls and young women.

The modern cozy mystery heroine is an amateur sleuth who operates in a world that now contains these more 'hardboiled' female detectives, and this makes them very different to the spinsters and other female detectives who were created in the 1920s and 1930s.

The 'hero's journey' Joseph Campbell wrote about in *The Hero with a Thousand Faces* (1949) and which has informed much of the theory of plot structure – including, to some extent, my own book *Plot Basics* – is heavily biased towards the quest story of a *male* hero. This model has been criticised for not reflecting the challenges faced by a *female* hero. Maureen Murdock's *The Heroine's Journey* (1990) and Carol Pearson and Katherine Pope's *The Female Hero in American and British Literature* (1981) offer detailed criticism of, and alternatives to, Campbell's model. I would recommend both books to anyone who plans to write about a female hero of any kind – or for anyone who is creating heroes who do not conform to the heterosexual male type.

While the modern cozy sleuth certainly owes a debt to the hard-boiled female detective, she doesn't share all of her qualities. Where the hardboiled detective is cynical and world-weary, the cozy sleuth has a much more optimistic outlook and exists in a world that is far removed from the 'mean streets' of the private eye. At first glance, the modern cozy mystery – with its no sex, no swearing, no violence taboos – might appear to be a retreat from the strong feminist ideals of the female detective Professor Heilbrum was celebrating. How do we reconcile their emphasis on domestic settings, pets, and 'feminine' hobbies such as baking and needlework with the image of a strong independent female hero? There's also more than a hint of the romantic comedy in many popular modern cozy mysteries. A number of successful writers in the genre write, or have written, romance novels and their heroines share many common traits. But the romance genre is as far as you can possibly get from feminist heroes. Isn't it?

The 'Romantic' Heroine

Janice A. Radway challenged accepted criticism of the genre romance in her book *Reading the Romance: Women, Patriarchy, and Popular Literature* (1984). It is, in part, an analysis of the romance genre based on interviews and polls of readers, gathering and evaluating data on what they feel makes a good romance. Her summary of what readers look for in a romance story heroine is:

- Intelligence
- Sense of humour
- Independence
- Femininity

These qualities are listed in order of importance, most important first. Critics of the genre have said that the heroine in a romance is typically passive and helpless, a victim needing a man to rescue her and give her life meaning: the heroine is a 'prize' that the hero wins at the end of the story. It shouldn't really come as any surprise that romance readers do not want to read about passive victims and trophy wives: rather, they want a heroine who is at the centre of the story, who is the main protagonist making the decisions, and then taking actions based on them. She may be vulnerable and occasionally make mistakes, but she is not a victim. An intelligent, independent woman with a sense of humour is an ideal heroine for the modern cozy mystery.

In *Writing the Romantic Comedy*, Billy Mernit says of the heroine: "We like 'em feisty, not feeble..." and says that the ideal heroine tends to go against the female heroine cliché by being "... an aggressive, active, on-top-of-it kind of woman. Where some degree of vulnerability is expected of most heroines, it's her unexpected resistance to this norm that makes our heroine attractive. We expect her to be, if not a feminist, inherently modern in her sensibility."

The modern cozy mystery, unlike the traditional whodunit, *can* feature a romance subplot or a continuing romantic story arc across the books in a series. But it doesn't *have* to. If romance is present, it is more likely to centre on the witty banter of a romantic comedy rather than what goes on between the sheets. And while sassy and witty heroines are popular, humour isn't essential for the modern cozy, though they do all tend to have a lighter tone than a traditional whodunit or hardboiled detective story. Like the hardboiled detective, the modern cozy sleuth can narrate her own story in the first-person, allowing her personality to come through in every word. The story could be told in the first-person by a Watson – though this is less common in the modern cozy. Or the story can be told in the third-person, often with the viewpoint restricted to that of the heroine and to her inner thoughts.

One of the best-known female detectives, and a forerunner of the modern cozy sleuth is Nancy Drew. She first appeared in *The Secret of the Old Clock* in 1930 and was the creation of Edward Stratemeyer, publisher of the Hardy Boys stories. The credited author, Carolyne Keene, was actually a syndicate of ghostwriters, the first of whom was twenty-four-year-old Mildred Wirt Benson. The original series ran from 1930-

2003, and there have been various spin-offs, continuing to the present day. Taking into account the cross-over stories where she appeared with the Hardy Boys, she's probably appeared in over 500 books. As a character, Nancy Drew is important if only because she was the first amateur sleuth that many readers – and writers – encountered during their pre-teen reading.

Character Archetype: The Carer

The Great Detective and the Spinster Sleuth are both examples of the Thinker character archetype. They are *outsiders* who observe the behaviour of others and think about its significance. But they never become emotionally involved in events. The Modern Cozy Sleuth may demonstrate some of this type of behaviour, but she is much more likely to be an empathetic character who interacts *with* other characters, rather than sitting outside the circle watching them. Like the romance heroine, she is likely to be someone in whom the Carer archetype is stronger than the Thinker. Caring or nurturing is typically – or stereotypically – regarded as a female trait, but the Carer archetype encompasses both male and female characters who help and support others. A Carer-sleuth is more likely to have an emotional connection with victims, suspects and witnesses than a Thinker-sleuth.

The Carer Archetype

Motivation: To help others; to nurture relationships

Behaviours: Responds to life with the heart rather than the head; is selfless and altruistic. Empathetic. May feel 'betrayed' if their help and love is not acknowledged.

Values: Relationships with other people; caring for and developing others to allow them to achieve their potential; love and self-sacrifice.

Weaknesses: Risks being a 'people pleaser' putting what other people want ahead of her own needs or safety. May lack assertiveness, and so allow people to take advantage of her.

Tends to see the good in people and ignore the bad. Values herself only in terms of how other people see her.

Needs: Lacks the strengths of both the Thinker and Warrior archetype; needs to plan more rather than acting on impulse; and needs to be more assertive, taking care of her own needs as well as helping others.

The cozy mystery sleuth is not necessarily an example of a 'pure' Carer archetype. If she also has qualities from the Warrior archetype, she will be more adventurous, fun-loving and possibly a little cynical. If she has qualities from the Thinker archetype, she will be more creative, self-expressive and possibly rebellious.

Intuition vs. Logic

There is a tendency to assume that a female detective will rely on *intuition* rather than logic – Dorothy L. Sayers criticised early female detectives for this. Intuition is defined as the ability to understand or know something immediately or instinctively without conscious reasoning; it is based on what a person *feels* to be true. Feelings and emotions are assumed to be *irrational* – the Great Detective in the Sherlock Holmes tradition eschews emotion, fearing it will 'pollute' his rational thought processes. I think the word intuition has so much baggage associated with it that we need something else. *Empathy* is a better term, if we apply it in the sense of being able to understand what someone else is feeling based on the knowledge we have about our own feelings. If we can understand why we feel as we do about certain situations, and how we act as a result of those feelings, we can recognise the actions other people take and attempt to deduce what feelings prompted their actions.

Emotional Intelligence

The term 'emotional intelligence' was first used in a 1964 paper by Michael Beldoch, 'Sensitivity to Expression of Emotional Meaning in Three Modes of Communication,' but achieved prominence as a result of Daniel Goleman's book

Emotional Intelligence: Why It Can Matter More Than IQ
(1995). Goleman's approach has been criticised within the scientific community but proved popular in the business community and more widely. In broad terms, Goleman says that emotional intelligence is the ability of a person to recognize and
label their own emotions and the emotions of others, to use
knowledge of emotions to guide thoughts and actions, and to
manage emotional responses in order to achieve desired goals.

In all likelihood, I think the modern cozy sleuth will employ
something close to this in order to balance the 'irrationality'
of her feelings and the rationality of her logical thought processes. She has feelings, and embraces them, but is aware of
their influence on behaviour – both her own and that of suspects and witnesses – and will apply her intelligence to take
account of this.

I will admit up-front that I have some issues with the theory
of Emotional Intelligence. I first encountered it in a work setting, where a director tried to use it to coerce people into
behaving in a way she thought they ought to behave. This was
a problem with that individual rather than the theory itself,
but it did cause me to go away and read up on the criticisms
of the theory, and as a result I was left with a great deal a
scepticism about emotional intelligence, whether it is something that can be 'improved' in an individual, and how it can
be measured.

I also have problems with some of the terminology used. The
use of the word 'intelligence' implies an opposite of 'emotional
stupidity' and the reference to a number of 'competencies' implies the possibility of 'incompetence' – neither of these seems
quite right when we are discussing human emotions. But having said all that, I think the model of emotional intelligence
does give us a framework we can use to explore how the
method used by the modern cozy sleuth differs from that of
the traditional Great Detective, so I'm going to go with it.

Personal Competence and Social Competence
In discussing empathy and human emotions we have to consider both the individual, the sleuth, and the people she interacts with in the story. I'm going to use a variation of Daniel

Goleman's model based on his book *Working with Emotional Intelligence* and a diagram of the model created by J. Maddocks and T. Sparrow of JCA Occupational Psychologists. The notes below are not intended as a true representation of Emotional Intelligence theory – you can get that from Goleman's writings – as I have taken only those parts that I think provide some insight into creating a sleuth for a modern cozy mystery story.

This model divides emotional intelligence into two parts: *Personal Competence* and *Social Competence*. As I said, I'd prefer a word other than 'competence,' but that's what we have. Other writers have referred to these two sides as *intra*personal and *inter*personal intelligence. The theory then explores these two aspects in terms of *awareness* and *management*.

Personal Competence – Self-Awareness and Self-Regulation

Self-awareness is all about knowing yourself. In the context of emotional intelligence, a self-aware person knows their own feelings and the potential effect those feelings can have on people around them. It means having an objective view of your own emotional state at any given time, and knowing how this might affect how you will react in a given situation. If you're having a bad day, you're likely to react in a different way than if you are having a good day. It also has an element of self-confidence, meaning that you know who you are and trust in your own values and abilities, no matter what the situation or how that situation makes you feel in the moment.

Self-Regulation – sometimes referred to as self-management – is the ability to control your emotions so that you don't act impulsively and solely on the basis of how you are feeling in that moment. It includes the ability to analyse and adapt to situations. Management or regulation is not the same as suppressing emotions or denying how a situation makes you feel, but it is about avoiding uncontrolled emotional outbursts and displays of temper. It's more of a zen thing.

When you are aware of your own emotions and able to manage them, you are then better placed to be able to interact with other people in a constructive manner.

Social Competence – Social Awareness and Relationship Management

Social competence is about interacting with others, including dealing with 'difficult' people and any conflicts that arise. It requires that the sleuth has respect for the other person and listens to them, seeking to put themselves in that person's position and understand their feelings and what lies behind them. It requires empathy and a willingness to communicate with other people in an open and honest way.

Social Awareness is about understanding other people and being able to recognise and empathise with their emotional responses. It is about reading the existing emotional dynamics of any given situation and being able to predict possible changes in these emotional responses. An individual might not be able to put into words what they are feeling or why, and conflicting emotions may mean that they put out mixed messages. A socially aware sleuth will be able to come to an understanding of what a person's words and actions really mean, and what is motivating them. And she will understand that communication is not all about speaking but is much more about listening.

Relationship Management is not about manipulating or controlling others to get them to do what you want. It is mainly about communication and about building the type of relationship needed in order to communicate effectively. Relationships require that trust is established – in this case, between the sleuth and the potential witness or suspect. If a person comes to respect the sleuth, that person is more likely to confide in her, to seek advice from her, to listen to her, and to take comfort from her. When a trusting relationship has been established, the sleuth is much more likely to learn who someone really is and what they really think.

The sleuth is able to get people to open up and talk about themselves, partly as a result of her natural curiosity and partly because she is genuinely interested in what the other person has to say. People like to talk about themselves – if they sense that the other party is actually listening to them. Our sleuth must be a good listener and she must be able to read non-verbal signs as well. Effective listening is not a passive activity, it is an active one. It requires that the listener be present in the moment and not be distracted by external events or their own internal thoughts.

But our sleuth isn't simply a sponge soaking up what the other person says: she must be able to communicate her own thoughts and feelings in a way that demonstrates she and the other person have things in common. There must be two-way communication. And it must be honest – lack of authenticity is a sure way to ruin a relationship and people are very good at spotting it. Effective communication requires honesty on the part of the sleuth – even when speaking the truth might give rise to difficult emotional responses in the other person. A socially aware person will be aware of the potential risk here and choose her words carefully, speaking the truth while avoiding or minimising hurt to the other person. The golden rule is always for the sleuth to ask: 'How would I like to be treated?'

When a sleuth has established a relationship with someone and engaged in genuine two-way communication with them, she is then in a position to let that person know what she wants. She can be open and honest with them, and the other person will respect that and be more likely to respond positively.

Despite her best efforts, the sleuth will occasionally find herself faced with a conflict situation. She will deal with it, if she can, by putting herself in the other person's position and trying to understand the feelings that have sparked off the confrontational behaviour. Based on this understanding, she will try and resolve the conflict.

The amateur sleuth has no official capacity to *compel* people to give her the information she needs to complete her investigation. She can only build relationships with people and encourage them to help. Some witnesses or suspects may open up to her immediately, others will be suspicious of her, and some will block her efforts completely. All she can do when she meets reluctance or direct opposition is try and convince the other person to change their mind. The amateur sleuth needs to be effective in the art of persuasion or influence. You cannot force someone to change their mind, but by understanding their feelings and motivations, you can persuade them.

Developing Others

I quoted Carolyn G. Heilbrum earlier in this chapter and one of the things she said about the new female detectives was that they acted as mentors for others. The Carer character archetype also embodies the idea of nurturing others and helping them achieve their full potential – it is the archetype where we find teachers as well as nurses. Developing others is also covered by Emotional Intelligence, which is often applied to help team members work more effectively together.

The Great Detective, as we saw earlier, likes to show off and prove that he is the most intelligent man in the room. He is also not above publicly belittling the efforts of his Watson or the police detectives. Our modern cozy amateur sleuth does not feel the need to behave in this way. As an emotionally intelligent person, she is aware of her own abilities and has a healthy degree of self-confidence. From this position, she is entirely comfortable encouraging others to achieve the best that they can. She is not afraid of a protégé outshining her and never feels envious or threatened by the success of others. She is pleased for them. The guidance and inspiration she provides will be authentic and unforced: she will have no ulterior motive and will not expect to receive anything in return.

For the same reasons, our sleuth is also happy to work *with* others to achieve a desired outcome: she does not feel the need to stand alone and aloof in order to prove that she is special and different. The cozy sleuth enjoys working with friends and other talented individuals, sharing the workload and feeling energised by those around her. Her emotional intelligence may make her an ideal leader, but she never feels the need to dominate the other members of the group and is happy to hand over the reins to anyone who is better able to lead in any given situation.

The modern cozy sleuth succeeds because she is able to build relationships and communicate. She is honest and reliable. And she is cheerful and a genuinely nice person to be around. Other characters should feel this and so should your reader.

The Investigation

The detective's investigation of the crime has three main phases:

1. Incrimination of the suspects – where the means, motive, and opportunity of each are explored.
2. Elimination (or exoneration) of suspects – where alibis are tested
3. Solution and revelation – where the true sequence of events, meanings of clues, and identity, motive and method of the murderer are finally explained.

1. Incrimination of Suspects: Means, Motive and Opportunity

Each suspect in the story, including the murderer, must be (a) capable of killing, and (b) capable of committing this particular murder; they must have a reason for wanting the victim dead; and they must have had physical access to both the victim and the murder weapon at the time the murder took place. They must have, in other words, the means, motive, and opportunity.

Means

How was the murder committed? What weapon was used, and how was it employed? We may also add the fact that a person must be physically capable of committing the murder, using the weapon that was employed.

Marie F. Rodell's advice, when it comes to the murder weapon, is to stick with the tried and tested: "The good old blunt instrument, gun, carving knife, or rat poison will do yeoman service; originality can better be expended on other elements in the story." It is dangerous for the murderer, she says, to try to be too ingenious when it comes to the murder method: the more complicated it is, the greater the risk that it will go wrong. For that reason, complex Heath Robinson murder devices should be avoided.

Obscure poisons and unlikely weapons such as blow-pipes should also be eschewed as they have all almost certainly been used before. Yes, real-life killings have been effected by poison injected from the tip of an umbrella and by polonium in a teacup, but unless you're writing comedy I'd follow Marie F. Rodell's advice and keep it simple. That being said, there is still an opportunity to add an element of mystery to the means by which the murder was committed. Rodell offers three options for doing this:

(i)   Some 'difficult and ingenious method' that makes it seem impossible that the murder could have been committed at all. Here she refers to the 'locked room' mystery, which we will explore later.

(ii)   A missing or disguised weapon, where the author then employs "... the Purloined Letter technique: the weapon is in full view, but its function as something else is so evident that it is not suspected as having been used."

(iii) Death was caused without use of a weapon and so appears to have been accidental. "A blow with a fist, a shove down the stairs, or the use of shock on a person with an admittedly weak heart would all come under this category."

Motive

Why was the victim killed? What motivated the killer to take his irreversible action? There must be a reason, and it must be believable.

As well as having a reason to kill, the murderer must also be sufficiently motivated to do so. That is, is the suspect mentally capable of committing it? Someone may have ample reason to want to kill someone, a motive, but be psychologically incapable of murder for that motive. In the heat of the moment, to protect ourselves or a loved one, any one of us is probably capable of murder. But not everyone has a temperament that allows them to plan a murder in cold blood.

A murderer is someone who decides to solve a problem in their own life by taking the life of another human being. Earl F. Bargainnier argues that it is a combination of egoism and moral immaturity that allows them to do this. In *Crooked House*, Agatha Christie has someone from Scotland Yard compare a murderer to a child who never learns to feel what is right and wrong. They are aware that murder is wrong, but they do not feel it in the same way as a normal person. The murderer believes that he or she is in some way special, that it is okay – necessary even – for them to commit murder. Their own needs or desires are more important than the life of another person. Edgar Wallace, in his autobiography, said that murderer is an act of criminal vanity. W. H. Auden uses the term 'demonic pride,' saying that the murderer "claims the right to be omnipotent."

The motives for murder are usually given as money (or gain), fear, revenge and love (or passion). In the 'classic' detective story the murderer is never a homicidal maniac or serial killer.

Gain is commonly seen in terms of wealth, usually a significant inheritance from a parent or spouse. But it could also be a rise in social status, or to gain a position of power. Often the murder victim is viewed as a barrier to be removed – because they are standing in the way of the murderer obtaining wealth, or of being able to enter into a desired relationship with someone. Or the murderer may simply want to prove to the world that he is smarter than everyone else and that he can get away with murder. Jealousy falls somewhere between the motives of gain and fear: the murderer may jealously guard something he has, fearing to lose it; or he may be envious of what he perceives others to have – things that he feels he deserves.

"The drive to power is one of the most potent human impulses..." writes Marie F. Rodell, say that this usually "...a compensation for some humiliation or sense of inferiority sustained in childhood or youth..."

Fear arises from the risk of losing something. The murderer may be afraid that his or her own life is at risk. He may fear for the life or wellbeing of someone he cares about. Or he may be concerned that his social status is threatened. He may be the victim of a blackmailer, seeking to put an end to this persecution. Or he may be concerned that a valued institution or principle is under threat.

Fear encompasses not only the undesired act itself, but also the *consequences* of that act: loss of prestige, of position, of money, or of a fiancé, for example.

The second murder in a novel is often motivated by fear of exposure for the first murder: the second victim is believed to have known something significant about the first murder that might lead to the murderer's exposure. Or they may have been trying to blackmail the murderer.

Revenge usually revolves around a desire to 'get even,' to gain compensation for some real or imagined wrong that the murderer has suffered. It may be a wrong that the law is unable or unwilling to punish, or which it does not even recognise as a legitimate wrong. There may have been some tangible loss – financial ruin or loss of a job, for example – or the murderer may have been the victim of some form of humiliation, and feel a need to restore his self-esteem. Revenge is 'punishment' for previous actions, and can be meted out to anyone the murderer feels has wronged him – even to the ne'er-do-well or philanderer who has brought shame to the family name. Revenge can also be linked with feelings of power, with the murderer seeing himself as some kind of avenging angel, taking the law into his own hands, and meting out 'just' punishment.

Where revenge is a motive, the murderer does not act in the heat of the moment, striking out in anger, but bides his time and carefully puts in place his place to 'get even.'

Love and/or sexual desire is at the heart of the 'crime of passion.' One of the so-called rules has it that love should be kept out of the detective mystery. Marie F. Rodell points out that in real life, the *crime passionel* is committed in the heat of the moment, and that the lover – or ex-lover – of the victim is easily identified as the murderer. This does not make for good detective fiction, which requires a premeditated murder and the need for investigation. But love can be used as a motive

where someone stands in the way of the murderer's happiness
– his lover's inconvenient husband must be gotten rid of. Or a
wealthy relative who holds the purse strings and requires one
or other of the lovers to enter into a marriage to a third party.
Or the blackmailer who knows something about the past of
one of the lovers. Rodell adds a final caution that "... crimes
arising from sexual perversions are used only in the most
lurid thrillers."

Motive is important because it is the reason *why* the murderer
took the life of another person. It must be strong. The murderer must fear the consequences of *not* committing murder
more than he fears the risk of punishment for murder. Of
course, as Marie F. Rodell writes, the murderer is convinced
he's too clever ever to get caught, so the balance tips in favour
of his reaching for the knife or poison.

An individual murderer's motivation can be a combination
of the above: his desire for revenge may be coupled with a wish
to gain a family inheritance, and/or the hand of a loved one,
taking these away from a despised rival.

Carolyn Wells offers some final bits of advice on the subject
of motives:

Keep it Simple – "Murder is the result of one of the most prim-
itive impulses in man; and though the working out of the plot
may be subtle, it is wise, so far as possible, to have the motive
simple, straightforward, and strong."

Make it Recent – "It is annoying to discover at the end of the
book that the motive is retaliation for a wrong done thirty or
forty years ago, as in *A Study in Scarlet* or *Hand and Ring*.
These, otherwise perfect and really great detective stories,
finally reveal motives which could not possibly be discovered
by the reader..."

Be Logical and Fair – "Let the motive be as carefully concealed as you like, but offer adroit hints and veiled allusions
that the astute reader may catch if he can, and when at last
the motive is revealed, let it be a logical and sound one, and,
above all, let it be adequate."

Opportunity

Did the suspect have access to the weapon used, and access to the victim – to the scene of the crime – at the time the murder took place? This is the simplest of the three, but is the one on which the alibis of most suspects hinge: they can prove that they were elsewhere when the murder took place.

2. Elimination (or Exoneration) of Suspects – Alibis

Alibi in Latin means *elsewhere*. In criminal defence proceedings, a defendant tries to prove that he was in another place at the time the offence in question was committed. In detective mysteries, each of the suspects tries to demonstrate that they were somewhere other than the scene of the crime at the time of the murder. If they can prove they were indeed elsewhere, then they do not have the necessary opportunity to have committed the murder. They may still have had access to the means – the weapon – and a motive for wanting the victim dead, but lacking the third vital component, they are eliminated from the list of suspects.

Unless, or until, their alibi can be proved false.

The Iron-Clad or Unbreakable Alibi

An unbreakable alibi – in real life – is one which the police are unable to disprove, and which stands up to cross-examination in court. In mystery stories, the convention is that an 'unbreakable' – or perfect or watertight – alibi is one which appears to be impossible to disprove, but which the detective must ultimately demonstrate is false. It became a cliché that the one character whose alibi appeared iron-clad was eventually proved to be the murderer.

Whole novels have been constructed based on the investigation of an unbreakable alibi. Sometimes a character is known to be guilty, but he will escape justice unless the detective can somehow disprove his alibi. These often feature a complicated series of events that the detective has to piece together.

An alibi does not have to be complicated to be 'unbreakable' – some of the best ones rely on a single simple 'fact': to disprove them, the detective must show how this indisputable fact (often the time of the murder), assumed by everyone to be true, is actually false. Once he has this clue, he can re-examine everything he has discovered, and piece together the sequence of what really happened.

Sometimes an alibi seems to be unbreakable because the suspect could not have been in two places at the same time. But when the detective discovers he or she had an unsuspected and unlikely accomplice, the secret is revealed and the alibi broken.

The novels of Freeman Wills Crofts often centre on the investigation of an unbreakable alibi, as do a number of Erle Stanley Gardner's Perry Mason stories.

3. Solution and Revelation – Clues and Red Herrings

"Clues are the traces of guilt which the murderer leaves behind." – Marie F. Rodell

"The plot is the skeleton, but the evidence and the deductions therefrom are the muscle and sinew. On the value and presentation of the evidence does the reader's interest depend. No matter how absorbing the puzzle, if the evidence and deduction be not full of action and surprise the story palls." – Carolyn Wells

Clues should be boldly planted but disguised as something else. The reader should see it easily, but not recognise it for what it is. Clues can either be tangible, such as a button or a footprint; or intangible, such as an action or a statement. What did the killer leave at the scene, or take away? A clue may be something that is suggestive, rather than providing concrete evidence.

There is a tendency to think of clues being things that are found at the scene of the murder, or obtained as part of the subsequent investigation, during the questioning of the suspects. But there may be clues from *before* the murder. The killer may have needed to make preparations for the act of murder, and these actions may have left behind clues. People may have witnessed certain activities in the days or weeks or months prior to the killing. Items may have been purchased or made. Skills or abilities may have been gained or demonstrated.

Clues need to be interpreted to ascertain their correct meaning: a clue may suggest an obvious meaning, but also have a second, less obvious, meaning. Marie F. Rodel: "A clue is seldom in itself a proof of guilt. It is the deductions which the detective makes from it which are significant; it is because of these deductions that that button eventually proves the murderer's undoing ... A good clue, then, is one which does in fact point in the right direction, but which seems at first to point in the wrong direction, to mean something other than it does, or to point nowhere at all."

The murderer may also leave behind *false* evidence in an attempt to draw attention away from himself or to incriminate someone else.

Fair Play

The detective must solve the mystery, discover whodunit, as a result of logical deduction based on the facts he has discovered during his investigation. There should be no inspired guesses, no luck, no coincidence. Nor should he flush out an unknown murderer through the use of a trap – though it is fair to trick someone into revealing their guilt, once the detective has deduced their identity.

Dorothy L. Sayers said that any fool can tell a lie, but the clever detective story writer will tell the truth in such a way that the reader is seduced into telling the lie for themselves. You want the reader to see your clue, but not see its significance; or better yet, you want them to see it and assign the *wrong* significance to it.

Fair play dictates that every clue discovered by the detective should be shared with the reader (and vice versa). Many writers break this rule. If the detective discovers a letter or some other document and says 'Aha, now I understand it all!' your reader is going to be more than a little miffed if the content of the document is not immediately revealed. The detective doesn't have to reveal what he has deduced about the document, but we should at least be allowed to share what it contains so we can see if we can work out its significance ourselves. If the clue can't be shared because it gives away the whole solution, you should then probably ask yourself whether it is the right clue to use: if you can only maintain the mystery by 'cheating' then your story may have a problem.

What provides the challenge for both the sleuth and the reader is the *significance* of the details, which the writer may, at times, hold back. This happens when the detective does not see the significance immediately or is waiting for some other evidence to corroborate his hunch.

Tangible Clues
"When not irrationally lugged in, shreds, ravelings, scrapings of dust from boot heels, or scraps of paper are much prized as fictional evidence." – Carolyn Wells

Traditionally, clues were physical objects left at the scene of the murder or, perhaps, taken from the scene. Fingerprints, footprints, fibres, hairs, and blood are also tangible clues. So too are bullet holes, stab wounds, marks on the body, and poison found in the body. The location in which the body is found and its physical condition can be clues. Financial records relating to the victim or one of the suspects can be a clue. Other clues can include the time it takes for a particular action to be completed – including the use of train timetables; and the distance between two points. Also, experiments to test whether a particular sound can be heard in a particular place.

The body of the victim may provide tangible clues. If the body was found in water, but there is no water in the lungs, they were almost certainly killed by some other means than drowning.

Intangible Clues
Eyewitness accounts; lies – of commission and of omission; discrepancies between the statements of suspects; phoney alibis; refusal to answer questions; confessions; accusations and other things said by people involved in the investigation are intangible clues. Certain actions may also provide clues: a nervous tick, or the fact that someone has fled the scene.

Other intangible clues include previously unrevealed relationships or connections between two characters.

Another form of intangible clue is the analogous clue: the detective sees or hears something unconnected with the case which provides an insight into the mystery at hand. He may, for example, see a workman use a lever or a pulley to move an object he couldn't lift without mechanical assistance, and apply a similar solution to the mystery of how the body of the victim was moved from A to B. This kind of 'flash of inspiration' is tricky to handle effectively, as there is a danger of the detective being seen to rely on luck to solve the mystery, breaking the rule of 'solution by detection not by coincidence.' If the analogous clue legitimately belongs within the setting of the mystery, such that the murderer may have gained his inspiration in the same manner, then this type of clue seems less of a cheat.

Psychological Clues

Marie F. Rodell writes that intangible clues may be of two types: "those revealing basic character traits, and those to do with behaviour patterns..." At their most obvious, clues may reveal traits such as sadism or squeamishness. But those relating to a suspect's feelings towards the victim are more complex. "A man who is jealous of his wife will be more apt to kill her lover than a man indifferent to his wife's behaviour," Rodell writes, while "a man who tries to arrange other people's lives for them is more likely to kill out of a rationalised conviction that he is doing good, than one who minds his own business."

One form of psychological clue is what is commonly known as a 'Freudian slip' – someone says or does something that reveals what they are really thinking but trying to hide. This could be a glance in the direction of a secret hiding place, or an involuntary movement, such as reaching towards a pocket where an item is hidden.

Hamlet employs psychological detective work when he determines to use a play, showing the events he believes occurred in the murder of his father, so as to see how his uncle – the main suspect – reacts to seeing the events reproduced.

The One True Clue

In the classic mystery story, there is generally one pivotal clue which holds the key to unravelling the mystery. There is a critical turning point at the end of Act II when the detective finally figures out the true significance of this clue. Usually, the clue will have been discovered early in the story and a particular meaning or significance ascribed to it. But it has a second, equally plausible meaning that the detective does not see until something causes him to re-evaluate it and look at it from a different perspective. Having done this, he is able to see the true significance of the other clues and to determine the true sequence of events. He is also able to understand the motive of the murderer, and so arrive at their identity. The *why* and *how* leads finally to the *who*.

The pivotal clue has an obvious initial meaning and a second true meaning that requires lateral thinking for its discovery. If this clue is taken at face value, then the version of events that the murderer wants people to believe seems the correct version; only when the clue is understood properly does it unlock the true version of events.

Only when this true meaning has been discovered can the detective say that all the pieces of the puzzle have 'fallen into place.' If he says it at an earlier stage in the story, he is on a false trail.

The 'one true clue' may be a fact that everyone assumes to be true, but which is finally proved wrong – the time of the murder, for example. Once the real time of death is established, everyone's alibis may need to be re-checked.

Hiding the Clues

Mystery writers use a number of techniques for sneaking in their clues, hoping that readers will miss their significance. This is often compared to the technique of *misdirection* – or 'sleight of hand' – employed by a magician. Clues must be presented while the reader is distracted and 'looking elsewhere.' The importance of the clue must be downplayed or it must be somehow camouflaged. Following is a list of possible methods of concealment.

Hidden in Plain Sight. Poe used this in 'The Purloined Letter,' and it can still be used today. The clue is visible to everyone at all times – they just have to spot it and recognise it as a clue.

Taken for Granted. Some things are so obvious that they are overlooked.

Hidden in a List. A list of items on a mantelpiece or a side table, or the contents of a bag, drawer, or pocket, includes a number of items, all of which are given the same degree of importance – but only one of them is actually significant. The reader and the detective must figure out which.

Too Much Information. Related to the above. Some characters just talk too much. If most of what they say is inconsequential, the reader tends to stop paying attention and so misses the one significant thing they say. You might also think in terms of 'The Boy Who Cried Wolf.' An ex-colleague whose father was a doctor told me of a patient who was something of a hypochondriac and always listed her ailments when she visited the surgery, but one day her list included a symptom never mentioned previously – spotting this the doctor followed it up and discovered she had an illness requiring urgent treatment.

Unreliable Witness. If the reader believes that a character is unreliable – because they have lied previously or because they are thought to be stupid – then everything that person says is likely to be discounted. But occasionally these people may be telling the truth. Things said by children sometimes fall into this category – 'From the mouths of babes...' as the saying goes.

Unremarked Incongruity. This is a variation on the list device: items are listed or a person or place is described, and within the details given one item is out of place, it doesn't belong. This fact isn't drawn to the reader's attention, it is just included in passing as just one more detail. What is the significance of the incongruous item or property?

A Clue of Two Halves. Sometimes an item or an occurrence does not gain significance in the investigation until it is paired with a second. On the night of the murder, a character changes into a black dress; during a conversation, she states that she never wears black. What she says and what she does are in conflict: this must have significance, but what is it? The greater the time between the revelation of the two parts, the less likely the reader is to spot the connection. This can be extended to a clue consisting of a chain of three or more parts, but this can be harder to manage effectively.

Delayed Reaction. Related to the above, but involving separate clues. Something noted early on may not become relevant until something else is learned later.

Delayed Significance. Related to the clue of two halves, this device has the detective or some other character noting a particular object or event – e.g. an item with a date such as a newspaper cutting or a photograph or a sporting trophy – which does not gain significance as a clue until a person related to the item makes a statement which contradicts the fact provided by the item: he says he did not meet the person in the photograph or did not visit the place it relates to until a much later date, for example. The detective may discover a document, the significance of which is not immediately obvious.

Incomplete Clues. If a character reveals something important, the reader will tend to believe that this person has told everything that they know, especially if the revelation is difficult or embarrassing for them. But they may not be telling all, and a half-truth is, by omission, still a lie. The astute detective (and reader) will be as much interested in what is not said as what has been revealed.

Hidden in the Action. If an amusing, entertaining, suspenseful or otherwise emotional event is being played out in a scene, a clue can be slipped in: it will not be noticed because other things are claiming the attention of the reader. Things said in anger during an argument fall into this category. However, the confrontation or other action of the scene must be relevant to the plot, otherwise it will stand out as a plant.

Before the Fact. One way to hide a clue is to introduce it before the murder takes place. This can be used a number of times in a story where the murder does not occur until the midpoint.

Humóur. Something said in jest is unlikely to be taken seriously by the reader.

Overshadowing. It can be effective to insert a clue after something dramatic has happened. This may be following a major turning point in the investigation – the discovery of a second body, for example – or it may be inserting a small, seemingly insignificant clue after the discovery of a big flashing neon clue. Or red herring. The reader's attention is caught up with the bigger event, and so they miss the smaller.

Relying on Assumptions. We all have stock reactions, stereotypes – if we are told that a vicar is present in a scene, we will in all likelihood visualise a white male past middle-age. An assumption is made. Such assumptions can be used to trick the reader. This example is crude, but the device can be used with considerable subtlety.

Absence of Clues
Poirot: Then there is the matter of the footprints in the flower-bed.
Giraud: But I see no footprints.
Poirot: No. There are none.   *(Murder on the Links)*

There are a couple of things to consider under this heading: the absence of some item or occurrence that would normally be expected to be found – why is it missing? And the complete absence of clues of any kind.

The corpse found with no signs of foul play – no injuries externally, no poisons internally – is one example of the latter. If it is murder, how were they killed? A person with no apparent life history – Who are they? Where did they come from? – is another.

'Missing' clues include things the murderer may have taken from the scene – Why were they taken? And an absence of clues to corroborate the generally accepted theory of what has happened: If the murderer climbed in through the window, why are there no footprints in the soil under the window?

Missing clues can also be hidden in lists – an inventory is given, and an item is missing: it is up to the reader to notice its absence.

An apparent absence of clues can be more of a challenge to the detective than a scene littered with bizarre clues requiring interpretation.

Red Herrings

A red herring is something that appears to be a clue, but isn't. It either distracts from the real issue or directs attention in the wrong direction.

The origins of the term 'red herring' as a distraction is thought to be related to the use of a kipper (a reddish-coloured smoked herring) to lay a false trail to lead hunting dogs astray. Some people have said that it was used by hunt saboteurs to disrupt fox hunts, and others that it was used by escaped convicts to confuse the hounds that were hunting them.

Red herrings, like real clues, can be tangible or intangible. People can also be red herrings: a character who has motive, means, and opportunity but who is not the killer is a red herring. So is someone who has a guilty secret they wish to protect – unconnected with the murder – which causes them to behave suspiciously. If there is more than one murder in a story, one (or more) of the corpses may be a red herring: the additional corpse is designed to distract reader and detective from the killer's motive for committing the 'real' murder – it is assumed that both were killed for the same reason, causing the detective to seek a relationship between the two which doesn't actually exist.

"Clues to disregard are those that come in pairs, such as an earring with a bloody fingerprint on it. That strains coincidence just a bit too much and is an obvious plant." – Matthew J. Mahler, 'Whodunit: A Guide to the Obvious.'

Another frequently used red herring is the *wrong victim*. The first murder victim was killed in error, having been mistaken for the intended victim. The detective then spends time looking for motivation which doesn't exist. As Carolyn Wheat says: "Whenever a mystery reader sees a character putting on someone else's coat, little bells go off in our heads and we're ready to bet that a *wrong murder* is about to be committed."

Some of the accepted conventions of the whodunit can also be used to provide red herrings. The iron-clad alibi is one such device: if someone has the perfect alibi, then the seasoned mystery reader knows to suspect them – the alibi is too good, and so is a red herring designed to deceive. Then there is the 'least-likely suspect,' someone who seems to be without motive, access to means, or opportunity – someone who couldn't possibly be the murderer. Red herring. And in a similar vein, there is the 'most likely suspect,' someone who seems far too obvious to be the killer – and who is probably eliminated as a suspect early on – but this is a double-bluff on the part of the writer.

A final note of red herrings: do not include too many of them, and do not have your detective spend too much time trying to discover the significance of the ones you do use. If you waste too much time on red herrings, your reader is likely to feel cheated. Red herrings used sparingly can be effective, but it is far better to confuse and mystify your reader through the use of real clues which can be interpreted in more than one way.

Deductions from Clues

"Circumstantial evidence is a very tricky thing," answered Holmes *thoughtfully. "It may seem to point very straight to one thing, but if you shift your own point of view a little, you may find it pointing in an equally uncompromising manner to something entirely different."* – 'The Adventure of the Boscombe Valley Mystery'

The detective may pick up a clue at the scene, but not examine it closely until later. This can add an element of intrigue or suspense. Especially if the item is (a) unusual or bizarre in some way, or (b) something apparently commonplace.

Telegraphing

Suspense relies on setting up a situation where the reader anticipates – desires or dreads – some outcome. But the flip side of this is accidentally giving away too much, 'telegraphing' a conclusion before you are ready to reveal it. This happens if you underestimate the reader and do not camouflage the clues sufficiently, or draw attention to them by referring to them repeatedly.

Overused Clues

Don't use these as clues, unless you can put a genuinely original spin on them or you're using one as a red herring. Obviously, if you're writing a parody, use all of them.

A button or brooch, usually found when the body is moved: the murderer missed it because it was hidden. A 'family' birthmark. An accent that slips. Cigarette ash or a cigarette butt. A glass with a fingerprint or lipstick on it. A cigarette butt with lipstick on it. Fibres of material of identifiable type and colour. Burnt papers. A diary or ledger with pages missing. A clock or watch that stopped at the time of the murder. A telephone call from an unidentified whispering voice. A dog that doesn't bark because it knows the intruder.

Other Clues to Avoid

Don't include clues that depend on obscure technical knowledge that the average reader does not have. If you need to include something of this nature, introduce the knowledge earlier in the story in an innocent context.

Keeping Track of Your Clues

Having chosen which clues are required, and the order in which they are to be presented, you then need to figure out where to place them on the plot line. Drawing out a chart or plotline and marking the placement of the clues will help you keep track of them, and help to ensure that you are not introducing something too soon if it relies on a previous item or occurrence. As well as noting the first appearance of the clue, you can also plot any follow-up or linking to other clues that may be required.

You also need to think about how you intend to misdirect the reader's attention when the clue is introduced: what else will be going on in the scene. Do not create a scene whose sole purpose is to introduce a clue: that risks drawing too much attention to the significance of the item introduced. Rather, have a scene which serves multiple purposes.

Sequencing

The clues are indications of the sequence of what *really* happened on the night of the murder. Their proper significance needs to be deduced by the detective, and their proper sequence needs to be identified. Consider them as stepping stones that the detective needs in order to reach the final solution.

To make things as difficult as possible for the reader and the detective, the clues should not first appear in their proper sequence – they should be so mixed up that it seems almost impossible to sort them into order. This is where two-part clues also come in handy – because (a) the reader has to spot both parts, (b) they have to figure out the connection, and (c) they have to decide where they fit in the overall sequence.

Something else to bear in mind is that a story needs to build in terms of reader interest – smaller clues coming before larger revelations. Clues are only one part of this, as we will explore later, as major turning points in the story are often related to deductions based on clues, rather than the finding of the clues themselves.

The discovery of a clue, the detective's deductions based on it – the different theories he comes up with to try and explain it – are a sequence that needs to be added to the plot. Several such sequences will overlap or supersede one another. Again you can work backwards from the correct interpretation of the clue, preceding it with theories that are tested and rejected, finally working back to the discovery of the clue itself.

Creating this mystification can end up causing confusion for the writer. This is why having the sequence of events – what *really* happened – plotted out is vital. Work backwards from the murder. Against this, you can indicate which clues relate to which occurrences and indicate which clues are related to other clues. Once you have that sorted, you can have fun mixing them up and inserting the red herrings, working forwards from the murder.

Something else you might want to try is writing the detective's final explanation of his solution before you write the rest of the story. Once you have that, you can plot backwards.

Plot Structures

We are going to deconstruct three basic murder mystery plots in detail:

(1) The 'Act I Murder'
(2) The 'Midpoint Murder'
(3) The 'Most Likely Suspect' or 'Innocent Accused'

After that, we'll look briefly at a couple of subgenres of the murder mystery: the *Locked Room* or Impossible Crime and the *Inverted Mystery*.

In the 'golden age' or traditional murder mystery, unlike most other genres, there is no subplot. There is no unfolding crisis in the detective's personal life that is unrelated to the murder. There is no romance between the detective (or the Watson) and any of the other characters in the story. This is one of the reasons why this type of novel tends to be relatively short – typically 55,000 to 65,000 words. Agatha Christie's novels in this genre are usually 50 to 55,000 words: this is the length she preferred, complaining that making them longer only meant including yet more suspects to be eliminated, which wasn't a good thing.

The modern cozy mystery *does* allow for a romantic subplot – involving the sleuth or other characters in the story – or for an ongoing romantic arc through a series of novels. With this type of novel, you can extend the length into the 70,000 to 75,000-word range, but since they need a light touch and a brisk pace, I would aim for shorter rather than longer. Look at some examples of novels of the type you want to write, and estimate their word-length based on an average number of words per line multiplied by lines per page and pages per book. Be careful about using a 'big name bestseller' as your model – their status and popularity often mean these authors are expected to write longer novels for their fans, often eighty- to a hundred-thousand words or more.

Today 60,000 words is about the lower limit for a novel, so we will use that as our 'ideal' model. I'm going to use the *four quarters plus midpoint and eight-sequences* model that I described in *Plot Basics*. In my own writing, I find an average chapter length of about 2,000 words works best, which gives me thirty chapters in a 60,000-word novel. This number is completely arbitrary. Agatha Christie had forty or more chapters in some of her novels, and I know a number of writers who are more comfortable with chapters of a thousand to fifteen-hundred words. Choose whatever works best for you. The total number of chapters really doesn't matter, as we'll be breaking the plot into eight sequences of approximately the same length. That's more than enough about numbers.

The Main Parts of a Murder Mystery

The fundamental parts of a murder mystery story are:

    a) A murder
    b) A victim, perhaps more than one
    c) The suspects, including the murderer
    d) A detective
    e) First part of the investigation: Incrimination of the suspects
    f) Second part of the investigation: Elimination of the suspects
    g) Final part of the investigation: Solution and revelation of whodunit
    h) Denouement – the restoration of order

The order of parts (a) to (d) can be varied depending on the story, but (e) to (h) will usually occur in sequence. The murder occurs in chapter one, or before chapter one, in a 'body in the library' type story, which we're calling an 'Act I Murder.' In other stories, the first murder does not occur until about the middle of the story – a 'Midpoint Murder.' As mentioned previously, the choice of Act I or Midpoint for the murder depends in part on how you wish the reader to view the victim. If they are dead at the beginning of the story, then they exist primarily to provide a corpse as an excuse for an investigation, and the only things we learn about them are what other people reveal during the course of the investigation. The reader has little emotional interest in the victim. With a midpoint murder, the reader gets to see the victim as a living person for half of the novel and sees them interacting with the suspects. This can give the murder itself more impact, especially if the victim isn't the person the reader expected to be killed. This is a choice you have to make depending on the story you want to tell.

The 'Most Likely Suspect' or 'Innocent Accused' plot is a variation on the Act I murder.

The Act I Murder Plot

This is the plot most people think of when they hear that a story is a 'murder mystery.' It begins with the discovery of the body and the introduction of the detective, usually in that order, and moves through a series of clearly defined stages. Agatha Christie's *Murder at the Vicarage* uses this plot sequence, as does *The Body in the Library*. I used it for my novel *Murder by Magic*.

Four Quarters Plus Midpoint
In *Plot Basics* I said that the basic structure of any plot was to set up a situation in the first quarter – the hero is presented with a problem or an opportunity for change ; he then makes two failed attempts to resolve the solution before a third and final attempt provides the climax and resolution. This 'rule of three' for attempts at resolving a situation is found in all types of story, from the 'Three Little Pigs' to Hollywood block-busters. Three is the minimum number of attempts to estab-lish a pattern, and anything more than three is overkill. In the murder mystery, the investigation will typically pass through three phases: each of these *may* include a failed attempt at an answer to whodunit? – but it doesn't have to. The 'failure' or crisis at the end of an attempt may come in the form of a twist that – for the reader and the Watson, but per-haps not for the detective – makes the situation seem more complex and further from a resolution than ever before.

Here is the basic breakdown of the four quarters plus mid-point for an Act I Murder plot:

(i)   A murder is committed and a detective introduced
(ii)   The detective investigates and clues point towards either a potential murderer or a vital witness.
        (Midpoint) The potential murderer or vital witness is killed

(iii)   The detective re-evaluates the evidence so far, investigates more, and proposes a second theory. But a twist makes it seem that the situation is even more baffling and impossible to solve.

(iv)   Final solution – the murderer is identified and brought to justice.

The midpoint doesn't *have* to be a second murder, it could be a different sort of plot twist that complicates the situation, but a second murder is very common at this point. The twist at the end of the third quarter *could* be a murder, as well as or instead of the midpoint murder. The complication at the midpoint or the end of quarter three could be that the person everyone thinks is the murderer turns out to have a cast-iron, 'unbreakable' alibi that the detective will then need to test. Or it could be a confession, possibly by some sympathetic character who the reader will want to be proved innocent.

Breaking the plot down into four quarters like this helps by giving a bird's-eye view of the *function* of each part of the story. In the broadest possible terms, it tells you what needs to go where. In the next section, we will divide each of the quarters to give us eight sequences, providing a more detailed view of what can go where.

If you are more familiar with a three-act structure, think of the first quarter as Act I, the second and third quarters (with the midpoint between them) as Act II, and the final quarter as Act III. Note that a 'quarter' is an approximate measure, rather than a strict mathematical one. The first 'quarter,' for example, is often longer than the final one.

Eight Sequences

The eight-sequence model was created by Frank Daniel at UCLA for teaching screenwriters how to break down their plots. It can be used for developing the plots of novels as well as screenplays. Here we'll look at how the plot of an Act I Murder mystery can be structured using eight sequences. Note that the details below are serving suggestions – things that *could* go in each of the eight sequences. Your story may require that a particular event occurs earlier or later than shown below – moving something into a sequence one below or one above is fine. If you are moving things further than that, I would suggest double-checking that this is absolutely necessary for your story. If you're including things a lot earlier than expected, you may be 'writing short' and need to look at what's missing; if you're including things a lot later, you may be 'writing long' and including unnecessary material. In the final analysis, it is your story and you can do whatever feels right – but if you're not following the guidance below, make sure you know that you *are* heading off the track and *why* you have chosen to do so.

Act I – First Quarter: Setting Up the Problem, Introducing Characters and Setting

Sequence 1: The body – usually discovered dead as the story opens, though there may be a prologue in which the murder is committed by some unseen person. In this type of plot, the corpse should be discovered as soon as possible – perhaps in the first scene, but certainly before the end of Act I. If the victim is shown before the murder, it is usually only in a brief scene. The discovery should be a dramatic scene – it should be shown as disturbing the equilibrium of the closed world of the story. The corpse should be discovered in unusual or intriguing circumstances. *How* the victim was killed, or how the body was left, may give a clue about why he or she was killed, or about the type of person the murderer was. Or the circumstance may have been deliberately arranged to disguise both these things, or perhaps even incriminate an innocent person.

Introduction of the detective. This may happen in Sequence 1 or at the beginning of Sequence 2. Have him (or her) do or say something clever and unexpected, establishing them as unique and interesting. Show them as being apart from the suspects in the story – they must be an *objective* investigator. Initially, establish them as enigmatic or quirky – do not reveal too much about them at this point: make the reader want to know more.

Show the world – the setting and milieu – in which the murder has occurred, and how the death has upset the balance of this world. Establish that it is a *closed* world, limiting the number of suspects that need to be investigated.

Sometimes a symbol is introduced early in the story – an image, an object, a person or an action which serves as a metaphor for what occurs in the story. The symbol may then appear at the end of the story, either in its original form or changed in some way, as an observation on what has occurred.

Sequence 2: The suspects and witnesses. These may have been present in the first sequence, but here the detective is introduced to them now that their roles as suspects or witnesses have been established. The closed circle of suspects will include the murderer, who must be present during Act I. We will probably also learn something about the victim during this sequence. Character personalities and the relationships between characters are introduced in broad terms. Initially, at least, the victim should be seen as an innocent person who didn't deserve to die, and the suspects should seem shocked and upset by his or her death. Reaction to the murder, discussion of the event, and speculation about the identity and motive of the murderer. Perhaps an accusation – or one implied. Perhaps there is one obvious suspect who is *too* obvious.

The detective's first impressions of the crime scene and events, and first gathering of clues. Often something occurs – or is hinted at – at the end of Sequence 1 or early in Sequence 2 that makes it clear to the reader that the crime is more complicated than originally thought, or that the investigation will be more dangerous. Or both. A hint at what is at stake for the unknown murderer and the detective.

Act II Part 1 – Second Quarter: The Investigation

Sequence 3: Questioning the suspects. The detective must try and establish who was where at the time of the murder and what the relationship of each suspect was to the victim. At this stage, we are interested in the broad details so that the detective and the reader can become familiar with the main cast. Witnesses who are not potential suspects can wait to be interviewed at a later stage – towards the end of this sequence or early in Sequence 4. The detective learns about each character from what they say about themselves, and what they say about each other. People also reveal their own characters in the judgments they make about others.

The detective will also observe the reactions and interactions of the suspects.

Revealing backstory. We also need to learn about the victim from the things that suspects say about them. The detective will gradually piece together details about the life, personality, and relationships of the victim. He may hear conflicting views about what sort of person the victim was. What enemies might they have had? Who might have benefited from their death? The detective may discover that the victim wasn't a nice person – which may widen the circle of the suspects who may have had reason to dislike them and therefore (perhaps) a motive for murder. A truly unpleasant victim may mean that the murderer wasn't necessarily a villain: the killer may have been a nice person who was *driven* to murder by the victim's actions.

The detective will explore the setting further. There may be physical clues such as maps, plans, or timetables.

The detective may begin to construct a timeline of events, showing who was where and in what order things happened. He may identify gaps that need to be filled by further questioning. He may also begin to notice discrepancies between the accounts of different suspects, flagging them up for further investigation.

Generally speaking, each suspect will be interviewed twice by the detective – once in Sequence 3 and a second time in Sequence 4 or 5. Each interview will be the equivalent of a chapter. In the initial interview, the detective will establish the basics about the character; and then after the first round of interviews are complete, he will compare the statements of each suspect and come up with some more detailed questions that he needs to ask each person in the second round of interviews. Using the numbers I outlined earlier, that means each major suspect will provide two chapters of around 2,000 words each. And you will have, probably, six main suspects. Any more than that and the interviews part of the story becomes too monotonous; less than that and you risk having too few suspects for the murderer to hide among – especially if you are planning to have a second murder and kill one of them off. You might also have some shorter chapters involving witnesses who are not suspects, and they will only get a single chapter each.

Each suspect will receive an initial assessment to see if they have means, motive and opportunity. Some characters may seem to lack one of these three, or have an alibi that demonstrates they were elsewhere at the time of the murder, and as a result may be – at least for the moment – ruled out as plausible suspects.

Sequence 4: This sequence will lead up to a major revelation or some other twist at the midpoint of the story. By this point, the detective will have gathered tangible clues from the location and intangible clues from the statements made by each of the subjects and witnesses. He or she can now make a first attempt at piecing things together and coming up with a theory about what happened on the night of the murder.

At this stage in the story, we are exploring what *seems* to have happened – putting together the sequence of events that the murderer wishes everybody to believe. Statements and clues are taken at face value and point in the direction the murderer wants them to point – away from him (or her). The best kinds of clues are those that *appear* to show one thing, but are later demonstrated to mean something different.

The initial round of interviews has shown some or all of the suspects to be behaving suspiciously. They have a guilty secret of some kind and want to avoid it being made public. The detective will need to establish which of these guilty secrets are connected to the murder, and which are red herrings. Currently, it is too early to tell – he must investigate further. For the time being, we want it to appear to the reader that any one of the suspects could be guilty. They must all have some reason – a motive – for wanting the victim out of the way.

Guilty behaviour by suspects may include destroying, or attempting to destroy, evidence. Or seeking to discredit

another witness or incriminate another suspect. Are they doing this because they are guilty themselves – of murder or
some other misdemeanour? Or are they seeking to protect
someone else?

One or more suspects may disappear – are they guilty, or
are they the victim of foul play? Have they fled because they
are in possession of vital evidence and are afraid of becoming
the murderer's next victim? The answer to a question like this
is what usually forms the dramatic revelation or twist at the
midpoint of the story.

The detective may form a first hypothesis – it may point to
one of the suspects being guilty or it may point to one of the
characters having vital evidence about the murder. Or he may
be talking to a character who is on the point of revealing a
vital clue to the murderer's identity or motive.

Midpoint: As we have already seen, this is typically a second
murder. And the person killed is either the person the detective thought was guilty, or it is the person who had a vital clue
about the murderer. There doesn't have to be a murder here
– you might want to save the second murder for the 'crisis' at
the end of Act II (which is the end of quarter three and the
end of Sequence 6). Instead, you might have an attack on the
life of the detective – a hint that he is getting too close to the
murderer; or a ploy by the murderer to make the detective
believe he is getting close to the murderer's identity when in
fact the murderer is framing someone else. Or the midpoint
twist could be a piece of evidence that seems to prove someone
the reader wants to be guilty is innocent, or someone they
want to be innocent is guilty.

Sometimes there may be a failed murder attempt here. The
murderer may stage an attempt on his or her own life, in order
to shift suspicion away from them. Or they may carry out a
second murder and make it appear that the second suspect
was killed by mistake and that the intended victim was the
murderer himself (or herself).

Whatever the actual nature of the midpoint twist, it serves
to derail the detective's first hypothesis – or it *appears* to
prove it wrong – and spins the story in a new direction. The

stakes are raised and the pressure on the detective to come up with a solution is increased: he must identify the murderer before someone else is killed.

Act II Part 2 – Third Quarter: Re-evaluation

Sequence Five: This begins with everyone's reaction to the events of the midpoint, including the detective's. It is often a period of confusion: the situation is even more mystifying than it was before. Things people thought they knew have been proved wrong. The detective's and/or his Watson's confidence is at a low point. If there has been a second murder, the detective may blame himself for making a mistake that allowed it to happen. He may feel that he has not been as ruthless and dispassionate in his methods as he is capable of being – he needs to raise his game.

This sequence requires a re-evaluation of everything that has happened so far. The detective knows that nothing can be taken for granted – nothing and no one can be trusted. The midpoint has shown that the reality of the situation is not what it appeared to be. Perhaps an assumption has been made that cannot be trusted – there is some key 'fact' that needs to be identified and reinterpreted. The detective may have misinterpreted clues or drawn mistaken conclusions, and as a result, has been taken in the wrong direction. Usually, this is exactly how the murderer has planned things.

Everything must be reassessed in the light of what was learned at the midpoint. And the detective must piece together any clues from the second murder with what he has from the first.

Sequences 5 and 6 are where alibis are retested. Before the midpoint, it may have appeared that one or more of the suspects had an unbreakable alibi, which meant they could not possibly have committed the murder. Now the detective knows he must see if he can find a weakness in this alibi.

The detective will question most of the suspects again, challenging them on the suspicious behaviours they demonstrated before the midpoint. Or challenging them on discrepancies in their account of events when compared to the account provided by another witness. This is also where the detective may learn that some relationships are not what they first appeared. A previously unknown relationship – between suspects or between a suspect and one of the murder victims – may come to light. One or more of the characters may not be who they appeared to be. Events that seemed to be unrelated may, in fact, be closely linked, or events which it was believed were related, or to have been consequences of one another, may, in fact, prove to be unrelated. Things begin to take on new meaning or new significance.

There is usually some event or clue at the end of Sequence 5 that moves the investigation forward. The detective learns something about someone or is able to give new meaning to an old clue or observation. His optimism about resolving the mystery is renewed.

Sequence 6: This sequence builds up to a major turning point at the end of Act II. In many genres, this turning point is a crisis and marks the hero's darkest hour. In the murder mystery, there is an event that appears *to the reader* to be a catastrophic event or major failure on the part of the detective – at which point the detective will announce that he now knows whodunit. The trick is to make this breakthrough on the part of the detective look to the reader like something that makes the mystery seem more confusing than ever before. The fact that the detective says 'I now have all the information I need' serves part of this function, as it leaves the reader thinking 'How can that be true? I still have no idea whodunit!'

Sequence 6 in most stories details the hero's second attempt to resolve his situation, and this attempt fails spectacularly causing the crisis of the story and paving the way for one final do-or-die attempt at the climax in Act III (Sequence 7). In a murder mystery, we may see the detective testing out a second hypothesis, which will fail because he still needs one final piece of evidence, or needs to reinterpret a clue he already has – we mentioned this in the section on *clues* as being a 'key clue'. This sequence often has the detective putting up a 'straw man' – a theory that he can then pull to pieces himself, forcing himself to re-evaluate every statement and piece of evidence – he's saying, 'This is what *could* have happened, but what other sequence of events could account for this evidence?' The second wrong hypothesis exists only to be discredited and lead him towards the correct one. Usually, there is one clue that forces him to abandon hypothesis two – it doesn't fit. This seems like a failure to the reader, but it provides the detective with the last bit of data he needs to explain everything. At which point he draws everyone together in the drawing room for the climax.

Act III: Final Quarter – Climax and Resolution, Explaining the Mystery, Restoring Balance

In the murder mystery, Sequence 7 is typically a lengthy explanation by the detective and Sequence 8 is a brief scene that demonstrates that balance has been restored to the world of the story.

Sequence 7: The drawing room scene. Logical deduction defeats the murderer. Traditionally the detective turns to each of the suspects in turn, explaining how they may have had a motive for the murder, but how their alibi or their lack of access to the means or lack of opportunity demonstrate that they cannot be the murderer. The detective may or may not reveal the nature of the person's guilty secret – if he doesn't reveal it publicly, he reveals it to the Watson or a police detective in private at another point so that the reader has all of the facts. The suspects are exonerated one by one until, by a process of elimination, the murderer is revealed. Or not. Sometimes all of the suspects appear to have been exonerated.

Sometimes the detective will initially appear to 'prove' someone is guilty – following the *apparent* meaning of the evidence, which the murderer wanted everyone to believe – but then suddenly show how this is wrong, and then show the real meaning of the evidence and reveal the true identity of the murderer. He presents the chain of events in their true sequence and explains the true meaning of the evidence, discounting its apparent meaning. His explanation demonstrates the murderer's motive and that he had the means and opportunity, and it disproves his alibi.

Ideally, the identity of the murderer will be a surprise to the reader, even though all of the evidence can be demonstrated to point to him (or her).

In some stories, it may be necessary to lay a trap for the murderer, to trick him into revealing himself, especially if there isn't currently sufficient evidence to prove his guilt. This should only be done where the detective has already deduced the identity of the murderer and needs additional proof: it is a cheat (at least in terms of the genre expectations of the murder mystery) if a trap is used to reveal the identity of a murderer that the detective has been *unable* to deduce from the evidence presented so far.

A full confession from the murderer is usually an anti-climax, as it draws attention away from the brilliance of the detective. Nor should his identity be revealed as the result of a stupid mistake he has made – he must remain a worthy opponent for the detective to the end. His one fatal flaw may be over-confidence or arrogance – he may slip-up because he has assumed that he is smarter than the detective.

Cornered and dangerous, the murderer may seek to escape. There may be a fight or a chase as the murderer seeks to avoid capture – but the detective and/or the police are prepared for this and his escape fails. In this type of story, the murderer must be brought to justice. He is punished in some meaningful and satisfactory way. In the 1930s, when a convicted murder's fate was to be hanged, the murderer was often permitted to take the 'gentleman's way out' and commit suicide. This allowed for a more dramatic ending than having him carted off in handcuffs to await trial.

Sequence 8: This brief sequence usually has the detective explaining a few final thoughts to his Watson or to the police detective. There may be some mention of what has happened – or will happen – to the other suspects: this is meant to show that the disruption caused by the murder has been resolved and equilibrium has been restored. Typically a young couple caught up in events as suspects can no go off happily hand in hand and become man and wife. Or the detective returns to the comfortable everyday surroundings of his own home. Justice has been served and all is now right with the world.

The Midpoint Murder Plot

In this plot, half of the 'evidence' relating to people and events is provided *before* the murder takes place. And instead of hearing second-hand accounts of the victim's speech and behaviour, we are able to witness it first-hand. We will not know the identity of the victim and may be led to believe that another person is the most likely to be killed. We may also see the murderer – whose identity is also not yet known to us – engaged in activities designed to demonstrate his innocence or inability to commit the murder. Agatha Christie's *Death on the Nile* follows this plot pattern almost exactly and is divided into forty-two chapters. I used it for my first mystery novel *The Sword in the Stone-Dead*.

Four Quarters Plus Midpoint

(i)   Characters – including the murderer, victim, and suspects – and setting are introduced. The detective is usually present from the start, but his appearance can be delayed until the second quarter.

(ii) The character of the victim and the nature of their relationships with other characters are explored.
      (Midpoint) A murder is committed. The detective may propose a first theory based on what is already known – what *appears to have happened.*

(iii) The detective interviews suspects and gathers evidence. This is an extension of the information already provided about people and events before the murder. He evaluates the evidence and proposes a second theory. But a twist – perhaps a second murder – proves this wrong.

(iv) Final solution – the murderer is identified and brought to justice.

Eight Sequences

Many of the events that occur in the Midpoint Murder plot are the same as those in the Act I murder, but they occur in a different sequence. They are included below in briefer form.

ACT I – First Quarter: Introducing the Characters and Setting

Sequence 1: Introduce the victim, murderer (or murderous couple), and major suspects as characters. Introduce the location and establish that there will be a closed circle of suspects. Introduce the detective. (This can be delayed until Sequence 2). The sequence will usually climax with a scene involving either the murderer or the victim, typically showing them either as a bully or as the bullied.

Sequence 2: Introduce more suspects. Explore the victim's character and his/her relationships with other characters – these scenes function, in part, as a replacement for the first round of suspect interviews in the Act I Murder plot. This sequence will often climax with an event foreshadowing murder. Perhaps a threat or an attempt on the life of the victim or murderer; perhaps the victim or murderer goes to the detective and asks for his help. The detective is drawn into the story in some way.

ACT II Part 1 – Setting Up the Problem, 'Rising Conflict'

Sequence 3: More about the detective – set him up as the ideal investigator; an outsider and a genius. The detective observes the suspicious behaviour of the suspects. The detective observes the behaviour of the person who will become the victim. Introduce the romantic couple – either as lovers or as people with the potential to be lovers by the end of the story. The climax of this sequence is an argument, confrontation, accusation, or an attempted murder. Perhaps an unsuccessful murder attempt – on the victim; or a fake attempt on the life of the murderer to divert suspicion away from him.

Sequence 4: More suspicious behaviour from the suspects, who may now mistrust each other following the arguments or violence in the previous sequence. The detective learns more about the relationships between the suspects and the victim. The murderer's alibi is established.

Midpoint – The murder. A corpse is discovered. Acts as the climax of Section 4.

ACT II Part 2 – Reaction to the Murder & The Investigation Begins

Sequence 5: Reaction of the suspects to the murder – a new perspective is established now that the equilibrium has been upset. Beginning the investigation proper – all are suspected. Establishing the limits of the closed circle of suspects. Was the earlier attempted murder or violence linked to, or a clue to, the actual murder? Establish what *seems* to have happened: the sequence of events that the murderer wishes everyone to believe is true.

The detective interviewing suspects – questioning them about their previously observed suspicious behaviour. Uncovering guilty secrets – are they relevant to the murder investigation? Establishing whether each suspect has means, motive, and opportunity to commit the murder. And also the facts relating to their alibi. The climax of the sequence is the discovery of an import clue.

Sequence 6: Closing in on one suspect – either they know something important about the murderer, or they are the person who seems most likely to be the murderer. The climax of the sequence may be a second murder. The person currently suspected of murder or the person who knows something significant is killed, or there is some other major setback to the investigation.

ACT III – Climax and Resolution – Announcing the Solution, Explaining the Mystery, Restoring Balance

Sequence 7: Reaction to, and investigation of, the second murder or major setback. The detective proposes a second hypothesis, based on evidence from the second murder or new evidence. He may discover a key clue – something that causes him to see events in a whole new light, and to re-evaluate everything that has gone before. The climax of the sequence occurs when the detective says he knows who the murderer is, and asks all of the suspects to join him in the drawing room, or some similar location.

Sequence 8: The drawing room scene – the detective begins his explanation, recapping the evidence, the clues, and explaining their significance. He explores the possible guilt of each of the suspects in turn, before eliminating them as the murderer. The climax involves the naming of the murderer; explanation of his guilt – the how and why. Capture of the murderer if he attempts to escape.

Aftermath of the climactic revelation – the murderer's fate. Perhaps the murderer is allowed to commit suicide. The lovers come together happily, a symbol of the re-establishment of the equilibrium of the story world.

The Most-Likely Suspect

or Innocent Accused Plot

This is a variation on the Act I Murder Plot, and as well as being used in a traditional or cozy mystery, it is often used in hardboiled or detective thriller plots, because it provides a greater opportunity for jeopardy and suspense than the other plots discussed here.

The historical detective novel *Aristotle Detective* (1978) by Margaret Doody uses this type of plot.

Four Quarters Plus Midpoint
Here is the basic breakdown of the four quarters plus midpoint for a Most-Likely Suspect / Innocent Accused:

(i)   A murder is committed and a suspect is accused. The detective is introduced.

(ii)   The detective investigates and clues point towards the most-likely suspect. Another possible suspect or a vital witness is identified.
       (Midpoint) The potential murderer or vital witness is killed

(iii) The detective re-evaluates the evidence so far, investigates more, and proposes a second theory. But a twist makes it seem that the most-likely / innocent suspect is guilty after all.

(iv)   Final solution – the real murderer is identified and brought to justice.

Eight Sequences

Act I – First Quarter: Setting Up the Problem, Introducing Characters and Setting

Sequence 1: The murder and discovery of the body. Introduce the location/crime scene. Witnesses may give chase as the murderer escapes. The immediate aftermath of the murder – the reaction of witnesses, friends and family. Discussion about the event, including speculation about the identity and motive of the murderer. Perhaps an accusation – someone who obviously stood to gain from the death, who openly quarrelled with the victim, or has an obvious motive for murder. This person may have been seen at the scene with the murder weapon in his (or her) hand, or they may have been seen running away from the scene. This 'obvious suspect' is either going to be an innocent person who is wrongly accused, or they may be the real murderer and trying to make it look like they are too obvious a suspect to be the murderer. The detective may be introduced in this sequence or in Sequence 2.

Sequence 2: Reaction to the accusation – friends, relatives, and enemies/rivals of the accused react. First reaction of the detective. The detective demonstrates his near-magical deductive abilities and agrees to take the case – he may initially be on the side of the victim and in opposition to the accused, or he may be on the side of the accused from the beginning.

First clues from the crime scene. The detective talks to witnesses and learns something about the victim. Typically, he discovers that the victim wasn't the popular figure that he (or she) appeared. Perhaps there are even members of the victim's own family that might have wished to see them dead. Revelation of backstory – of the victim, the suspects, and the accused.

More clues discovered or statements taken as the detective investigates further. Perhaps a first glimmer of hope for the accused – the first hint of a possible alibi.

Act II Part 1 – Second Quarter: The Investigation

Sequence 3: More and deeper investigation: more potential enemies of the victim identified – people other than the chief suspect had a motive for the murder. Perhaps hints of a debt owed to or by the victim. Or of a 'vendetta' – a revenge that was 'owed.' Or of a wrong suffered by the victim or caused by them. Or of some important rival or enemy they – or the accused – may have had.

A positive step – an enemy of the victim identified and some clue that this person may be the murderer, rather than the accused. If he wasn't on the side of the accused before, the detective will now agree to help prove them innocent.

A negative step – some damning evidence or revelation, or perhaps even a confession, that seems to prove the accused guilty after all. Perhaps there is some secret the accused has kept from the detective who was trying to help him – even though the two of them were meant to be working together and trusting one another.

Sequence 4: Proof of the accused's secret/guilt – or an admission from the accused himself or someone close to him, and it is worse than the detective feared. The accused has lied to protect this secret – if his lies are made public, he will appear even more guilty in the eyes of his accusers. The accused may be prepared to sacrifice himself – his life and/or his reputation – in order to protect his lover. He may know that the lover has a guilty secret, or may only suspect that they do.

Reaction by the detective and others to the previous discovery/revelation. The whole situation for the accused looks much darker than before. And the stakes may have been raised, with the accused's lover now being at risk too. The detective may begin to suspect that the accused is guilty after all, and must convince himself to try and remain objective.

Detective may discover that the accused has an actual enemy – someone who hates the accused and has a motive for destroying his life, rather than just regarding him as a convenient scapegoat for the murder. This may provide the first inkling that someone else has a strong motive for murder. More clues and information gathering are required as a result.

There may be discussion of some apparently trivial matter or clue which will become very significant later. An attempt may be made on the life of the detective, the accused, or the accused's lover. The detective may be injured trying to protect the accused or the lover, or when he tries to chase the attacker. If the accused really *is* guilty, this attack may have been faked to divert suspicion away from him and rebuild the detective's belief in his innocence.

Midpoint: A significant setback. A witness who has vital information that could prove the accused innocent may go missing or be murdered. Or a witness may be found who can prove that the accused's alibi – or the lover's alibi – is false. Or someone may come forward with evidence that the accused committed an earlier, unrelated crime, blackening the accused's reputation and making it seem more likely that he could be the murderer after all. Or another suspect who appeared to be a strong suspect for the original murder may be killed.

Act II Part 2 – Third Quarter: Re-evaluation

Sequence 5: Re-evaluation of all that has gone before in the light of the midpoint revelation/discovery. The detective may try to get one or more witnesses to recall seemingly insignificant details that might cast a new light on events. Was anything out of place at the murder scene? Anything missing? Anything there that shouldn't have been? Perhaps someone recalls seemingly unconnected events or exchanges of dialogue that happened immediately before the murder. These clues can probably be interpreted in two ways – either supporting the accused or damning him, depending on how they are read.

In the light of the damning evidence revealed, or supporting evidence lost, at the midpoint, the other suspects turn on the accused. They try to undermine the detective's belief in his possible innocence. They may try to interfere with the investigation or try to persuade him to stop helping the accused.

Discussion between the detective and the accused – and the detective becomes more sure of the accused's innocence because of what he says – and because of the attempts by others to prove his guilt. The detective rededicates himself to proving the accused innocent.

Sequence 6: The detective may help the accused avoid capture or arrest – effectively breaking the law himself. Or he protects the accused from the vigilante justice of the other suspects. This further strengthens the bond between accused and detective. The accused may reveal more of his backstory, relating to his relationship with the first murder victim. There may be things he knows that he doesn't want to make public because they would tarnish the reputation of the dead man.

The detective learns more about the original victim. The victim may have been blackmailing one or more of the suspects. Or may have had some other type of hold over the fate of one or more people. There may also be more evidence that supports the accused's account of the nature of his relationship with the victim.

Having taken the side of the accused, the detective may be challenged by the other suspects – accused of bias or lack of objectivity. These actions may serve to distract the detective from his investigation. There may also be action against the detective by a third party who is in league with the murderer – or who is acting independently because they don't want the accused to be proven innocent. This misfortune serves to increase reader sympathy for the detective, especially if he is an amateur sleuth. It also serves to demonstrate the increasing odds he faces.

More speculation on the identity and motive of the murderer also acts as a distraction. Depending on the accused's motives at this point, he may distract the detective with unrelated problems.

Another clue, perhaps related to the murder weapon or method – the 'means' – and who owned it or had access to it. Perhaps a denial from the owner of the weapon, or of the person known to have taken it, borrowed it, or had access to it. The weapon or poison or whatever may have been stolen recently or lost. Other minor clues are uncovered, tangible or otherwise, but the detective still has no idea how they all fit together.

Usually, there is a crisis of some kind at the end of Act II/end of Sequence 6. The detective may put forward a hypothesis and name a murderer – only to be proved wrong when that person is themselves murdered. Or perhaps the detective has identified someone who can prove the accused's alibi and has persuaded them to speak out – only for them to be murdered before they can reveal what they know. Or perhaps the detective discovers this witness, and they admit what they know, but they refuse to speak out and help the accused because of some personal vendetta they have against him.

Act III: Climax and Resolution – Announcing the Solution, Explaining the Mystery, Restoring Balance

Sequence 7: The detective recognises the true meaning of the 'key clue' – is able to place events in their true sequence, and understand the real meaning of all the evidence gathered. The crucial evidence is usually something overlooked in Act I: something that appeared to be of little consequence at the time it was first disclosed, but which takes on a new meaning as a result of what was revealed at the midpoint. The detective knows whodunit, but now he must prove it – hatches a plan to uncover an important clue, or to persuade a reluctant witness to speak.

Sequence 8: The drawing room or courtroom scene – unmasking the guilty. Explanation of the mystery. Restoration of balance to the story world – usually in the form of a romantic relationship being confirmed.

The Locked Room Mystery
or 'Impossible' Crime

The locked room mystery is a subgenre in which a murder is committed in seemingly impossible circumstances. The murder has taken place in a location – the 'locked room' – which no person could have entered or left. Either it is a physically locked room or a place that has been under constant surveillance. When the murder is discovered, the situation is such that the murderer seems to have vanished into thin air. The detective must discover *how* the crime was committed. This type of story is sometimes referred to as a *how*dunit because whodunit is pretty much a secondary question. We can broaden the scope of this category to include other 'impossible' situations in which murder is committed. For example, a victim is discovered lying in the snow, shot at close range, but with no footprints to be seen other than his own.

Dorothy L. Sayers' Lord Peter Wimsey novel *Have His Carcase* (1932), has a murder victim discovered on a rock, surrounded by wet sand which shows no footprints: the body seems freshly killed, yet fisherman on a boat nearby swear nobody approached the rock. Edgar Allan Poe's 'The Murders in the Rue Morgue' (1841) is a locked room mystery. The earliest examples at novel-length are Israel Zangwill's *The Big Bow Mystery* (1892) and *The Mystery of the Yellow Room* (1907) by Gaston Leroux. A number of Arthur Conan Doyle's Sherlock Holmes stories make use of the locked room or impossible crime: the novels *The Sign of Four* (1890) and *The Valley of Fear* (1914), and the short stories 'The Adventure of the Speckled Band,' 'The Adventure of the Crooked Man,' and 'The Adventure of the Resident Patient.' *Locked Room Murders and Other Impossible Crimes: A Comprehensive Bibliography* (1991) by Robert Adey lists over 2,000 short stories and novels, including notes on the nature of the crime and – in a separate section, so as to avoid spoilers – their solutions.

The Appeal of the Locked Room Mystery

In his article 'Maybe You Better Not Lock the Door' in *Murder Ink* (1978), Gordon Bean describes the appeal of this type of 'impossible' murder mystery: "Reading a locked room mystery, you enter a world reminiscent of a fantastic magic show: Men walk through walls, slither through keyholes and vanish like pricked soap bubbles. And not only do you experience magical effects, you are fooled by magical methods as well. Not trapdoors, secret wires, mirrors – these are just gimmicks. Rather, I am speaking of suggestion and misdirection, psychological devices the magician – along with his literary equivalent, the locked room writer – uses to coax your mind down a prescribed path of 'logic' which ends in paradox."

Donald A. Yates in his essay 'The Locked Room,' refers to the various 'rules' that have been formulated for writing mystery stories, and says: "... there is among these themes one in particular which most perfectly embodies the special generic characteristic of strict limitations. It is the classic problem which makes the purest appeal to logic for its solution; it highlights the 'closed' nature of the detective tale and is, unquestionably, its most traditional expression. It is the plot idea which has come to be referred to as 'the locked-room mystery.'"

If we're honest here, the locked room story is a gimmick story and is really a short story idea told at novel length. The main point of interest is how a person came to be murdered in a room that the murderer could not get into or out of without being observed, and so appears to have disappeared into thin air. The set-up describes the 'hermetically sealed' room and the murder (or discovery of the body), and the climax is the explanation of how the crime was committed and made to look like an 'impossible' crime. Of course, if we are being *brutally* honest, this applies to all classic murder mysteries. Several of Agatha Christie's novels are based on ideas she first tried out at short story length.

The appeal of the locked room mystery lies in not in discovering whodunit, but rather how it was done.

First Lock Your Room...

The first requirement of the locked room mystery is – unsurprisingly – a locked room. You need to establish that the room was locked from the inside so that the murderer could not possibly have exited from it after he had completed his wicked crime. Here's how Sir Arthur Conan Doyle set things up in the Sherlock Holmes story 'The Speckled Band':

... the door had been fastened upon the inner side, and the windows were blocked by old-fashioned shutters with broad iron bars, which were secured every night. The walls were carefully sounded and were shown to be quite solid all around, and the flooring was also thoroughly examined, with the same result. The chimney was wide, but is barred by four large staples...

All locked room stories will have a similar description – you need to demonstrate that any possible way out of the room was locked. If the window isn't barred, it is either too narrow to permit its use for escape, or it is screwed shut, and there are no signs of the putty having been tampered with, since removing a pane of glass and then fixing it back into place with new putty would be a dead giveaway. Walls are checked for hidden doors and secret passageways, and the floor and ceiling checked for trapdoors. The room is shown to be – to use Dr. Fell's preferred term – hermetically sealed.

The use of secret entrances or hidden passageways is considered to be a cliché – so old that it was first used in Biblical times – and a cheat. So are duplicate keys and the use of bizarre and unlikely mechanical devices.

The Locked Room Lecture

"I like my murders to be frequent, gory, and grotesque." Dr. Gideon Fell, *The Hollow Man*

John Dickson Carr's *The Hollow Man* (1935, published in the USA as *The Three Coffins*), is regarded as one of the best examples of its type, and its Chapter 17 contains the 'Locked-

Room Lecture' given by the detective hero Dr. Gideon Fell. This is quoted in texts about mystery stories, and in many later locked room mysteries, including Anthony Boucher's *Nine Times Nine* and Clayton Rawson's *Death from a Top Hat*.

Dr. Fell presents his explanations under two headings: (i) where death occurs in a sealed room "from which no murderer has escape because no murderer was actually in the room..." and (ii) where the murderer was in the room and seems to have passed through a locked door or window.

(i) The Murderer was Not in the Room

(1) The victim's death proves *not* to be a murder at all, but rather a series of coincidences resulting in an accident which looks like a murder. Before the room was locked, a robbery or some other attack, or just a tripping accident occurred – furniture was broken or some other damage resulted, making it appear that a struggle had taken place. Later, after the room was locked, the victim was wounded, stunned, or killed while alone. Events which took place before and after the locking of the room are assumed to have taken place at the same time and after the door was locked. The cause of death is a blow to the head which looks as if it was caused by a blow, but was actually the result of a fall or some other accident - occurring in the locked room or before the victim entered. Dr. Fell names two early examples, but we shall not include spoilers here.

(2) The death *is* murder, but the victim has been compelled in some way to kill himself or engage in an activity that causes his accidental death. The compulsion may be the result of a haunting, by hypnotic suggestion, by some sort of drug or poison, or by gas fed into the room from outside. The chemical may cause the victim to behave violently, destroying the furniture and making it appear that a struggle has taken place.

(3) The death is murder and it was achieved by some sort of mechanical device already planted in the room, hidden undetectably in some innocent-looking piece of decoration or furniture. The trap may have been set recently or put in place long ago by someone who is now dead. Examples given by Dr.

Fell include a gun-mechanism concealed in the telephone receiver, which fires a bullet into the victim's head as he lifts the receiver. There is a pistol fired by a piece of string pulled tight by the expansion of water as it freezes. A clock that fires a bullet when it is wound. Or "the ingenious grandfather clock which sets ringing a hideously clanging bell on its top, so that when you reach up to shut off the din your own touch releases a blade that slashes open your stomach." There are other mechanisms that release falling or swinging weights, or undetectable poisoned needles, all triggered in some way by the unwitting victim himself. Among the more bizarre suggestions are a "bed that exhales a deadly gas when your body warms it" and a variety of items wired to deliver a lethal electric shock, including a tea urn.

(4) The victim's death was suicide but he staged it to make it look like murder. This is often achieved by having the weapon disappear in some way. A man stabs himself with an icicle, which melts before his body is discovered. A man shoots himself with a gun which is then whisked away up the chimney on a piece of elastic when his dead hand releases it. The gun might also be attached by string to a weight hanging out of a window which then drags the gun away and deposits it in water or a snowdrift.

(5) The death was a murder, but it took place at a time *before* the door was locked. The murderer (or someone else) then impersonated the victim, making it appear he was still alive sometime after his death and so allowing the murderer to provide himself with an alibi.

(6) It is a murder which was committed by somebody *outside* the room, but which has been made to look as though it must have been committed by somebody inside. Fell gives as an example an icicle fired as a bullet from outside. He also includes methods that he says could equally have occurred under (3) such as poisonous snakes or insects hidden inside the room before it was locked. The doctor then says: "... for the greatest long-range murder ever committed in a locked room, gents, I commend you to one of the most brilliant short detective

stories in the history of detective fiction. (In fact, it shares the honours for supreme untouchable top-notch excellence with Thomas Burke's, 'The Hands of Mr. Ottermole,' Chesterton's, 'The Man in the Passage,' and Jacques Futrelle's, 'The Problem of Cell 13.') This is Melville Davisson Post's, 'The Doomdorf Mystery'..." – and the long-range assassin is the sun. Again we shall avoid spoiling the ending.

(7) Finally, there is the murder that is the reverse of (5): the victim is presumed to be dead sometime *before* his murder actually occurs. The victim lies in the locked room asleep - either naturally or drugged. Knocking on the door does not rouse him, and the murderer loudly says that he suspects foul play. The murderer breaks open the locked door and gets in ahead of everyone else, and at that moment commits the murder. Everyone assumes the victim was dead before the door was opened. Dr. Fell says that Israel Zangwill was the originator of this particular method.

(ii) The Murder was in the Room – and Vanished!

Dr. Fell dismisses chimneys as a way of escaping from a locked room: "...chimneys, I regret to say, are not favoured as a means of escape in detective fiction – except, of course, for secret passages. There they are supreme ... But the murderer who makes his escape by climbing up is very rare. Besides being next to impossible, it is a much grimier business than monkeying with doors or windows." He then moves on to ways in which doors may be tampered with to make it look as though the murderer somehow passed through a locked door:

(1) Tampering with a key that is still in the lock. Fell says this is an old-fashioned method and too well-known to be effective today. Perhaps the most obvious variation is where the stem of the key can be gripped with pliers from outside and turned to lock the door after the murder. Other methods include threading string, or a metal bar attached to string, through the key so that the murderer can pull on the string to lock the door when he is outside and then pull the string free and dispose of it.

(2) Another way to exit through a locked door is to remove the pins of the hinges without unfastening the lock or bolt and then reinstating the pins. This only works if the hinges are accessible from outside the room.

(3) Tampering with the bolt. Again, string can be used, with some make-shift mechanism involving pins or paperclips, to shoot the bold from outside the door.

(4) Tampering with a falling bar or latch. Something is used to prop up the latch as the murderer exits and then removed once he is outside. This might be as simple as something that falls away when the door is slammed or as complex as an ice cube that melts and allows the latch to drop.

(5) A simple illusion. The murderer locks the door from the outside but allows people to believe that the door has been locked from within. The door is broken down and while everyone else's attention is taken by the sight of the body, the killer puts the key into the lock on the inside. Fell also suggests that other methods might be used where string is used to get the key back into the room before the door is opened.

Dr. Fell rounds off his lecture with a few comments on tampering with windows: "I can tell you several brands of funny business with windows if they're only locked. It can be traced down from the earliest dummy nail-heads to the latest hocus-pocus with steel shutters. You can smash a window, carefully turn its catch to lock it, and then, when you leave, simply replace the whole pane with a new pane of glass and putty it round; so that the new pane looks like the original and the window is locked inside."

And finally, he dismisses the 'human fly' who can walk on a 'sheer smooth wall' to each an inaccessible window – and who would need to start from somewhere and end somewhere, either on the roof or the ground below – and would presumably have left some evidence of his presence in one of those places.

In Chapter 14 of his novel *Nine Times Nine,* Anthony Boucher has his characters discuss the methods listed by Dr. Fell, summarising them as falling into three categories:

(a) The murder was committed before the room was locked.
(b) The murder was committed while the room was locked.
(c) The murder was committed after the room was broken into.

In Search of the 'Model' Locked Room Plot

The same half-dozen or so novels are typically named in discussions about the locked room sub-genre:

The Big Bow Mystery by Israel Zangwill (1892)
The Mystery of the Yellow Room by Gaston Leroux (1908)
The Canary Murder Case by S. S. Van Dine (1927)
The Hollow Man (vt. *The Three Coffins*) by John Dickson Carr (1935)
The Chinese Orange Mystery by Ellery Queen (1934)
Nine Times Nine by Anthony Boucher (originally under the name H. H. Holmes) (1940)
Death from a Top Hat by Clayton Rawson (1938)

These novels do not all follow one of the 'model' plots as closely as other murder mysteries, though the ones that do are – I believe – the better for it.

Israel Zangwill's *The Big Bow Mystery* is a short novel at under 42,000 words, and would probably be a better story if 10,000 words were cut from that length. It has twelve chapters, and the murder occurs in the first, meaning that it is close to following the 'first act murder' plot model. It also features elements of the 'innocent accused,' in that the victim's fellow lodger is accused of the crime, and tried for it. Suspense in the final act arises as the amateur detective must prove the accused man's innocence before he is sent for execution. The explanation of how the locked room murder was achieved, and the revelation of the identity of the murderer, occur in the final chapter.

Gaston Leroux's *The Mystery of the Yellow Room* also has a 'first act murder' plot, but with a variation in that the victim is severely injured but not killed. The attack on her occurs in a locked room – and instead of a second murder, there are actually two additional attempts on the same victim's life.

John Dickson Carr – under his own name and his pseudonym Carter Dickson – is regarded as a master of the locked room mystery, and *The Hollow Man* is usually cited as a classic of the subgenre. Its 85,000 words are divided roughly into three – the first third concerns a locked room mystery; the second part another 'impossible' murder that occurs in the middle of a snow-covered street in front of witnesses, and the final third features the much-quoted Dr. Fell 'lecture' on locked room mysteries along with the explanation of the methods used in the first two murders and a naming of the murderer. If I was being ungenerous, I'd say that this was two 30,000 word stories made into a novel through the use of back-story and the lecture.

Ellery Queen's *The Chinese Orange Mystery* tells of the investigation of only a single murder and is close to the traditional structure of a whodunit. But the bizarre circumstances in which the body is discovered, and the equally bizarre explanation of these circumstances, mean this is too much of a curiosity to serve as a model for other writers. Better is Queen's *The King is Dead* (1951) in which a James Bond-like villain is threatened with death by an unknown assassin, and is killed in a locked room. The murder occurs after the mid-point, and the final third of the novel concerns the discovery of how the murder was carried out – though Queen 'cheats' somewhat in that this isn't strictly speaking a locked room mystery from which the murderer 'disappears.' The novel does come close to following the 'mid-point murder' plot structure.

Another novel sometimes included in a 'locked room' list is Edgar Wallace's *Four Just Men* (1905), but this is actually an 'inverted' mystery story – and we'll look at those separately.

The Inverted Detective Story

In the traditional detective mystery, a murder is committed, the detective investigates, and at the climax of the story he reveals how and why the crime was committed, and the identity of the murderer. Not for nothing is this type of story known as a *who*dunit. The inverted mystery story makes no secret of the identity of the criminal – they are often revealed at the beginning. The story then concerns how the detective proves the murderer guilty. Or the whole story is told from the murderer's point of view – he is the protagonist, not the detective – and we see how he plans and carries out his crime, and/or how he got away with it. Or not.

Invention of the inverted mystery story is usually credited to R. Austin Freeman and to his short story collection *The Singing Bone* (1912, vt. *The Adventures of Dr. Thorndyke*). Ellery Queen wrote: "Dr. Freeman, a man of true scientific curiosity, posed himself the interesting question: Would it be possible to write a detective story in which, from the outset, the reader was taken entirely into the author's confidence, was made an actual witness of a crime and furnished with every fact that could possibly be used in its detection? In other words, reverse the usual procedure: let the reader know everything, the detective nothing. Would the reader, in possession of all the facts, be able to foresee how the detective would solve the mystery? Or would the reader be so occupied with the crime and its concomitant drama that he would overlook the evidence and still be dependent on the detective to find how the case could be cracked?"

In an essay titled 'The Art of the Detective Story,' Freeman himself said: "Some years ago I devised, as an experiment, an inverted detective story in two parts. The first part was a minute and detailed description of a crime, setting forth the antecedents, motives, and all attendant circumstances. The reader had seen the crime committed, knew all about the criminal, and was in possession of all the facts. It would have seemed that there was nothing left to tell. But I calculated that the reader would be so occupied with the crime that he would overlook the evidence. And so it turned out. The second part, which described the investigation of the crime, had to most readers the effect of new matter."

The stories in *The Singing Bone* all detail the detective's scientific methods as he tries to prove the guilt of a criminal identified at the beginning of each story. The detective's processes - the 'how' of the detection - is more important to Freeman than the 'who.' The television series *Columbo* of the 1970s used a similar approach. Freeman's first novel, *The Red Thumb Mark* (1907) uses the 'innocent accused' plot, shifting the emphasis from the *who* to the *how* – there are only a couple of possible suspects, and there is little doubt from early on who the culprit is: the fun comes in the explanation of how the crime was committed. This sort of story has been dubbed a 'howcatchem,' which I think is a term that really doesn't deserve to catch on. The Ellery Queen quote above is taken from an introduction to Roy Vickers' story collection *The Department of Dead Ends*, originally published in 1947. Queen said that Vickers was "the most brilliant manipulator of the 'inverted' method."

Because this type of story concentrates on *how* a particular crime is committed, these stories like the locked room mystery, are sometimes referred to as howdunits. In locked room and other impossible crime stories, the mystery is in how a murder was committed. The inverted detective story is more concerned with 'will it succeed?' or 'how will it be achieved?' In some stories of this type, we learn at the beginning that a certain crime is to be committed, and then we follow the means by which it is carried out. The structure of the plot is then similar to the Act I Murder, but instead of seeing the detective slowly piece together what happened, we see the criminal commit the crime in 'real time.' In Edgar Wallace's *Four Just Men* (1905) we meet the criminals at the beginning, we learn what murder they plan to commit, and the story then concerns their plans for achieving it and the police's attempts to prevent them. A locked room murder occurs in the final act, and the explanation of the crime is very briefly handled. *Malice Aforethought* (1931) by Frances Iles (Anthony Berkley Cox) features a husband who is planning to murder his wife. Cox wrote that he was more interested in "the story of a murder than the story of the detection of a murder." He wanted to write about the psychology of his characters, rather than follow the scientific methods of a detective. Marie Belloc Lowndes wrote a different sort of inverted mystery novel, *The Chink in the Armour* (1912, vt. *The House of Peril*), which is an account of a crime seen from the point of view of the victim.

In other stories of this type, as Freeman says above, the planning and carrying out of the crime occupies the first half of the story, and the then the second half follows the detective trying to discover how it was done and identify the culprit. In this case, the plot is more like that of the Midpoint Murder.

As a result of its emphasis on the process involved in committing the crime, the inverted detective story has also been linked with other genres such as the criminal caper story and the crime thriller. And in featuring the murderer as a protagonist, it is a forerunner of the 'psycho-thriller' which gained popularity in the 1940s and 1950s.

Putting It All Together

Practical Application

Where Do You Begin?

Where you begin depends on what you've already got:

- an interesting or unusual murder method
- a curious circumstance in which a body is discovered
- a victim you want to murder
- a varied group of suspects
- a suitable location
- a fascinating clue
- an unexpected murderer

Any of these could be the initial spark for your detective mystery. Compare what you already have with the list of fundamental parts of a murder mystery and see what gaps you need to fill. Then refer to the relevant sections of this book that cover how to create them. As a reminder, the fundamental parts of a murder mystery story are:

(a) The murder
(b) The victim
(c) The suspects – including the murderer
(d) The detective
(e) First part of the investigation: Incrimination of the suspects
(f) Second part of the investigation: Elimination of the suspects
(g) Final part of the investigation: Solution and revelation of the identity of the murderer
(h) Denouement – the restoration of order

Then decide which of the three types of plot you want to use Act I Murder, Midpoint Murder, or Innocent Accused. If you don't know which to choose, start with Act I Murder and start putting the things you brainstorm into that structure. As you create characters and events and location, it may become apparent that you don't want to have your victim murdered right at the beginning, because you want to write scenes with them as a living person. In that case, switch to a Midpoint Murder structure and try that out. Or if it looks as though you have a suspect who is going to be unjustly accused of the murder, try the Innocent Accused plot structure. The great thing about plotting your novel first is that you can experiment – and even make mistakes – without it costing you weeks or months of work.

As you continue to think about different scenes that could occur in your story, remember that in the detective mystery two opposing views are represented. The first is that crime pays because if the murderer is brilliant and ruthless he can escape justice. If he gets away with the murder – then this negative point of view is proved correct. The opposing, positive, viewpoint is that justice will prevail if the detective is brilliant and tenacious. As the story progresses first one side of this 'argument' seems to prevail, and then the other:

(a) a murder is committed and the killer flees the scene – he may get away with it (negative)
(b) a detective arrives on the scene and discovers a clue which may lead to the discovery of the murderer's identity and/or motive (positive)
(c) more 'clues' left by the murderer mislead the detective into suspecting the wrong person (negative)
(d) the detective learns that someone holds an important clue (positive)
(e) the murderer kills this person before they can reveal the vital information to the detective (negative)

And so on. This is a contest between detective and murderer, with the advantage passing back and forth between them, and the stakes being raised each time.

I-dunit

After I had researched the 'model plot' for a Midpoint Murder mystery, I set out to test it by writing a novel based on that structure. Over a period of about three months, I completed *The Sword in the Stone-Dead*. I was quite pleased with how quickly I wrote it – until I discovered that Agatha Christie wrote her first Poirot novel in about two weeks! I have written a full account of how I created that novel – including the notes I created for myself as I went along, from the initial idea, through the creation of the characters, to the final revelation of the who and how of the solution – and have included it as an appendix. I include it as an example not because it is a good murder mystery – that is not for me to judge – but because it is a novel where I know how and why every choice was made and how every part was put together.

Have a look at Appendix 1 and you'll see how I used the information presented in this book to create a full-length novel: I hope you find it useful and that you will be able to adapt my methods for your own use.

How Will You Do It?

Use the model plot structure to see what elements you have already created in your own notes, and what elements you still need to develop. Start with the four quarters so that you always have an overview of what function each part of the plot serves. Then copy the headings for each of the eight sequences of your chosen plot structure onto a separate sheet of paper and put them in a ring-binder – or create files for them in whatever software you use for writing and put them in a folder – then add your own notes into each sequence as you develop them. Try and work out what your climax for each sequence is going to be, based on the suggestions in the 'formula.'

Create a page for each of your characters write down who they are and what their guilty secret is, and begin to think about their relationships with the other characters. Think about the two chapters that each suspect will appear in and consider what they are going to reveal in the first one, and what they are going to hold back until the second. Think about what characters are going to say about each other and what this may reveal about their relationships. And then as your notes grow, start to think about the sequence that will most effectively present what you have – begin to think in terms of separate chapters within each of the eight sequences.

The more of this preparation you do, the easier you will find the actual writing of the book. Based on my own mistakes in doing this, I would strongly advise you to pay particular care to your preparation of the two sequences that follow the mid-point – many books, including those published by well-known professional writers, get bogged down in sequences five and six. It's almost as if writers lose their way at this point, and have to spend some time figuring out how to get back on track. Partly this is because it isn't easy to figure out what this part of a novel is actually supposed to achieve. Hopefully, the plot models in this book will help you to determine that and provide your readers with chapters that don't wander in a fog while you figure out what comes next.

Know and Love Your Genre

If you're going to write in the murder mystery genre – or any genre – then it should be because those are the types of story you know and love. If you try and fake it, even with all the information I have given you here, readers will know. They will know their genre better than you do, and they will know that you haven't done your homework. If you've been reading murder mysteries and cozies for years, you're probably on safe ground. If you are relatively new to the genre, you will need to extend your knowledge by reading classic and modern examples. You need to know what has been done before and you need to be able to separate the clichés (which you should avoid) from the conventions (which you need to follow): hopefully, this book will help you understand the conventions.

I've included two appendices that may help you extend your reading – the first, Appendix 2, covers the stories published before the golden age of the 1920s and 1930s when the conventions were still being established; the second covers the golden age itself. They may point you in the direction of writers you haven't encountered before and whose work you will enjoy. If you're looking for more modern examples, especially of the modern cozy mystery, I would suggest looking in the categories on Amazon or one of the other online booksellers.

Appendix 1:

Writing *The Sword in the Stone-Dead*

Under a few broad headings below I have brought together the main notes I made while preparing my first murder mystery novel. They were all handwritten on sticky notes and scraps of paper, and the brainstorming process happened in a haphazard manner as I jumped from one idea to another and back over a period of a couple of weeks. I've presented them here in a more coherent form, trying to show how my ideas developed and how I used the process outlined in this book to both generate the necessary material and to structure it into a workable plot. I stayed fairly close to my 'guidebook' for this first attempt – for my second and subsequent ones I took a more relaxed approach.

Setting

The first notes I made were on the setting: *People brought together for a party at a country house, inn or hotel.* I knew I needed an isolated location and a small group of people to act as suspects. *No telephones working. No other house within five or six miles. Dangerous countryside around – old lead mines. Rocks. Cracks in the ground.* I think I went a bit overboard there: all you really need to do is tell the reader the location is isolated, and they'll accept it – it's part of the willing suspension of disbelief you get with this genre. I also wrote: *Catering by a butler and four staff, plus cook? Mobile catering company. After the food is served, the staff disappear, driving away. Leaving the other cars disabled or the other cars are gone.* I used some of those ideas in the finished draft. An important note that I wrote down early on was: *Something a bit Gothic about the location – a Victorian folly like a mini medieval castle. Ghost story related to it.* Originally, I was thinking

about having a Shakespearean theme to the party the suspects were attending, but that was a bit clichéd – the fake
medieval castle inspired the idea of a King Arthur and the
Knights of the Round Table theme. I had been looking for
something to emphasise the Englishness of the location, and
that fit the bill nicely.

Characters

I'd been re-reading Agatha Christie's novels and the published extracts from her notebooks, so I started off listing the
types of characters she often used:

- The demanding hypochondriac and her put-upon
  niece, husband or son
- The 'frog-eyed' colonel (this is the phrase Christie
  used in her notebooks)
- The vampy widow/divorcee
- The horsey woman
- The effete young man
- The plain, poor girl with low self-esteem
- The attractive young couple

The trick then was to come up with my own versions of these
stock characters. Starting off with the Shakespearean theme,
I decided to make some of them actors. And the temporary
name I gave to one of them was 'Falstaff' because that gave
me a picture in my mind of the big, loud actor I wanted to
create. He became Leo Fulbright in the first draft. Thinking
about who the murder victim might be, I asked myself: *Who
might have power over these suspects? Who might have
wronged them all?* All of the suspects would need to have some
kind of relationship to the victim; they must all have been
persecuted by him (or her) in some way, such that they all
potentially had a motive for murder. My original thought was
that Fulbright would be the murder victim, killed at the midpoint of the story. Making him a father, husband and theatre
director would put him in a position where he would have
relationships with, and perhaps power over, the other suspects. Here's my first attempt at a cast list:

- Falstaff / Fulbright – overbearing, egomaniacal, greedy, demanding, angry, controlling, sometimes self-pitying. Actor / director?
- His younger lover – a wannabe actress, younger than Fulbright's daughter. Was his daughter's friend?
- His ex-wife – hypochondriac, highly-strung, alcoholic.
- His daughter – plain, poor, low self-esteem. Put-upon – looks after 'invalid' mother.
- Dashing young man – attracted to the daughter. Fast car. At odds with Falstaff who doesn't want his daughter dating anyone because he wants her to look after the ex-wife.
- Falstaff's sister – the horsey woman.
- Sister's lover – Marlene Dietrich.
- Ex-husband of Falstaff's lover – an actor; alcoholic. Faded matinee idol. Falstaff tries to pair him up with ex-wife.
- The Detective – music hall performer; conjurer/magician. Singer.
- Falstaff's driver – becomes the detective's Watson.

You can see that I'm still thinking in terms of types and stereotypes here, but most of these people ended up in the first draft. I liked the idea of Fulbright's sister having a female lover who dressed as a man, but that didn't quite work out in the end – it made the lover too much of an interesting character for me and her role was too small to allow that. I shall save her for another time.

The Detective
My earliest thoughts about the detective were that he would be a debonair gentleman magician and that he would team up with a more working-class driver/assistant. I wanted there to be a strong hint that the two would become romantically involved – but this would be kept very low-key given that in the mid-1930s – the time period I had chosen for my story, homosexual relationships between men were still illegal. There have been discussions – some more serious than others

– that both Sherlock Holmes and Hercule Poirot might have been gay. There is also the possibility of a 'bromance' between any two male detective partners – I just wanted to make it a reality for once.

Below are my original notes for the character, who I named *Benjamin Vickery*. There are a few ideas that I didn't use. The debunking of psychics and spiritualists was an idea I stole from the life of Harry Houdini. James Randi was also an inspiration for the character.

- *Former music hall magician – The Great Vicari*
- *Songwriter*
- *Hidden secret*
- *Gave up magic after a tragic accident killed his assistant – magic apparatus went wrong*
- *He's the magic advisor on the film – to an old character actor who is playing Merlin*
- *Vickery is an accomplished magician – but also loves to see spiritualists and so-called psychics debunked. His mother was conned by a spiritualist who claimed to speak to the 'ghost' of his father.*

One thing I usually do when thinking about a character is to put down the names of two or three actors to help me 'see' the character and – more importantly – to pick up the tone and rhythms of how he or she might speak. These aren't actors I imagine playing the character in a film – the names are just an early tool to help me 'find' my character. For Vickery, I had in mind William Powell, Vincent Price and Basil Rathbone. In the second Great Vicari novel, I had a country named Rathbania after the Sherlock Holmes actor. I had Noel Coward and Cole Porter in mind, I'm sure, when I added that the detective was also a singer. In the end, he didn't sing at the party, as I had other characters do it instead.

I decided that my detective would be a retired stage magician and to give him a bit of enigmatic backstory I thought that he would have retired because his assistant – and lover – was killed when a stage illusion went terribly wrong. He has been a recluse since then but occasionally agrees to help people investigate minor mysteries. I decided that he would have been present at the party because he was acting as 'magic advisor' on the film to an old actor who was playing Merlin. And also because Fulbright had asked him to investigate some threatening letters he'd received – along the lines of 'I know what you did.' Again, this helped to set Fulbright up as a potential murder victim.

My detective needed a name, and I thought something Italian might suit a stage magician. Here's my list of possible names.

Almondi	Ravenwood	Firedrake
Almondo	Rookhaven	Orsino
Altieri	Rookwood	Reynaud
Damiani	Ludavico	Sangster
Damiano	Malchus	Tempesti
Danziger	Mauriac	Tallon
Davenport	Morante	Dragan
Drexler	Vicari	
Fulbright	Vincenzo	

'Fulbright' I gave to the pompous actor. 'The Great Vicari' had a nice ring to it for a magician and I thought it would be fun to say that his name was really 'Vickery' and that he was probably from Yorkshire, despite his faint foreign accent. When you're writing about England in a period before the Second World War, you have to have an awareness of the class system. I wanted my detective to be able to interact with both the 'upper' and 'lower' classes – making him a theatre performer and (possibly) a foreigner gave me that freedom: he would be treated with respect, because he dressed and spoke properly, but regarded as 'not quite a gentleman.' I stole that from Hercule Poirot, of course. For a similar reason, I made the driver-Watson character (possibly) Irish rather than English.

The Murderer and the Victim

Having come up with a basic cast, I could start asking questions about them and think about the web of relationships between them. The fundamental questions are obviously *Who will die?* and *Who will kill them?* As I mentioned above, I initially thought that Leo Fulbright would be the victim.

Who is the murderer? I wrote that at the top of a notebook page and listed the possibilities: Fulbright's young lover; his ex-wife; his daughter; the dashing young man; his sister; the young lover's ex-husband... everyone except the victim and the detective was a potential suspect. I even gave my almost-Watson character, Fulbright's driver, a reason to hate his current employer. In a murder mystery, you also have to consider the possibility that two of the characters are joint murderers. Agatha Christie came up with some interesting pairings in her novels, putting together the two people you would think least likely to be working together. I thought that the young actress and her ex-husband or ex-lover might be in cahoots, and that their relationship was not as 'ex' as they let people believe.

During one brainstorming session, I had the idea of having my theatre actors be involved in the 1930s British film industry. This allowed me to think of Fulbright and his soon-to-be-ex-wife in terms of the great acting partnerships of Laurence Olivier and Vivien Leigh or Elizabeth Taylor and Richard Burton. I made Fulbright an actor-director and the party that everyone was attending then became a private celebration for cast and crew at the end of the first week of filming on his latest project. I made the film an adaptation of the King Arthur story. And Fulbright's lover became a young actress making her debut opposite him as Queen Guinevere. The fact that he had chosen her over his usual acting partner, his wife, would create a nice sense of conflict between the three characters. Fulbright would be throwing the weekend party to demonstrate his power as the 'king' – he became 'Leo the Lion' for that reason – and there would also be a rumour that he was about to announce his engagement to the younger actress. If the other leading male actor was the ex-lover of the young actress, that would give him a reason to hate Fulbright too. I was thinking all of this with the idea in mind that someone was going to kill the obnoxious and pompous Leo Fulbright.

Having, in my own mind, set Fulbright up as the victim with lots of potential enemies, I then thought it might be fun to have someone else murdered instead. Everyone would think he deserved to die, only he doesn't. Leading the reader to expect one victim and then killing another is something you can do in a Midpoint Murder plot. It helps keep things fresh. *Is Fulbright the victim?* I wrote, *Or is his young lover?* Having decided to kill her, I then had to think about what motives the other suspects might have. Her ex-husband/lover would obviously be upset that he was dumped in favour of Fulbright. Fulbright's wife would hate her for stealing her husband and the starring role of Queen Guinevere. I also needed a motive for Fulbright wanting his young actress lover dead.

Perhaps she has refused to marry him? Or he has cast her in the film, only to discover that she is a terrible screen actress? The King Arthur film is a vanity project for Fulbright, and he has invested his own money in it – and now it is going to be a disaster. But if the young actress is killed, he can replace her *and* use the attendant publicity of a murder to promote his film. I thought I'd have the first weeks 'rushes' do to be screened at the party and then have the film reel disappear, fuelling rumours that the young actress was terrible in the scenes shot so far.

The poor actress's fate was sealed – I decided she would be found dead in the fountain in the courtyard, stabbed. Here are my original notes on her character, who I named *Eleanor Trenton:*

- *The Actress – Ex-lover of Teddy Kimball; thought to be Fulbright's mistress.*
- *Pale, beautiful – somewhat insipid. Quiet, seemingly frail, nervous. Quite intense.*
- *Seems to need constant assurance.*
- *Appears to have hidden depths – to be enigmatic – but isn't. What you see is all there is.*
- *Cold, frigid. Fulbright expected to melt her heart – find the fire beneath. But didn't.*
- *Guinevere*

Another early page of notes on this character – who was named Elspeth Tiernan right up until the final draft – reads: Perhaps there are no notes on Elspeth – she drifts through the first part of the story like a ghost, existing only to provide the first corpse? Does Vickery ever speak to her? Perhaps some brief notes on her relating to the film – and in the introduction of her father [her uncle, Sir Geoffrey] and her monstrous little brother. She was inspired, in part, by Gwyneth Paltrow and Cate Blanchett.

The Suspects

As a separate exercise I listed my characters and gave each of them a 'guilty secret.' They would each have something to hide and this would cause them to behave suspiciously during the investigation. Below are the notes on each of the suspects, including their guilty secret. When I wrote these, I had not decided who the murderer would be.

The Actor – Leo Fulbright.

I imagined him as a blond giant with a big bushy beard. A lion. At one point, I thought that he might have purchased the fake castle where the party took place and thought about calling the novel *Death at Fulbright's Folly*. I later used 'Fulbright's Folly' to refer to the motion picture he was trying to make. Here are the notes:

- *Big, blond bear of a man – booming voice, red face. Full beard. Pipe.* (I changed the hair from blond to red – for the fiery temper cliché and the make it easy for Vickery to recognise his sister)
- *Commands the theatre stage, but needs to tone down his performance for the camera.*
- *Likes food and drink – getting fatter.*
- *King Arthur.*
- *Moves his ring to his middle finger, like a knuckle-duster, when he's angry.*
- *Guilty secret: financial difficulties; has misled his major investor*

Actors I was thinking of for Leo Fulbright were: *Orson Welles, Brian Blessed, Kenneth Brannah*. As I wrote the first draft I also had in mind British actor James Robertson Justice.

The Actor's Ex-Wife – Margot McCrae
'Margot' I think came from Dame Margot Fonteyn and 'McCrae' from Joel McCrae – I must have been trying to think of names with showbiz connections. The image of a Victorian widow in black lace was nicely theatrical. In the 1974 film version of *Murder on the Orient Express*, the one with Albert Finney as Poirot, Dame Wendy Hiller plays Princess Natalia Dragomiroff as such a character. Two other actresses helped inspire her – Dame Diana Rigg, who had just appeared as the aunt in *Game of Thrones* and is one of my favourite actresses, and Dame Maggie Smith. I seemed to have taken to heart the idea that 'there is nothing like a dame.'

- *Hypochondriac – invalid following riding accident. Requires her daughter to be her 'nurse.'*
- *Has a scar on her cheek from a back-handed slap from Fulbright's ring*
- *Bitter, sarcastic*
- *Pale, severe features. Dark eyes like little chips of jet. Lines at the corner of her eyes and in her top lip – as if pursed in pain.*
- *Dresses in black like a Victorian governess. Dress with a high neck to hide wrinkles. Black gloves to her elbow. Hair drawn back – severe. What is that hairstyle like a circle on the back of the head – Chignon?*
- *She played opposite Fulbright – they were mesmerising, sparks flying, sexual undertones. Think Bogart and Bacall, Burton and Taylor.*
- *Great theatrical roles for women? – What was her signature role?*
- *She has recently been asked to play Lady Bracknell – "...hardly a stretch, is it?"*
- *She was previously married – to a politician? 'I think one should have at least one husband who isn't an actor.' Began an adulterous relationship with Fulbright. Married Fulbright so that 'Linette would have a father – I certainly didn't marry him for his money!'*

- *Does she blame Fulbright for her riding accident? Or is she just bitter because her injury meant she had to slow down? 'Fate eventually found a way to tame me.'*

After a bit of research – I may have Googled 'great stage roles for women' – I decided Margot's 'signature' role was Medea. The *Wikipedia* entry gave me enough details for what I needed.

- *Margot played Medea in a brief run of Euripides' play – a barbarian, the 'warrior princess' of her day.*
- *Medea helped Jason slay a dragon. She killed Jason's second wife with a poisoned robe and crown. She killed her own children by Jason.*
- *Medea – famous scenes? – She calls Jason a craven villain for being unfaithful to her – she killed the dragon so he could get the golden fleece. If he leaves her, she cannot go back home – having killed her brother. Having killed Jason's new wife and her father, she – in a chilling scene – decides whether or not she will kill her children.*
- *One of the characters – Fulbright when he's drunk? – always greets her "All right, m'dear" because of her role. Ironic – patriarchal. "He's completely oblivious."*
- *Poisoned clothes burning flesh from bones. A mother murdering her children. Hair dishevelled – face gleaming with sweat – eyes wild. It was all a bit grim for modern audiences. Fulbright was Jason?*
- *Fulbright refused to appear opposite her in* Macbeth *after that – so she had to make do with* Much Ado.
- *Guilty Secret: She is not the invalid she pretends. Does it to get Fulbright's money. She has a scar on her cheek – back-handed slap from his ring. She is also still in love with her husband, despite his philandering*

Two things should be obvious from the above notes: the character of Margot started to take on a life of her own, and I came up with more details than I ever used in the story. I think she turned out to be a more interesting character as a result. And her dialogue with Vickery, as they watch the party and offer a commentary, was a lot of fun to write. I'd love for those two to team up again in a future story.

The Sister – Veronica Fulbright.

She was 'Emily' well into the first draft, but I did a search and replace and changed it. I had another character whose name began with 'E' and the general advice when it comes to names is not to have names that begin with the same latter, or names that are otherwise similar – avoid having a Milly, a Lily and a Billy in the same story! There were no actresses for her – she was the 'horsey woman' stock character – perhaps a young Margaret Rutherford?

- *Fulbright's older sister. He had her locked up – committed – took control of the money their father left them. She's out now, but dependent on him.*
- *A butch, horsey sort of woman. Wears men's tweed trousers and jacket. Highly polished men's brogues, glossy like horse chestnuts. Vickery expects her to take a pipe out of her pocket.*
- *Hair is red and curly – white mixed in with it. Ruddy complexion – no make-up. Freckles. Bright blue eyes.*
- *Good singing voice.*
- *Guilty secret: Fulbright had her committed – took control of the money his father left her. She's out now – but dependent on him. Why was she locked up? 'I tried to kill my brother.' Also has been secretly meeting the lover her brother forbade her to have a relationship with*

The brogues popped into my head – I saw some like them when I was very young, and the shiny brown leather did make me think of horse chestnuts – 'conkers' to me then – at the time.

The Daughter – Linette Fulbright

- *Plain in comparison to her glamorous mother. Low self-esteem. Put-upon.*
- *Mother needs her companionship.*
- *Father needs her to look after her mother.*
- *Has secretly married or become engaged) – without her parents' permission.*

To begin with, Linette was a typical stock character – a plain young woman who is trapped in the position of having to care for an older relative who is a hypochondriac. But the character of Margot turned out not to be a self-pitying invalid, and so Linette got to take on the role of 'bright young thing' instead. 'Linette' I took from a character in an Agatha Christie novel.

- *Young, bright, attractive – but living in the shadow of her two famous parents.*
- *Had to grow up quickly – to survive the turbulent relationship of her parents, and to deal with their emotional ups and downs; their need for attention.*
- *When her mother suffered a riding accident, Linnie had to act as nursemaid. A role that she fears she will have to play for the rest of her mother's life. She doesn't want to become one of those bitter spinsters – who devote their lives to caring for some ungrateful hypochondriac and end up at fifty with nothing to show for it.*
- *Guilty secret: Resents having to look after her mother. Secretly married against her father's wishes.*

The Dashing Young Man – Oliver 'Ollie' Garvin.

- *Photographer. Fast car. Attracted to Falstaff's daughter. At odds with both of Linette's parents.*
- *Has secretly married Linette – they are planning to disappear for their honeymoon.*
- *He's young, brash. Works for a newspaper – wants to be a proper journalist. Takes photographs for the society column.*
- *Guilty Secret: Wanted to marry daughter – but Fulbright forbade it. He married her anyway. And he took photographs that Fulbright is using against Kimball.*

Originally, I thought Garvin was a bit of a charmer, the sort of character that Jude Law might play. But in the writing, he became more like the Jimmy Olsen character from *Superman*, and I tended to see him as Justin Whalin who played Olsen in *Lois and Clark*.

Fulbright's Rival – Edward 'Teddy' Kimball

- *Matinee idol gone-to-seed. Alcoholic.*
- *Falstaff had tried to pair him up with Margot – needs someone to look after her.*
- *Afraid his time has passed. Desperate to prove he still has attraction – as an actor and a lover.*
- *Effete young man is his lover?*
- *Falstaff has photographs of them – or letters. Blackmail.*
- *Kimball once romanced Falstaff's wife? Falstaff now humiliating Kimball – revenge.*
- *Kimball is better-looking than Fulbright – more popular – great voice, also a better actor.*
- *Falstaff said he was doing him a favour – as a villain, he's in his first character role. It will assure his future as an actor.*
- *Teddy hit a newspaper photographer outside a bar? – He was drunk.*
- *Guilty secret: Humiliated by Falstaff – lost his wife / fiancé to him. Found out about it in a gossip column. Made to look a fool in some other way. Small part in latest film – as a cuckold. An alcoholic with a violent temper; also caused Margot's riding accident out of revenge*

The Effete Young Man – Arthur 'Artie' Delancey

I decided to take Agatha Christie's 'effete young man' and make him an effeminate one: *Murderer's accomplice isn't a woman – it is a young female impersonator. He has effeminate gestures, a feminine laugh. The murderer blackmailed him into it – has incriminating photographs or letters or both.* I tried to make this plausible by saying that the young man would double for the young actress in horse-riding scenes in the King Arthur film. Because homosexuality was illegal, gay men could be blackmailed and this meant that a murderer could compel the impersonator to do his bidding. I also thought this young man might have a crush on the matinee-idol actor (Fulbright's rival) and that there might be some suggestion of a scandal involving the two of them.

- *Female impersonator. Dreams of showbiz glamour – afraid it will be as sordid and shabby as the life he knows.*
- *Playing a minstrel in the film – he is Kimball's 'assistant' – supposed to be keeping him on the wagon.*
- *Has a legitimate singing career – in Gilbert and Sullivan?*
- *Performs in drag under another name – in an illegal gay bar?*
- *Played female parts in Shakespeare at an all-boys school. Tried to persuade Fulbright to mount an all-male production of Shakespeare – bringing back a tradition. Fulbright didn't think the public would be receptive.*
- *Legal position of homosexuals in the mid-1930s?*
- *What stories had recently been in the press?*
- *What was the 'gay underworld' like?*
- *Use of Polari? Other gay slang.*
- *Being blackmailed by Fulbright. Is the murderer's unwilling accomplice.*

The Driver – Malloy

This character was always intended to team-up with the detective and act as his Watson. Originally, he was a Scot named 'Jamie McHeath,' but I wanted Leo Fulbright to refer to him as 'Molly' so changed his name to Malloy. Marlon Brando played Terry Malloy in *On the Waterfront* and he was one of the actors I had in mind for this character. Strong but sensitive was the feeling I was looking for here.

- *Ambulance driver during the First World War* (technically he's probably too young to have done this, so I never referred to it)
- *Appears to know the detective – both men say 'he helped/assisted me once before'*
- *Guilty secret: Bullied and humiliated by Falstaff. Calls him 'Molly' – 'My name's Malloy.' "I disobeyed him once – learned not to do it again," Malloy says, touching his jaw which was bruised by Fulbright's ring.*

Dickie Bannister – Older Actor

The old character actor playing Merlin. I made no notes him – he just appeared as I started typing his dialogue. I named him Jerry Bannister to begin with – then after finishing the first draft realised having a character called Jerry and one called Margot might make people think of the British sitcom *The Good Life,* so Bannister became Dickie. The name came from Richard Attenborough, but in my mind, I saw Bannister more as a cross between John Gielgud and Ralph Richardson, with a hint of cockney stand-up comic thrown in. And of course, he was a stereotypical theatrical 'luvvie.' Guilty secret: is the writer of the poison pen letters

The Nobleman – Sir Geoffrey Atterbury
Margot's ex-husband. Soon to be Fulbright's business partner. Owner of the Victorian folly where the story is set. And uncle to the actress Eleanor Trenton. No notes on him – he was intended to be a minor character, and essentially a stereotypical member of the 'upper class.' Guilty secret: had an unhealthy relationship with his sister; has transferred his affection to her daughter, his niece, Eleanor Trenton

Timothy
Eleanor Trenton's monstrous little brother. No notes on him – he was another stereotype, who ended up providing a bit of comic relief in a couple of scenes. He has no guilty secret as such. But I did give him a morbid fascination with the crime, so readers might think it could be possible he was a killer.

Plot

I said earlier that in a mystery story of this type, there are two versions of events – there is what *really* happened and there is the sequence of events that the murderer wants people to believe happened. It is the detective's job to see through what *appears* to have happened and to find the truth. Early on, then, I had to begin thinking about these parallel versions of events. *What version of events does the murderer want people to believe? What is the murderer's alibi?*

A scream is heard at 'X' time – and a splash – and everyone believes that to be the time of the murder. But the murder took place earlier (or later) than the scream. The murderer has an

alibi for the (apparent) time of the murder: he was with other guests and heard the scream at the same time they did.

This is an old idea and has certainly been done before with gunshots and has probably been done with a scream. I added a 'splash' as the victim fell into the pond/fountain just for a bit of extra detail. *How was the scream faked?* I asked in my notebook. *Not a recording – too obvious a trick.*

I also thought that the dead actress would need to be seen walking around *after* she had been murdered – to support the murderer's alibi – which meant that someone would have to impersonate her. I initially thought this would involve someone in a duplicate Queen Guinevere costume, but eventually settled on a red dress instead.

A clue – a button or brooch from her costume. But there doesn't seem to be one missing from her costume. A clue that there is a duplicate costume.

Detective sees Falstaff move the ring to a middle finger – like a knuckleduster – when he's angry.

The detective can pick pockets – when he sees Falstaff pick something up and secrete it in his pocket, he takes it. It is a button from the Queen's costume.

I knew that I also wanted to try and lead the reader to believe that the belligerent bully, Leo Fulbright, was going to be the murder victim – he *had* to be, because everyone hated him. This meant that in the first half of the novel, I concentrated on revealing the characters mainly through their relationships to him. But at the same time, I had to have them all interact with the real victim in some way.

The pre-planning stage where all of the above notes were created, is a bit like going out and gathering all of the ingredients that you need for a recipe. Or all of the materials you need for a DIY project. It's like an artist preparing a canvas and mixing colours, or a sculptor preparing the clay. The basic plot outline – the Midpoint Murder plot or the Act I Murder or the 'Innocent Accused' – give you a good idea of what materials you need to gather and prepare.

Much of the character material I created I knew would need to be revealed in dialogue. There is a lot of dialogue in a murder mystery. The detective interviews witnesses and suspects, and gradually pieces together all of this information about the people involved and their web of relationships. It is important that characters reveal who they are through what they say – or don't say – and how they say it. Since the murder would not occur until the middle of the story, I had my detective finding things out about people during casual conversations at the party. I gave Vickery a minor mystery – some poison pen letters sent to Fulbright – so he had an excuse to be there and to be asking questions.

In a 'mid-point murder' story, important clues are given *before* the murder takes place. And a lot of those clues are revealed – or hidden – in what people say. The psychology of the characters is what we're after – what are they like? Why do they behave in the way they do? What are their values? Their fears? Their hopes? And hidden in what they say will be brief flashes of something they are hiding – some dark secret they don't want to reveal, but which leaks out.

Each major character has an introductory scene – or their introduction may be split across a couple of scenes – in the first half of the novel, and then a second scene after the midpoint that serves to complicate things and make them seem to be behaving suspiciously because of the dark secret they are keeping.

As we are going to give each character a couple of major scenes – splitting information about the character between the two, we have two options that can help increase the confusion during the second half of the novel. We can either introduce a character and make them likeable in the first scene, and then reveal a darker side of their personality in the second – making the detective and the reader suspect them more. Or we can show them to be an unpleasant character in the first scene, but then reveal some undeserved misfortune which has turned them into this unlikeable person – again, this misfortune can serve to make them seem a more likely suspect.

Mixed up with all this are the red herrings – the guilty secrets that cause people to behave suspiciously, even though they are not the murderer, and the false clues the murderer plants to direct attention away from himself. Each character has their own little story – a mystery of their own – that the detective must uncover in order to be able to eliminate them as a murder suspect. He must understand the real reason for their guilty behaviour, in order to show that they are not guilty of murder.

While the psychology of each character – *why* they behave as they do, their motivation – is important, the people in the purest form of murder mystery only really exist as a function of plot. They are an obstacle the detective must tackle on his way to uncovering the truth. For this reason, the murder mystery can be regarded as perhaps the most plot-oriented of the story genres: it is almost pure plot.

By the Numbers

Agatha Christie thought that the ideal length for a murder mystery novel was between fifty and fifty-five thousand words. Any longer than that, she said, and you just had to pad them out with more suspects. Fifty-five thousand words is on the light side for a modern novel, so I picked sixty thousand as my target length. The final draft of *The Sword in the Stone-Dead* turned out to be just under 65,000 words, though the first draft was under 50,000.

Christie favoured short chapters – 1,500 words on average. My personal feeling – and it is only that – is that this is a little short and makes the reading experience a bit choppy. Two to three thousand words suits me better. For that reason, I chose to divide my 60,000-word novel into twenty-four chapters of 2,500 words. Some would be longer, and some much shorter, but that was to be my average. If you fancy writing shorter chapters, go for it. Choose whatever length works for you – the *proportions* I use below can be used for any number of chapters.

If we take the commonly held theory that the beginning, middle and end sections of a story – Acts I, II and III – should be of the ration 1 : 2 : 1 – that is, the middle section is twice the length of the beginning and end sections, we can divide our 24 chapters as follows:

Act I – The Beginning – Chapters 1 to 6
Act II – The Middle – Chapters 7 to 18
Act III – The End – Chapters 19 to 24

Our midpoint will be between Chapters 12 and 13

That already gives us some kind of structure to work within, but that middle section – all 30,000 words of it – seems a long stretch, even with our murder at the midpoint to aim for. We can use Frank Daniel's 'eight sequence' approach to break our three acts down into more manageable chunks. Act I will consist of two sequences, Act II four sequences, and Act III two sequences. Each sequence will be three chapters long. Personally, I think eight chunks is a far as you need to go in breaking down a plot – you can assign a function to each of these eight sequences without the whole thing becoming too detailed and restrictive.

Plot Structure Overview

ACT I

Sequence 1 (Chapters 1-3) – Introduce setting and major characters – argument or confrontation, or a threat of murder revealed.

Sequence 2 (4-6) – Introduce minor characters – expand on major characters. Climax: Argument, accident, or murder attempt.

ACT II

Sequence 3 (7-9) – Suspicious behaviours; victim's behaviour/relationships; an unsuccessful murder attempt, threat, or accident. Or a disappearance or arrival.

Sequence 4 (10-12) – Investigation the climax of Sequence 3. Establish murderer's alibi.

Midpoint – The murder and discovery of the body.

Sequence 5 (13-15) – Beginning of investigation. Climax: A confession or an accusation. Or a clue of 'obvious' guilt.

Sequence 6 (16-18) – Murderer eliminated as a suspect. Closing in on one suspect – believed to be the murderer or someone who knows something. Climax: Second murder.

ACT III

Sequence 7 (19-21) – Investigating second murder – which is the final clue. Drawing room scene part 1. Elimination of some minor suspects. Guilty secrets explained/exposed. Climax: Detective says he knows whodunit.

Sequence 8 (22-24) – Drawing room scene part 2. Explanations and justice served. Restoration of equilibrium.

I knew I was going to have to write about each of my characters several times during the course of the novel – their introduction, their first interview with the detective, suspicious behaviours, perhaps a second interview with the detective, and then a final bit in the 'drawing room scene' where they are exonerated (or not). To help keep track of them, I made myself a Cast List, so I could make sure I remembered them all and gave them their proper coverage. On it, I also included a reminder of each person's guilty secret.

Having made all sorts of bits of notes about my setting and characters, I could start to fit them into the structure and begin working out the sequence of my plot. As I was making notes and writing longer sections of dialogue, I found that characters would often refer to something from another chapter, and I had to keep notes for myself along the lines of 'This must go after Malloy has searched the pond.' I also tried to vary things by not having long sections of interviews one after the other, breaking them up with something with a little more action or description.

I've said this before, but in the interests of honesty and to provide context I repeat it here: I hate plotting out a story before I write it. I like to discover the story as I write – I'm effectively telling myself a story as I go. If I've plotted out every twist and turn beforehand, the story is already told and I lose interest in it. The downside of this is that I begin a lot of stories that I never finish because I don't know what the hell I'm getting myself into. And have no way of getting myself out of the corners I write myself into. In coming up with a model for the structure of a murder mystery story, I wanted the best of both worlds – I wanted something that would give me guideposts from beginning to end, so I always knew what direction I was heading, and would have pointers if I started to feel like I was getting lost. But at the same time, I didn't want to know in advance the exact nature of the climax or twist that was called for at any particular point.

Knowing that there *was* a structure gave me the confidence to set-off and start telling my story without having set down every little detail in advance.

This approach may not be perfect, and I made some mistakes along the way that made the first draft pretty weak – especially in the second half of Act II – which I'll tell you about later. But I did end up completing the first draft in two and a half months, working evenings and weekends, and a rewrite of the second half of the novel in an additional couple of weeks. Three drafts in total – handwritten, typed, and rewritten – in three months. That's the quickest I'd ever completed a full-length novel.

I had my characters and setting. I knew who was going to be murdered at the midpoint, I knew who my second victim would be and why they would be killed. I knew I wanted to try and trick the reader into thinking that someone else was the prime candidate for being the first murder victim, so that the murder itself wouldn't seem too obvious when it finally came. But I didn't know who my murderer was.

And I didn't decide who it was until I had written most of the first half of the story, and some of the second half. And even when I did decide, I actually chose a different character than the one in the final version of the novel. It is both a strength and a weakness of the classical murder mystery novel that any of the suspects could turn out to be guilty. And with a few minor changes in the second half of the story, you

can have a different character altogether be the murderer.
Agatha Christie occasionally took one of her short story ideas
and rewrote it as a novel – with a different character revealed
as the murderer. I think it is also possible that Agatha Christie sometimes wrote to the midpoint of her novel before she
decided which of her characters would prove to be the culprit.
There's probably more fun to be had in setting things up so
that the reader suspects all of the characters, than there is in
untangling the whole mess and deciding who the real killer
is.

Once I did decide whodunit, I only had to go back and make
a few minor changes in the chapters I had already written to
plant clues for the final solution. And I knew what these
changes needed to be because I wrote the detective's explanation in full before I'd finished writing the rest of the second
half of the novel. Once I knew the name of the killer, everything had to work towards that final explanation, so writing
it sooner rather than later seemed like the right thing to do.

Plotting in Parts

Before I started the actual writing of the novel, I plotted out
the first six chapters – Act I – of the novel. I find it helpful to
have an idea of what I need to include in a chapter. And –
more importantly for me – what I should *not* be including. Yet.
In the past, I tended to write first drafts that were way too
short – or which died around the midpoint because I couldn't
see that there is enough material to sustain the rest of the
work. Part of the problem was that I included too much material too soon, rather than pacing it properly and building up
to the major scenes. Having grown up watching Hollywood
action movies in the 1980s, my sense of story has always been
that things should happen quickly, one after the other, bang-
bang-bang. That sort of story needs a lot of incident and a lot
of dialogue – but in the classic murder mystery, there are relatively few major incidents and a much more gradual revealing of what is actually going on. There is a lot more tease and
a lot less bang.

Plotting out the first six chapters according to the plot structure model forced me to hold back from revealing too much too

soon. My plan originally was to introduce a major suspect in each of the first six chapters, along with some hint about their guilty secret. But I found that I didn't need a whole chapter for each character, and also that mixing between and overlapping the introductions of the main characters was much less artificial.

Act I – Chapters 1 to 6

Sequence 1

(1)   Introduce Fulbright, Margot and Vickery.
Introduce the (exterior) setting – the folly.
Introduce the situation – the banquet and the house party. Arthurian costumes of guests.
The arrival of the bus.
Fulbright is obnoxious – sends driver to collect Eleanor Trenton.
Ollie's arrival – Fulbright angry: Ollie was supposed to be there to photograph the guests arriving – Fulbright isn't spending all this cash for there not to be a record of it in the society columns.

(2)   Vickery and Margot in the courtyard – discussion of the history of the folly. Fulbright's monetary problems – the film.
Fulbright acting like a tyrant.

(3)   Arrival of Eleanor Trenton – Margot's catty remarks.
Vickery's observations on Linnie's engagement to Ollie.
Margot is rude to Artie Delancey

Sequence 2

(4)   Margot on Ted Kimball
Frostiness between Kimball and Fulbright
Awkwardness between Kimball and Eleanor – 'Daddy stole her from Teddy,' Linnie says.
Introduce the interior of the folly – establish that the main guests are staying in rooms. Establish that the location is isolated. No telephone.

Fulbright talking about the film industry – rude to the screenwriter. Mention of Korda and Hitchcock. Comments on the old aristocracy versus the new (film stars)

Entrance of Veronica, Fulbright's sister.

(5)   Veronica speaks to Vickery – draws his attention to Malloy.

Arrival of Sir Geoffrey – he is hard-up and is going to need new money to keep his estate.

Beginning of the banquet – Vickery draws attention to the heated discussion between Kimball and Delancey.

Margot apologises for being rude to Delancey – sort of.

(6)   [Early on I had an additional character, Sir Geoffrey's daughter – she thought actors were terribly glamorous, and she had a crush on Teddy Kimball. But I soon merged this character with the actress Eleanor Trenton.]

There is a power failure, so the reel of the film cannot be shown. Malloy is sent off to obtain oil for the generator.

Supporting characters leave on the bus. Caterers leave in their van.

Fulbright announces that the film has been stolen – later discovery of burnt film in the ashes of the bonfire.

I had intended to write more detailed notes for each chapter – but in the end only wrote notes for the first three chapters:

Chapter One

Open with a description of the 'castle' – gatehouse and fountain. A medieval scene, with a banquet being prepared. A hog being roasted over a fire in the courtyard. A bonfire being lit. Musicians in a corner of the courtyard. Serving people in medieval costumes.

Then once the scene is set – the arrival of the 20th-century vehicles: a coach; a Rolls Royce; a motorcycle; a sports car. Chaos, smoke, and noise. And the arrivees in Arthurian costume.

The arrival of Leo Fulbright – obnoxious, arrogant, over-bearing. Demanding everything is done his way.
The arrival of Fulbright's wife, Margot – dialogue to establish.
The arrival of Vickery – aloof, enigmatic; demonstration of his abilities.

I also made notes of some of the images I wanted to create in the first chapter:
Orange flames of a bonfire – casting shadows of people moving on the limestone walls.
The tower silhouetted against a red sky as the sun sets.
A coach pulls into view – red and cream, gold lettering – belching blue smoke. The bus pulls away – the honking of a horn as other vehicles pull into the driveway – crunching gravel.
A bright blue two-seater sports car nipping in – the wrong way around the fountain, narrowly missing the departing coach.

Chapter Two
Inside the folly – description of the interior, including the main hall with the banqueting table. The main table is King Arthur's roundtable.
Introduce other characters – in dialogue between Margot and Vickery?
The banquet.
Layout of the folly and its grounds. History of the folly.
More of Vickery's detective abilities.
More of Fulbright's obnoxious behaviour.
Relationship triangle – Fulbright, Margot, and the young actress Eleanor Trenton.
2nd Relationship triangle – Fulbright, Eleanor Trenton, and Ted Kimball.
Hints that 'Fulbright's folly' may be an apt description of the film as well as the 'castle.'

Chapter Three
About the movie and the cast. The film studio.
Rumours of problems with the filming – Eleanor lacks the screen presence for Guinevere?

An argument between Leo Fulbright and Ted Kimball. Kimball challenges Fulbright to a duel with swords. Fulbright accepts – overpowers Kimball, humiliates him.
Vickery makes a comment about this being a mistake.
A screen is put up in the hall to view the rushes of the movie – but the electric generator fails, plunging them into darkness. Whistles etc. like a restless movie audience.
The caterers have gone, and so have the guests who arrived on the coach.
Malloy is sent to fix the oil-fired generator – but it has failed because there is no oil – it cannot be fixed.
They go out into the courtyard – heat and light from the bonfire. Some guests go up to bed with candles.
Malloy and Vickery know each other.
Malloy sent to fetch oil for the generator – from a garage in a village ten miles away.

I also made a few brief notes for the next nine chapters, taking the story up to the midpoint and the murder:

Chapter Four
Set-up character of the 'victim' – a tyrant.
The victim and catalyst character interaction – setting in motion events that will lead to midpoint murder.
Introduce other significant suspects – and establish some relationships between suspects.
Relationship triangles – jealousies.
Plant other significant information – relating to guilty secrets.

Chapter Five
Introduce another significant suspect. And a hint of a guilty secret.
And another suspect – and their guilty secret.

Chapter Six
Introduce final suspects and behaviours.
Breakfast the next day. Fulbright is angry – he has discovered another poison pen letter. He's angry at Vickery for not having solved this problem. And he's suspicious of everyone else – because one of them is sending him the letters. Vickery is

suspicious because Fulbright is not sharing the full contents of the letters. He believes the full letter accuses Fulbright of being guilty of some crime – the cause of the letter-writer's desire for revenge. Vickery thinks he would be able to identify the letter-writer if he knew the full content of the letters. But Fulbright refuses to acknowledge there is more to the letters than he has already revealed.

With the murder held off until the end of Chapter Twelve, having the detective investigate a minor, possibly unrelated, crime keeps the story moving.

Act II

Chapter Seven
First signs that all is not well – relationship problems.
A threat.
Suspicious behaviour – someone covering their own guilty secret, or trying to cover up for a character they care about.

Chapter Eight
Someone asks the detective for help – to stop bullying/persecution. Or to solve a minor mystery.
Detective urges a suspect to forget thoughts of revenge – it will not end well for them. Try and forget old rivalries. But the suspect is too bitter.
This person is either (a) too obvious to be the murderer, or (b) making himself appear too obvious to be the murderer.
Something happens that will be significant later.

Chapter Nine
Detective discusses revenge/bullying with the victim – victim admits to guilt/deserving revenge. Seems afraid. Also makes a threat of his/her own.
Detective muses on the fact that he's heard three sides of the relationship triangle – but which is true?

Chapter Ten
Daughter complains about overbearing mother/parents – the unfairness.
Hints that something dramatic will happen.

Detective becomes aware of the guilty secret of a suspect.

Chapter Eleven
More suspicious behaviour, occasioned by a guilty secret.
Perhaps an argument. Or an accident – which may be an attempted murder. The would-be victim may actually be a victim – or they could be the murderer setting themselves up to appear innocent – i.e. they are the target of an attempted killing, so they cannot be the murderer when an actual murder occurs.

Chapter Twelve
A mysterious event – minor – e.g. something goes missing (or is found).
An argument.
The murder.

I had initially thought that the second six chapters of the novel would be a chapter relating to the suspicious behaviour of each of the six main suspects. But again, I found that mixing things up was a much more natural way of telling the story. Those six chapters basically show the relationship of each of the characters with Fulbright, and with the first victim, Eleanor Trenton. I had listed a number of arguments and revelations that could be included in these chapters – in no particular order:

- Veronica Fulbright out shooting pigeons – she's a good shot.
- Arrival of Sir Geoffrey – he's the last major suspect to appear, though he has been discussed by other characters.
- Discovery of the latest poison pen letter – and the consequences of the discovery.
- Fulbright discovers that Linnie is engaged – throws Garvin out of the house.
- Fulbright asks Margot to help fund his film – she refuses.
- Ted Kimball decides to quit the film. Garvin gives Kimball the negatives of the incriminating photographs. Or Linnie does.

- An argument between Fulbright and Eleanor Trenton – Linnie has shown her the photographs; told her how Fulbright had Kimball followed.
- Veronica Fulbright meets secretly with someone – possibly her old lover.
- Establishing the murderer's alibi.
- Margot with Kimball.
- Margot with Sir Geoffrey.
- Ted Kimball drinking at breakfast time.
- Sir Geoffrey arguing with Eleanor Trenton.
- Evening meal and entertainment. Artie Delancey singing.
- Argument between Kimball and Eleanor Trenton.
- Argument between Margot and Eleanor Trenton.
- The body is discovered.

Once you have a murder victim, you need to think about who might want them dead and why – what is their motivation. My first notes on motivation related to people who would want to cause harm to Fulbright, and people who might want to stop his King Arthur film from being made:

People who want revenge on Fulbright:
Ollie Garvin – obstacle to love; Linnie will inherit
Linnie Fulbright – as above
Ted Kimball – professional and love rival
Sir Geoffrey – for past humiliation

People who want to stop the film being made:
Margot McCrae – because she's not Guinevere
Veronica Fulbright – because Leo Fulbright is spending the family inheritance
Linnie Fulbright – as above

Do Artie Delancey and Dickie Bannister have motivations? [I wasn't sure.]

Having decided on Eleanor Trenton as the first victim, the obvious question to explore was: Who wanted her dead?

Margot McCrae – She was jealous – because Eleanor has 'stolen' her husband and the leading role in his film.

Veronica Fulbright – To 'punish' her brother for taking away her lover – she will take away Fulbright's lover as he did hers; and also to put an end to the film, which is 'wasting' the family money.

Linnie Fulbright – Wants to sabotage her father's happiness, as he has done for her and Ollie Garvin; and she wants to put an end to the film, which is wasting the money she might otherwise inherit from her father. Also, it was Eleanor that told Leo Fulbright about the secret engagement – so she was responsible for Fulbright turning on Ollie.

Ollie Garvin – As above.

Ted Kimball – He was humiliated when Eleanor left him for Fulbright.

Artie Delancey – He was jealous of Eleanor's role as Guinevere: wanted to take her place.

Sir Geoffrey – Because Eleanor is the image of his dead sister – and he has feelings for her that he cannot act upon.

Leo Fulbright – because she is terrible in the movie, and this might ruin him financially; and because she has spurned his advances.

My aim was to make Leo Fulbright look like the 'obvious' suspect. Is someone framing him? Either because they want to escape blame for the murder, or because they want revenge on Eleanor and Fulbright? Or perhaps Fulbright *is* guilty, and he's trying to set things up to make it look like he is being framed.

I knew that Artie Delancey was going to be the second victim, at the end of Act II, so I had to set him up – either as a possible murderer or as someone who knows something important, but who is killed before he can reveal it.

I wrote several pages of notes detailing how Dickie Bannister was the murderer – he killed Eleanor Trenton because she had 'stolen' Margot's role as Queen Guinevere. Dickie is totally devoted to Margot – he hates the way Leo treats her and wanted to punish Leo as well. In the end, I wasn't convinced by this argument – but it did provide me with the solution to the mystery of the poison pen letters – Dickie Bannister was guilty of sending those to Leo.

I made some very brief notes about what I thought should be in each chapter for the second half of the novel:

Sequence 5
Beginning the investigation
The actual murderer eliminated as a suspect
Climax – A confession, an accusation, or a clue of 'obvious' guilt

Sequence 6
Investigation of the confession/accusation/clue – something is not quite right.
Closing in on someone – the number one suspect, or someone who knows something important to the investigation
The second murder – the number one suspect, or the person who knows something, is the victim.

Sequence 7
Investigating the second murder
Eliminating minor characters as suspects – at the same time exposing their guilty secrets
The second murder is the final clue. The detective reassesses everything in the light of this new clue and finally knows whodunit.

Sequence 8
Drawing Room scene part 1 – Eliminating innocent suspects – at the same time exposing their guilty secrets
Drawing Room scene part 2 – Explanation of how the crime was committed and by who.
Resolution – Restoration of equilibrium. Justice is served. Lovers off into the sunset.

There were a few more detailed notes on Chapters 13 through 15:

Chapter 13
- Aftermath of the discovery of Eleanor Trenton's body.
- Malloy is sent to fetch the doctor and the police.
- The arrival of the doctor.

- The local inspector is unable to attend – he's in hospital with a broken leg. An inspector is being sent from across the county, but he will not arrive until midday.
- It is suggested that – while they wait – Vickery should conduct an investigation.

In the first draft, Inspector Debney does not appear until the final chapter, after Vickery has solved the mystery. I will explain later why I decided that this didn't work and why I eventually decided to have the Inspector turn up in Chapter 13.

Chapter 14
- There is some reluctance to accepting Vickery as a detective – but eventually, all agree.
- The doctor's initial examination of the body – Eleanor was stabbed from a low angle with the long-bladed weapon – probably a sword.
- The replica of Excalibur is discovered to be missing from the stone.
- The red button found at the scene of the crime did not come from Eleanor Trenton's red dress.
- She also had a fragment of cloth or a piece from a watch chain clutched in her hand.
- Vickery wants Malloy to search the pond for the missing murder weapon.

Chapter 15
- Excalibur is missing and so is Artie Delancey.
- Artie watched Malloy searching the pond – but when Malloy tried to speak to him, Artie bolted.
- Malloy speaks to Artie briefly – Artie agrees to meet him later at the summer house near the lake.
- Need to establish alibis for each of the suspects – who was where at the time of the murder – i.e. just after midnight.
- Artie knows something or has something to hide.

It was about this point that I decided it was time to figure out the true sequence of events on the night of the murder and to begin to write the final explanation. I started with a series of questions:

- What time does Eleanor Trenton sing?

- When does she leave the drawing room? Why does she leave? Because she feels unwell – because something was put in her food or drink, causing her a headache or stomach upset? Or does Artie say something rude about her singing?
- What time does Kimball leave the drawing room? Artie sings again while he is gone. Or Bannister does.
- When Kimball leaves, Artie seems about to follow him – then changes his mind. Seems lost in thought – doesn't want to sing again. Bannister sings instead.
- Vickery performs a magic trick – or 'assists' Bannister in performing one.
- What time does Kimball return?
- When does Artie leave the room – and reappear (outside or on the stairs?) as Eleanor Trenton? He is seen by several people. Artie even mimics her singing voice?
- When does Fulbright leave the room and why? Margot sends him on an errand.

I had a couple of goes at writing the detective's final explanation of whodunit – the how and why – before I was happy with it. As I wrote it, I made note of things I needed to go back and insert of 'fix' in earlier chapters to make them consistent with the explanation.

The 'drawing room scene' traditionally requires each suspect to be considered in turn, their possible guilt explored in terms of means, motive, and opportunity/alibi. They are then exonerated until only the real murderer remains. Sometimes the real murderer is apparently cleared early in this sequence, but the spotlight falls back on them again and their guilt is finally exposed.

I made a list of the characters in the order in which I wanted them to be accused and exonerated. I wrote each piece – and then shuffled them around into an order that I felt worked better once they were written. Along the way I also had the detective explain the solution to the mystery of the poison pen letters, before exposing the murderer.

Part of the explanation is the significance of the various clues, and the discounting of the red herrings (or false clues).

I thought at the beginning that there should be five or six clues and a similar number of red herrings. If I'm perfectly honest, I think clues relating to people – their motivations and their relationships – are much more interesting than physical clues such as footprints or cigarette ash. Here are the clues and red herrings I ended up with – this list changed several times during the course of writing the novel:

The Clues
- The red button – none were missing from Eleanor Trenton's red dress, therefore there was a second dress.
- Female impersonator who was going to double for Eleanor in the riding scenes in the movie.
- The poison pen letters – indicating that Fulbright is guilty of some recent crime and must be punished.
- Dickie Bannister's apparent infatuation with Margaret.
- Margot's accident wasn't an accident.
- Relationship between Artie Delancey and Ted Kimball.

The Red Herrings
- Fulbright's anger/violence
- The scream and the time of the murder
- The threats on Fulbright's life
- The burnt film and rumours of bad acting by the leading lady
- The guilty secrets of the innocent characters

Where I Went Wrong – Evaluating the First Draft

Before I share with you what I got wrong and how I fixed it, I'll show you one final tool I used to help me evaluate my first draft. It's really only another quick run-through of the eight sequences of the story, showing how they begin and end. I used it to force myself to check my draft manuscript against the model plot structure – and this helped me identify what was wrong with it. This, along with a chapter by chapter listing of what happens where, also helped me found my way around my manuscript when I needed to find scenes that I needed to rewrite or places where I needed to insert clues.

For each sequence, I listed the beginning and the climax:

Sequence Summary

Sequence 1 – Chapters 1 to 3. Begins with arrival of characters and setting. Ends with Vickery is a detective investigating threats against Fulbright.

Sequence 2 – Chapters 4 to 6. Begins with introduction of minor characters. Ends with film has been stolen – by the writer of the poison pen letters?

Sequence 3 – Chapters 7 to 9. Begins with Emily shooting pigeons and arrival of another letter. Ends with Fulbright attacks Garvin.

Sequence 4 – Chapters 10 to 12. Begins with Kimball attacks Garvin's car. Ends with Kimball's performance of the Limerick Hamlet and a scream at midnight.

Sequence 5 – Chapters 13 to 15. Begins with discovery of Elspeth's body. Ends with Fulbright is (too) obviously guilty.

Sequence 6 – Chapters 16 to 18. Begins with Fulbright accusing Kimball – but Kimball has a perfect alibi. Ends with Malloy searches the pond – no murder weapon there, but he does find an empty sack.

Sequence 7 – Chapters 19 to 21. Begins with the discovery of Artie's body. Ends with Bannister confessing to murder.

Sequence 8 – Chapters 22 to 24. Begins with Bannister being cleared of murder, but guilty of letters. Ends with Kimball is guilty; justice is served; equilibrium is restored.

It is often said that once you have completed your first draft, you should set it aside for a while – ideally a couple of weeks at least – so that you can come back to it with an objective eye and so see its faults more clearly. I don't know if this is true of all writers, but when I have finished something – and often before I've finished it – I have a nagging, almost subconscious feeling that something is not quite right. Or perhaps very wrong. And if I leave my subconscious to do its thing, I'll eventually know where the story is failing and – if I'm lucky – how to fix it.

I set the print-out of *The Sword in the Stone-Dead* aside for four days. I should have been able to enjoy seeing that nice neat pile of paper in the ring-binder – a complete draft of a book that never existed before. But instead, all I was aware of was that damned nagging feeling.

After four days, I sat and wrote myself a single side of notes:

Notes on First Draft
- Sequences 5 and 6 are weak / too short.
- Sequence 7 is too short.
- These sequences should deal with the actual investigation of the murder, and the first sequence of the explanation.
- Sequences 5 and 6 are investigation / incrimination.
- Sequence 7 is the first sequence of exoneration.
- Need to structure the investigation – from the discovery of the body to the drawing together of the suspects in the drawing room.
- Need to summarise/highlight everyone's suspicious behaviour, and their motive for wanting Eleanor Trenton dead before moving on to opportunity/alibi.
- Need to introduce physical evidence
- Need to establish (apparent) sequence of events – What happened, in what order, at what time. Who was where at what time – evidence to support this? Including: When was Eleanor last seen alive? What time was the scream heard?
- Also, what happened in the hour before the scream – Who was where? Who saw them?
- Sequence 7 establishes what seemed to have happened. Why the murderer is innocent.
- Sequence 8 explains what really happened. Why the murderer is guilty.

These notes covered the major defects of the draft – I thought there might also be a problem with the opening paragraphs, and decided that I should revisit those too. More on that shortly.

Bearing in mind that each of the eight sequences of the novel should have been around 7,500 words in length, here is what the word counts looked like for my first draft:

Sequence 1 – 9,690 words
Sequence 2 – 8,730
Sequence 3 – 4,900
Sequence 4 – 5,050
Sequence 5 – 3,350
Sequence 6 – 8,400
Sequence 7 – 4,700
Sequence 8 – 5,000

The first half of my novel was 1,600 words or so under target – I could live with that. The second half of my novel was 8,500 words short – that was more than the equivalent of a whole sequence missing.

Sequences 5 and 7 obviously had problems. Sequence 3 being short didn't worry me too much, as the first two sequences were long. And Sequence 8 as the last sequence is traditionally shorter anyway. But 5 and 7 needed work. Part of my problem was that in Sequence 5, Chapter 13 was only 350 words and I had no Chapter 15. Chapter 15 was a blank page.

Apart from a severe word shortage, the one thing that really bothered me about the draft was the way I had handled the absence of the police following the murder. I hadn't really come up with a plausible reason for having the Inspector severely delayed, such that my amateur detective had to take over the investigation of the murder. My location wasn't remote enough to make keeping the police away for six hours or so a reasonable proposition. I tried tweaking my timescales this way and that, but no matter what I did, I couldn't escape the feeling that I was cheating. In the end, I took the most sensible route and had the police turn up right after the murder, and I had my amateur detective in conflict with the official Investigator. Then I had my Investigator accuse an innocent character that everyone else liked so that they all pleaded with my amateur detective to investigate and discover the real murderer. Making those changes didn't actually force me to alter much of what I had previously written.

The mistake I had made with Sequence 5 was that I hadn't treated it as the beginning of a murder investigation. Because my detective had been questioning people about poison pen letters, Sequence 5 just seemed like more of the same. I hadn't followed my own plot framework for this sequence of the story. Having the Inspector turn up altered the dynamic, and helped me to see the amateur detective's investigation in a new light, and got me back on the right track.

I wrote a new Chapter 13 and wrote the missing Chapter 15, and ended up with a Sequence 5 word count of something like 8,300 words.

I left Sequence 7 pretty much as it was, and concentrated on fixing the second half of the 'drawing room scene' in Sequence 8. I'd skimped on the explanations here – as I'd told myself in my notes on the first draft, I needed to summarise and evaluate the evidence, exploring first in the light of what seemed to have happened, and then in the light of what had really happened. Fixing this added around 2,000 words. Having done this and filled in a few bits of missing description earlier in the story, I was pretty much done.

Apart from that one final problem that I didn't want to admit. But that was now giving me that damned nagging feeling. The first couple of pages of a story are the most important ones you write in any story. If you can't capture the attention of the reader in those opening paragraphs, they will put the book aside and probably never pick it up again. You've lost a customer. I had originally imagined the opening of *The Sword in the Stone-Dead* as a long tracking shot along a windy road through trees, up a gravel drive, to where the Victorian folly was silhouetted like a medieval castle against a red sunset. I wanted it to be like the opening shot of a creepy movie. I'd even written the first couple of paragraphs of the first draft in the present tense like a movie script – but ditched that because (a) most readers have probably never read a movie script, and (b) using something other than past tense risks making the reader uncomfortable – they might think you don't know how to write, or think the book is some weird experimental *avant garde* shit. But I liked my slow sweepy opening shot – it was like something from an Orson Welles movie – or so I kidded myself.

On the night I was printing out a copy of the manuscript for a friend to read, I abandoned my mistaken belief in that opening and cut it to about a third of its original length and got good old Leo Fulbright up on screen much sooner. Sometimes you really do have to kill your darlings – especially when they stink like a week-old corpse.

Postscript: My trusted first reader told me she thought the opening paragraphs were a bit short and that I should have included more description there. I reinstated some of what I'd cut.

Appendix 2:

A History of the Mystery

Before the Golden Age

The traditional mystery story as we know it has its origins in three short stories written by Edgar Allan Poe: 'The Murder in the Rue Morgue' (1841), 'The Mystery of Marie Rogêt' (1843), and 'The Purloined Letter' (1844). In these, he created the first 'Great Detective,' Auguste Dupin. Dupin was the model for Arthur Conan Doyle's Sherlock Holmes, who first appeared in 1887, and everyone else who came after. Poe did not describe his hero as a 'detective' – the word wasn't really used before the mid-1850s. Poe's hero was an amateur rather than an official investigator.

Poe is believed to have been inspired by the partly ghost-written memoirs of Eugène François Vidocq (see below), a former criminal who became the founder and first director of the crime-detection Sûreté Nationale in Paris, and also created the first private detective agency. Another possible influence is thought to have been Voltaire's *Zadig* (1747), in which the main character demonstrates analytical skills similar to those of our favourite detectives, though these skills can themselves be traced back to much older texts.

Historical Antecedents
The earliest stories in which a character demonstrates detective-like skills are so old as to be un-dateable, having been told by storytellers centuries before they were ever written down. Some argue that these are examples – like the Riddle of the Sphinx – of 'puzzle' stories, rather than detective stories, but the two are closely related, so I think it is helpful to be aware of them.

Aesop's Fables possibly date from 500 or 600BC, and include the story of 'The Fox and the Sick Lion,' in which the lion asks the fox why he does not come to visit him in his cave, to which the wily fox replies: "Because I can only see tracks going in, but none coming out."

From the *Apocrypha* (chapter 13 of the Book of Daniel) we have the story of Susanna. Susanna is falsely accused of meeting a lover when she refuses to have sex with a couple of old men who have been spying on her while she bathed. She is arrested and about to be put to death, when Daniel interrupts the proceedings, saying that the two old men should be questioned to determine whether or not Susanna is innocent. The two men are questioned separately and are asked under what sort of tree Susanna supposedly met her lover: one says a mastic, the other an oak. These types of trees are so different that the two men must be lying: Susanna is saved, and her false accusers are put to death.

Chapter 14 of the Book of Daniel gives us the story of Bel, which challenges the worship of idols, and provides one of the earliest examples of a 'locked room mystery.' The priests claim that Bel is a living god, but Daniel challenges this, saying Bel is merely a bronze and clay statue. If Bel is not living, then who eats the food and drink that is left out for him every night? The priests ask the King to seal the entrance to the temple: if the food is consumed at night, then Bel lives and Daniel should be put to death; if the food is not consumed, the priests should die. Daniel proves to the King that the food is not eaten by their god: he scatters ashes on the temple floor, and in the morning, shows the King the footprints that reveal how the priests and their families enter the temple through a secret door and consume Bel's food at night. The priests and their families are put to death, and Daniel is permitted to destroy the statue of the idol. The two stories about Daniel possibly date from 200 to 500 BC.

Dated around 440 BC are *The Histories* by Herodotus, which include the story of Rhampsinitus and the Thief, an early account of a master criminal and an agent of the law in close conflict:

King Rhampsinitus has a hoard of gold hidden in a specially-built, impregnable treasury. On his deathbed, the builder of the treasury tells his two sons of a secret way into the building: they enter the treasury on several occasions and fill their pockets. Aware that his hoard is diminishing, the King sets a trap for the thieves. One of the brothers is trapped, with no hope of escape, so begs his own brother to cut off his head so that he cannot be identified. Angered by the discovery of the headless corpse, the King orders it to be impaled on a stake and displayed in the marketplace: anyone who displays grief in front of the body is to be arrested.

The mother asks her surviving son to retrieve his brother's body: if he refuses, she will go to the King and tell him the truth. The young thief is left with no choice. He devises a plan to get the guards drunk so he can take his brother's body. Again the King is angered that he has been outsmarted by the thief, and is determined to catch him. He orders his daughter to pretend to be a 'maid' in the royal brothel. She is to speak to the men who visit and ask them to reveal their darkest secret: whoever tells her about stealing from the treasury will be arrested.

The young thief visits the princess, but is suspicious, and brings with him the right-arm of his dead brother. He tells the princess of his thefts, but when she seizes his arm, she finds herself holding the arm of the dead man, and the thief flees. Impressed by the ingenuity of the thief, King Rhampsinitus decides to pardon him, and offers his daughter's hand in marriage. The princess and the thief marry.

In her book *The Techniques of the Mystery Story* (1913) Carolyn Wells lists one of the tales of The Visakha as an early example. Visakha was chief among the female lay disciples of the Buddha, and demonstrated her wisdom and rational thinking in a number of ways, including this one, taken from *Tibetan Tales: Derived from Indian Sources* (1906):

When a householder dies, there is a dispute between two women as to which is the mother of his child. Initial investigations bring no conclusion, and so Visakha offers this solution:

"What need is there of investigation? Speak to the two women thus: 'As we do not know to which of you two the boy belongs, let her who is the strongest take the boy.' When each of them has taken hold of one of the boy's hands, and he begins to cry out on account of the pain, the real mother will let go, being full of compassion for him, and knowing that if her child remains alive she will be able to see it again; but the other, who has no compassion for him, will not let go. Then beat her with a switch, and she will thereupon confess the truth as to the whole matter. That is the proper test."

A similar story is told of Solomon, who suggests cutting the child in two and giving the women half each, knowing that the true mother would give up her child rather than allow him to suffer such a fate.

Another story often mentioned in relation to the detective story is 'The Three Princes of Serendip,' versions of which are known in Persia, India, and in the Talmud. These date from possibly 200 to 1,100AD but could be based on earlier oral traditions.

Fearing that their education has been too sheltered and privileged, King Giaffer sends his three sons out into the world. Arriving in the land of the Sultan Beramo, the princes pause to rest at the side of the road and observe the land around them.

"A camel has passed this way, laden with honey on one side and pickles on the other," said one brother.

"Indeed, and it was lame, blind in one eye, and missing a tooth," said another.

"And it carried a woman on its back," said the third.

Overhearing these words, the owner of the camel descended on them and accused them of stealing his camel. They were taken before the Sultan for him to pass judgment on them.

The princes protested their innocence, saying they had never even seen the camel. But how could this be true, given the details they were able to describe? In reply, the princes explained how they had come by their knowledge:

"We saw that the grass had been grazed on only one side of the road, and because there were pieces of chewed grass on the road the size of a camel's tooth, we inferred they had fallen through the gap left by a missing tooth. The camel's tracks showed three clear feet, with the fourth being dragged, indicating that it was lame.

"Flies had been attracted to something sweet that dripped on the one side, and not to the drips on the other, and from this we observed that one half of the load was sweet honey, and the other sour pickles. And where the camel had knelt, we saw the imprint of a foot belonging to the woman it carried."

Having demonstrated the source of their knowledge, the Princes were judged innocent by the Sultan.

This story of the three princes is quoted as inspiring part of Voltaire's philosophical novel *Zadig, or The Book of Fate* (1747).

"Young man," said the chief eunuch to Zadig, "have you seen the queen's dog?"

Zadig modestly replied: "It is a bitch, not a dog."

"You are right," said the eunuch.

"It is a very small spaniel," added Zadig; "it is not long since she has had a litter of puppies; she is lame in the left forefoot, and her ears are very long."

"You have seen her, then?" said the chief eunuch, quite out of breath.

"No," answered Zadig, "I have never seen her, and never knew that the queen had a bitch."

Before he can explain himself, he is asked if he has seen the King's horse:

"It is the horse," said Zadig, "which gallops best; he is five feet high, and has small hoofs; his tail is three and a half feet long; the bosses on his bit are of gold twenty-three carats fine; his shoes are silver of eleven pennyweights."

"Which road did he take? Where is he?" asked the grand huntsman.

"I have not seen him," answered Zadig, "and I have never even heard anyone speak of him."

Of course, our hero is accused of stealing both the dog and the horse, and has to explain his way out of this predicament:

"I saw on the sand the footprints of an animal, and easily decided that they were those of a little dog. Long and faintly marked furrows, imprinted where the sand was slightly raised between the footprints, told me that it was a bitch whose dugs were drooping, and that consequently she must have given birth to young ones only a few days before. Other marks of a different character, showing that the surface of the sand had been constantly grazed on either side of the front paws, informed me that she had very long ears; and, as I observed that the sand was always less deeply indented by one paw than by the other three, I gathered that the bitch belonging to our august queen was a little lame, if I may venture to say so."

And:

"With respect to the horse of the king of kings, you must know that as I was walking along the roads in that same wood, I perceived the marks of a horse's shoes, all at equal distances. 'There,' I said to myself, 'went a horse with a faultless gallop.' The dust upon the trees, where the width of the road was not more than seven feet, was here and there rubbed off on both sides, three feet and a half away from the middle of the road. 'This horse,' said I, 'has a tail three feet and a half long, which, by its movements to right and left, has whisked away the dust.' I saw, where the trees formed a canopy five feet above the ground, leaves lately fallen from the boughs; and I concluded that the horse had touched them, and was therefore five feet high. As to his bit, it must be of gold twenty-three carats fine, for he had rubbed its bosses against a touchstone, the properties of which I had ascertained. Lastly, I inferred from the marks that his shoes left upon stones of another kind, that he was shod with silver of eleven pennyweights in quality."

We can follow the trail: from the Princes of Serendip to *Zadig*, to Edgar Allan Poe, to Arthur Conan Doyle's Sherlock Holmes.

Apart from the stories mentioned above, there are very few others that might be considered as early examples of the detective mystery story. There are many stories in which the adventures of criminals and ne'er-do-wells are recounted, but few in which the successes of an investigator are celebrated.

In the sixteenth century, the 'picaresque' novel, following – in autobiographical fashion – the escapades of rogues, thieves, brigands, prostitutes, and other trickster types, were popular in first Spain, and then through the rest of Europe. *Lazarillo de Tormes,* published anonymously in 1554, is regarded as the first example, and Thomas Nashe's *The Unfortunate Traveller* (1594) is an English novel in this tradition. This type of fiction inspired Daniel Defoe's accounts of the lives of pirates and thieves in the 1700s, as well as his novel *Moll Flanders.* Henry Fielding's *Jonathan Wilde* (1743) is a novel based on the life of another well-known criminal.

In the second half of the eighteenth century, Gothic fiction captured readers' imaginations. Horace Walpole's *The Castle of Otranto* (1764) is the first of this type, and the popularity of this genre continued well into the nineteenth century, when Charles Maturin's *Melmoth the Wanderer* (1829) was published. But the detective story proper did not appear until those stories by Edgar Allan Poe.

Why was detective fiction not written before the appearance of Poe's short stories? In an introduction to *Crime and Detection* (1926), E. M. Wrong wrote: "Why was there no flowering under the Roman Empire? ... Perhaps a faulty law of evidence was to blame, for detectives cannot flourish until the public has an idea of what constitutes proof, and while a common criminal procedure is arrest, torture, confession, and death." This is certainly one reason why detective-type heroes did not appear: you cannot be a detective until there is a system of justice within which an investigator can function. There may have been investigators during the Spanish Inquisition and during the witch-hunts conducted from the 1400s to the 1800s, but these can hardly be said to have delivered justice, and were much closer to Wrong's Roman Empire than to our modern legal system.

There is also the matter of reader, or listener, sympathy. The law, until relatively recently, was designed to protect the property and rights of those wealthy enough to own property: ordinary people were more likely to be victims of the system, rather than beneficiaries. Little wonder then that stories about rebels and rogues were popular, from Robin Hood to Dick Turpin. In England, the justice system had little interest in the affairs of common folk until the laws governing who was permitted to vote in parliamentary elections were amended in the 1830s.

François Eugene Vidocq (1775–1857)

As mentioned above, the memoirs of the French criminal turned detective Francois Eugene Vidocq are also cited as one of the inspirations for the creation of Edgar Allan Poe's detective C. Auguste Dupin. Before he had reached the age of 18, Vidocq had been a thief, stable boy, carnival performer, soldier, and deserter, and had challenged more than a dozen people to duels, and killed two of them. He was an accomplished swordsman and went on to gain a reputation as a womaniser. He was imprisoned for assaulting a soldier, and escaped captivity on more than one occasion. His life as a criminal continued until he was thirty-four years old, and then he offered to become a police informant. In prison, he spied on fellow inmates and reported what he had learned to the authorities. Finally freed from prison, he worked as a police spy outside, using his familiarity with those in the underworld to earn their trust, and their secrets.

Vidocq organized an informal plainclothes unit, which he called the *Brigade de la Sûreté* (Security Brigade). The police department quickly appreciated the value of these agents, and Vidocq's brigade became an official unit under the Prefecture of Police. A year later, Napoleon Bonaparte signed a decree that made them a part of the state police, and they became known as the *Sûreté Nationale*, with Vidocq as their first leader. Many of Vidocq's men were ex-criminals like himself. He trained the men himself and, according to his autobiography, was himself a master of disguise.

Vidocq served the police for eighteen years, but following changes in the political regime in France, he found himself out of favour and submitted his resignation. Vidocq set up in business with a paper-mill, but was soon bankrupt. He returned to the *Sûreté* briefly, but then left and set up his own private police organisation: the first private detective agency. He also wrote a short autobiography, that was expanded to four volumes with the help of ghost-writers.

It is hardly surprising that such a colourful figure would inspire writers, both during his own lifetime and later. Honoré de Balzac drew on the character of Vidocq for several stories, most notably Jacques Collin, alias Vautrin, in the series that made up *La Comédie Humaine*. *Le Vautrin* (the wild boar) had been Vidocq's nickname during his teenage years. In *Les Misérables*, Victor Hugo drew inspiration from Vidocq for both the criminal Jean Valjean and Police Inspector Javert. And Alexandre Dumas used him as the model for his policeman Monsieur Jackal in *Les Mohicans de Paris*.

Vidocq is mentioned in Herman Melville's *Moby Dick,* and in Charles Dickens' *Great Expectations*. He also inspired Émile Gaboriau, creator of Monsieur Lecoq, a character who was one of the first to apply scientific methods to investigations, and who may have been one of the inspirations for Sherlock Holmes.

Edgar Allan Poe (1809–1849)

To say that Edgar Allan Poe created the classical detective mystery genre in the space of three short stories, 'The Murder in the Rue Morgue' (1841), 'The Mystery of Marie Rogêt' (1843), and 'The Purloined Letter' (1844), sounds a bit unlikely. A fourth Poe story that is also sometimes grouped with the Dupin stories as an example of an investigator at work, 'The Gold Bug' (1845), is really only a puzzle story. Looking at the three Dupin stories, what did Poe bequeath us?

In a piece titled 'The Contributions of Edgar Allan Poe,' Robert A. W. Lowndes notes that the first thousand or so words of 'The Murder in the Rue Morgue' are effectively an essay on analysis, and concludes that "...today's reader does not need it at all." I agree with him, because once you're past it and the story proper begins, we meet C. Auguste Dupin, the first detective, even though he is never called such. The story is told in the first person by an unnamed narrator, who first meets Dupin in an obscure library, where both are searching

for the same 'very rare and very remarkable' book. Falling
into conversation, the narrator soon learns that:

*"This young gentleman was of an excellent, indeed of an
illustrious family, but, by a variety of untoward events, had
been reduced to such poverty that the energy of his character
succumbed beneath it, and he ceased to bestir himself in the
world, or to care for the retrieval of his fortunes."*

Becoming better acquainted over time, and finding that he
and Dupin have much in common, the two decide to share
lodgings:

*"... and as my worldly circumstances were somewhat less
embarrassed than his own, I was permitted to be at the expense
of renting, and furnishing in a style which suited the rather
fantastic gloom of our common temper, a time-eaten and grotesque mansion, long deserted through superstitions into
which we did not inquire, and tottering to its fall in a retired
and desolate portion of the Faubourg St. Germain."*

These two men, we know already, are eccentric or perhaps
Bohemian in their tastes, and Dupin is something of an enig-
matic character: we are intrigued by him. We have our hero,
and his friend, the narrator. Doctor Johnson and his Boswell.
Similar partnerships were used for Holmes and Watson,
Poirot and Hastings, and a whole host of others.

Soon we learn that Dupin has a 'peculiar analytic ability'
and that, to him, most men 'wore windows in their bosoms.'
By way of demonstration, we see him appear to read the narrator's thoughts, and then go on to explain the process by
which he came to his startling observation. This 'mind-reading' trick is something Holmes does to Watson, and others
have used it too.

In 'The Murders in the Rue Morgue,' we also see Dupin, the
amateur investigator, describing the short-comings of the
police, saying that although they are "much extolled for acu-
men," they are in fact "cunning, but no more. There is no
method in their proceedings, beyond the method of the
moment ... The results attained by them are not unfrequently
surprising, but, for the most part, are brought about by simple
diligence and activity. When these qualities are unavailing,

their schemes fail." Dupin's professional rivalry with the Prefect of Police, named only as G—, is a forerunner of that between Holmes and Inspector Lestrade.

Visiting the Rue Morgue, the narrator observes Dupin "...examining the whole neighborhood, as well as the house, with a minuteness of attention for which I could see no possible object." Asked later if he noticed anything peculiar about the scene of the crime, the narrator admits that he did not. Dupin implies that he did, and then says: "It appears to me that this mystery is considered insoluble, for the very reason which should cause it to be regarded as easy of solution – I mean for the outré character of its features." The police find extraordinary crimes such as this one difficult to solve using their usual methods, but to Dupin, the peculiar features make the solution more obvious. He tells the narrator that he has arrived at the solution, and awaits only one more piece of information to verify his findings. He does not reveal what the solution is. As Lowdnes writes, in this type of story, "... the murder or mystery is almost always an extraordinary one, not susceptible to the usual routine of diligence and cunning which at its best results in the solution of most crimes."

There follows a long explanation of the evidence Dupin discovered, and of its probable meaning, showing that he found things which the police failed to spot. This leads up to a final confrontation which resolves the mystery and proves the solution. Having trapped the man he wished to speak to, Dupin does not turn him over to the police: he is more concerned with learning the truth of what happened, than in seeing someone behind bars. And having learned the whole story, Dupin tells the police only sufficient detail to ensure they release a wrongly arrested man. Truth and justice are served, though the full processes of police and legal system are not followed.

In 'The Mystery of Marie Rogêt,' Poe uses the detective and his powers of 'ratiocination' to explore a true murder mystery that was unsolved at the time he wrote the story. Much has been written about whether or not Poe did, in fact, solve the true mystery in his story, but that does not concern us here.

Lowdnes points out that the story adds seven more 'firsts' in the genre:

    i.   Dupin becomes the first detective in a series of stories

    ii.   The professional police come to the amateur detective for help

    iii.   Dupin solves the case without leaving the house, becoming the first 'armchair detective'

    iv.   Dupin solves the case based on official data and newspaper accounts, and the only person he questions is the Prefect of Police

    v.   In this second appearance, Dupin is presented as eccentric, rather than truly bizarre

    vi.   Dupin gives the police all the information they need to find and arrest the culprit but takes no part in events once the solution is known

    vii.   While discussing the case, Dupin challenges popular notions about crime

'The Purloined Letter' is probably the best, and most popular, of the three stories. The mystery is presented quickly: an important letter has been lost, the police know who took it, but they have been unable to find it in the man's quarters. When the Prefect of Police tells Dupin of the problem, the detective tells them they must look again.

The Prefect returns sometime later: the letter has still not been found. Dupin asks if a reward is offered for its return, and is told fifty thousand francs will be given. Dupin asks the Prefect to write out a cheque for the amount and then hands over the letter. Dupin then explains to the narrator how he deduced the location of the letter, and what actions he took to recover it. Along the way, he reveals something of his own backstory.

'The Purloined Letter' introduces a few more 'firsts,' according to Lowdnes, including the fact that the mystery involves the security of the nation, and so includes an element of political intrigue. And there is some humour in Dupin's treatment of the Prefect. In all, Lowdnes enumerates thirty-two 'firsts' within the three stories, so perhaps the claims made about

Poe being the father of the detective mystery story are not over-exaggerated.

In a final side note, since this is a chapter on the links between earlier works and later ones: In 'The Murders in the Rue Morgue,' Dupin criticises the methods of Vidocq, a figure who undoubtedly inspired Poe; and in *A Study in Scarlet,* Sherlock Holmes is critical of the methods employed by Dupin, who must have served as an inspiration for Arthur Conan Doyle. This tradition of one detective casting judgment on the methods of another was continued by later authors, as if it was an expected part of the game. Hercule Poirot, and others, mock the Sherlockian obsession with types of tobacco ash.

After Poe – Wilkie Collins and Charles Dickens

Over forty years separate the publication of Poe's stories and the first appearance of Sherlock Holmes in *A Study in Scarlet* (1887), and if you look at what was published during that time, one thing is obvious: Poe might have invented the genre, but it didn't achieve immediate popularity with readers. But there are a few things that were published during those intervening forty years that are worth mentioning.

Wilkie Collins' (1824-1889) *The Woman in White* (1860) is often said to be one of the first mystery novels, though it belongs more to the genre of 'sensation novels,' which are closer to Gothic fiction and thrillers than to detective mysteries. The hero, Walter Hartright, a young art teacher, does engage in some investigative activities, but he's not really a detective hero. The story is told from multiple viewpoints – Collins himself likened it to a number of witnesses giving evidence at a trial – and so lacks the focus that we usually find in a classic mystery.

1868 saw the publication of Collins' *The Moonstone*. T. S. Eliot described it as "the first and greatest of English detective novels," in an article titled 'Wilkie Collins and Dickens' in the August 1927 issue of the *Times Literary Supplement.* In an introduction to the Oxford University Press World's Classics edition of the novel published in March 1928, he amended this to "the first, the longest, and the best of modern English detective novels." In the same introduction, he also wrote: "Modern detective writers have added the use of fingerprints and such trifles, but they have not materially improved upon either the personality or the methods of Sergeant Cuff." Eliot also claimed that the genre was 'invented by Collins and not by Poe,' though this may be stretching things. Dorothy L. Sayers rated the book too, writing in her introduction to *The Omnibus of Crime* (1929): "Taking everything into consideration, *The Moonstone* is probably the very finest detective story ever written." And G. K. Chesterton, in 'The Victorian Age in Literature,' called it "probably the best detective tale in the world." This one *is* a detective story, then, but its links to the Gothic and 'sensation novel' traditions are still obvious.

The *Wikipedia* entry for *The Moonstone* lists the 'firsts' it contains in terms of detective novels:

- English country house robbery
- An 'inside job'
- Red herrings
- A celebrated, skilled, professional investigator
- Bungling local constabulary
- Detective enquiries
- Large number of false suspects
- The 'least likely suspect'
- A reconstruction of the crime
- A final twist in the plot

As well as Sergeant Cuff, it features Franklin Blake, an amateur, who is an early example of the 'gentleman detective.' Wilkie Collins' 1875 novel *The Law and the Lady*, features a heroine who sets out to prove that her husband is not guilty of poisoning his first wife – an early example of an amateur female detective.

Wilkie Collins met Charles Dickens in 1850 and the two became good friends. A number of Collins' stories, including *The Woman in White* and *The Moonstone* were published in Dickens' magazines. The two also worked together on two plays and two short stories. As we will see, there are also links between Dickens and Edgar Allan Poe.

Charles Dickens (1812-1870) also dabbled in the mystery genre. *Bleak House* (1852-53) features the character of Inspector Bucket, who carries out several investigations during the story, including that of the murder of Mr Tulkinghorn. He is notable in being one of the first detectives in English fiction. The character is believed to have been based on Inspector Charles Frederick Field of Scotland Yard. Dickens wrote articles about the Inspector and the work of the detectives for his magazine *Household Words*.

Dickens' novel *Barnaby Rudge* (1840-41) is a historical novel, comparable to the works of Walter Scott, set during the anti-Catholic Gordon Riots of 1780. It is not a mystery novel, but part of the plot does centre on the identity of the murderer of Reuben Haredale. While the novel was still being serialised, Edgar Allan Poe wrote an article for the *Philadelphia Sunday Times,* exposing the secret Dickens was keeping from his readers, and identifying the murderer. Poe was also fascinated by Grip, the raven that accompanies Barnaby everywhere – it was based on Dickens' own pet raven, also called Grip – and it is thought that he was the inspiration for Poe's famous poem, *The Raven*.

Charles Dickens' final novel, *The Mystery of Edwin Drood*, was unfinished at the time of the author's death, leaving the identity of the murderer a mystery.

Emile Gaboriau (1832-1873)

L'Affaire Lerouge (1866, translated as *The Widow Lerouge* or *The Lerouge Case*) was Gaboriau's first mystery novel and it introduced his detective Lecoq, who would feature in four further novels: *Le Crime d'Orcival* (1867, *The Mystery of Orcival*), *Le Dossier No.113* (1867, *File No. 113*), and *Monsieur Lecoq* (1868, *Lecoq the Detective*). The novels were influenced by Edgar Allan Poe's Dupin stories and have also been described as being in the 'French sensational' tradition. Gaboriau was a journalist who drew on his knowledge of the French justice system and the criminal milieu of nineteenth-century Paris for his fiction, which included a number of other crime novels without a mystery element.

Lecoq, drawing on elements from Vidocq and Poe, was a master of disguise and adept at using the scientific method for analysing physical clues. *Monsieur Lecoq* opens with a detailed examination of the crime scene, from which the detective deduces what occurred and provides a description of those involved. Arthur Conan Doyle cited Gaboriau as an influence in the creation of Sherlock Holmes, and the loosely connected first and second parts of *Monsieur Lecoq* – the first concerning the investigation and the second being an account of the events that led up to the crime – may account for the two-part structure of *A Study in Scarlet*.

Anna Katharine Green (1846-1935)

Anna Katharine Green's 1878 novel *The Leavenworth Case: A Lawyer's Story* introduced New York detective Ebenezer Gryce nine years before the appearance of Sherlock Holmes. According to *The Oxford Companion to Crime and Mystery Writing*, it introduced such "familiar conventions as the body in the library, the wealthy man about to change his will, the locked room, the use of ballistics evidence, a coroner's inquest, a sketch of the scene of the crime, and a partially burned letter..." The novel was influenced by the work of Emile Gaboriau. Wilkie Collins wrote to the author praising her inventiveness and depiction of strong female characters. Green went on to write a total of twenty-nine detective novels and four collections of short stories. In three of her novels, Gryce is assisted by a nosy spinster sleuth, Amelia Butterworth, who Agatha Christie credits as being an inspiration for Miss Marple. She also created a younger female amateur detective, Violet Strange.

Sir Arthur Conan Doyle & Sherlock Holmes

Sherlock Holmes made his first appearance in the novel *A Study in Scarlet*, published in *Beeton's Christmas Annual* for 1887. Sir Arthur Conan Doyle (1859-1930) would go on to write fifty-six short stories for *The Strand* magazine, and three further novels: *The Sign of the Four* (1890); *The Hound of the Baskervilles* (1901–1902); and *The Valley of Fear* (1914–

1915). The character of Sherlock Holmes was explored in detail in the chapter on The Great Detective.

Appendix 3:

A History of the Mystery

The Golden Age

The 'golden age' of the traditional or classical mystery story is generally regarded to be the period from about 1918 to 1939. *The Oxford Companion to Crime and Mystery Writing* defines the golden age of the short story to be from the first appearance of Sherlock Holmes in 1887 to the end of the Second World War, and for the novel it says the 'fullest flowering' occurred between the two world wars.

It would be impossible to cover the whole of the golden age in the space of a few pages: whole books have been written on it – I would particularly recommend Julian Symon's *Bloody Murder: From the Detective Novel to the Crime Novel - A History*; A. E. Murch's *The Development of the Detective Novel*, or Howard Haycraft's *Murder for Pleasure: The Life and Times of the Detective Story* to those wanting an account of the history of the genre. In this chapter, I will highlight a few writers and their fictional detectives that anyone working in this genre ought to be aware of.

Short Stories
G. K. Chesterton (1874-1936) is the creator of Father Brown, a Roman Catholic priest who appeared in fifty short stories, collected in five volumes: *The Innocence of Father Brown* (1911), *The Wisdom of Father Brown* (1914), *The Incredility of Father Brown* (1926), *The Secret of Father Brown* (1927), and *The Scandal of Father Brown* (1935). Dismissed by many he encounters as 'unworldly,' Father Brown is a character who relies on intuition, an understanding of human psychology, and a deep knowledge of theology and moral teaching.

Chesterton also wrote an article 'How to Write a Detective Story' (1925) and served as the inspiration for another writer's detective.

Ernest Bramah (1868-1942) gave us Max Carrados, a blind detective whose other senses were more sensitive to compensate for his loss of sight. He appeared in three collections of stories – *Max Carrados* (1914), *The Eyes of Max Carrados* (1923), *Max Carrados Mysteries* (1927) – and one novel, *The Bravo of London (1934).*

Jacques Futrelle (1875-1912) wrote about – Professor S. F. X. Van Dusen, aka 'The Thinking Machine,' who solves impossible and locked room crimes. The stories are collected in *The Thinking Machine* (1907, vt. *The Problem of Cell Thirteen*) and *The Thinking Machine on the Case* (1908, vt. *The Professor on the Case*). There is also a novelette *The Haunted Bell* (1909) and a novel *The Chase of the Golden Plate* (1906). The Thinking Machine is aided by a newspaper reporter, Hutchinson Hatch, who gathers information for him – a type of relationship developed by Rex Stout in his Nero Wolfe and Archie Goodwin stories. Futrelle died aboard the Titanic.

Arthur Morrison (1863-1945) chose a common man Martin Hewitt, a solicitor's clerk who employs common sense and keen eyesight, as his sleuth rather than an eccentric 'Great Detective.' His exploits are collected in *Martin Hewitt, Investigator* (1894), *Chronicles of Martin Hewitt* (1895), *Adventures of Martin Hewitt* (1896) and a collection of connected stories *The Red Triangle* (1903).

Baroness Emmuska Orczy (1865-1947) left her sleuth unnamed: the Old Man in the Corner was perhaps the first 'armchair detective' – solving crimes brought to him without needing to leave his seat in a London tearoom. He features in thirty-eight stories collected in *The Case of Miss Elliott* (1905), *The Old Man in the Corner* (1909), and *Unravelled Knots* (1925). Best known as the creator of *The Scarlet Pimpernel*, Orczy also created one of the few female detectives of the period, *Lady Molly of Scotland Yard* (1910).

Melville Davisson Post (1869-1930) wrote a series of stories about an unscrupulous lawyer, Randolph Mason, but is best remembered for his creation of Uncle Abner, a rugged, Bible-quoting country squire who travels the lawless lands of 1850s Virginia dispensing justice. The stories are collected in *Uncle Abner, Master of Mysteries* (1918), which includes the story 'The Doomdorf Mystery,' regarded as a classic locked room mystery.

Novels

Margery Allingham (1904-1966) published her first whodunit, *The White Cottage Mystery,* in 1927, but her popular 'silly-ass sleuth' Albert Campion first appeared in her second novel *The Crime at Black Dudley* (1929, vt. *The Black Dudley Murder*). In a series of eighteen more novels and twenty short stories, Campion is assisted by his manservant Magersfontein Lugg – an uncouth former burglar – and courts Lady Amanda Fitton, who eventually becomes his wife.

H. C. Bailey (1878-1961) created Reggie Fortune who first appeared in the collection *Call Mr. Fortune* (1920) and eleven more collections and nine novels followed, ending in 1948. He is a pathologist and consultant to Scotland Yard.

E. C. Bentley (1875-1956) wrote two detective novels – *Trent's Last Case* (1913, vt. *The Woman in Black*) and *Trent's Own Case* (1936) – and a collection of short stories, *Trent Intervenes* (1938). *Trent's Last Case* is regarded as one of the best examples of the golden age novel, and was written – in part – as a reaction against the eccentricities of 'Great Detectives' such as Sherlock Holmes.

Anthony Berkeley (1893-1971) – pseudonym of Anthony Berkeley Cox, who also wrote as Francis Iles. As Berkeley he wrote a series of novels about amateur detective Roger Sherringham, beginning with *The Layton Court Mystery* (1925). He said that he was more interested in the psychological aspects of a detective story rather than the puzzle. As Francis Iles, he published three novels: *Malice Aforethought* (1931), *Before the Fact* (1932) and *As for the Woman* (1939). The first two of these are regarded as examples of the 'inverted' detective story. *Before the Fact* was filmed as *Suspicion* by Alfred Hitchcock, but the ending was changed.

Earl Derr Biggers (1884-1933) created Charlie Chan, a Honolulu police detective, whose first appearance was in *The*

House Without a Key (1925). Written, in part to, to counter the 'yellow peril' stereotype of such villains as Fu Manchu, Charlie Chan later came to be regarded as something of a stereotype himself, more as a result of the success of the films in which the character appeared than the novels.

Nicholas Blake (1904-1972) – pseudonym of Cecil Day-Lewis who wrote twenty detective novels between 1935 and 1968, the first being *A Question of Proof*, reportedly written because he needed £100 to mend his cottage roof. His detective Nigel Strangeways appears in all but four of Blake's mystery novels. He is an amateur gentleman sleuth whose nephew is Assistant Commissioner at Scotland Yard. In his early appearances, Strangeways is said to have been modelled on W. H. Auden.

Leo Bruce (1903-1979) – pseudonym of Robert Croft-Cooke. Sergeant William Beef is a working-class village policeman who later turns private detective, whose adventures are told by the long-suffering Lionel Townsend. Beef appeared in eight novels, beginning with *Case for Three Detectives*(1936) and the last published in 1952, and several short stories. Bruce also created Carolus Deene, an amateur detective who is a wealthy history master at a public school who featured in twenty-three novels from *At Death's Door* (1955) to 1974.

John Dickson Carr (1906-1977) published his first detective novel, *It Walks By Night*, in 1930. His best-known character is Dr. Gideon Fell, who first appeared in the 1933 novel *Hag's Nook*. Regarded by many as the master of the 'impossible crime,' Carr's *Three Coffins* (1935, vt. *The Hollow Man*) features a chapter on the locked room mystery which is often quoted in texts on mystery fiction. The twenty-three novels about Gideon Fell are noted for their eccentric characters, colourful locations and strange atmospheres. Fell himself is said to have been modelled on Carr's favourite writer, G. K. Chesterton.

Agatha Christie (1890-1976) wrote her first detective novel, *The Mysterious Affair at Styles,* during a two-week period in 1916 and it was published in 1921. It introduced the character of Hercule Poirot, who would appear in a total of thirty-four novels and more than fifty short stories, collected in five volumes. Miss Jane Marple's first appearance came in the short story 'The Tuesday Night Club' in 1927 with the first novel, *Murder at the Vicarage* in 1930. Miss Marple appeared in twelve novels and twenty short stories.

Edmund Crispin (1921-1978) – pseudonym of Robert Bruce Montgomery. His detective Gervase Fen, an eccentric Oxford don, appeared in nine novels and two short story collections. The first novel was *The Case of the Gilded Fly* (1944) and the last was published in 1977. A final short story collection was published after the author's death. *Wikipedia* says his books "... are written in a humorous, literary and sometimes farcical style and contain frequent references to English literature, poetry, and music. They are also among the few mystery novels to break the fourth wall occasionally and speak directly to the audience."

Freeman Wills Crofts (1879-1957) published his first detective novel, *The Cask,* in 1920. It centred on unravelling an 'unbreakable alibi,' and it is considered a classic of its type. A 1940 edition contains an introduction by the author describing the novel's creation. Crofts' subordination of character to plot led Julian Symons – in *Bloody Murder* – to say he was representative of the 'Humdrum school of detective novelists.' The detail with which his plots are constructed led Raymond Chandler to describe Crofts as 'the soundest builder of them all when he doesn't get too fancy.' His detective, Inspector Joseph French of Scotland Yard first appeared in *Inspector French's Greatest Case* (1925). Crofts wrote three collections of short stories and thirty-four novels, thirty of which featured Inspector French. He also wrote an article titled 'The Writing of a Detective Novel' (1937).

E. X. Ferrars (1907-1995) – pseudonym of Morna Doris MacTaggart Brown who also wrote as Elizabeth Ferrars. Wrote more than seventy books during her career, most in the 'cozy' tradition, including those in a country house or theatrical setting. She did not have a single detective, but created several recurring characters: Toby Dyke is a Lord Peter Wimsey-like upper-class twit who appeared in five novels during the 1940s; Andrew Basnett was a retired professor of botany in eight novels from 1983-1995; Jonas P. Jonas an elderly amateur detective appeared in a series of short stories; and Virginia and Felix Freer an estranged wife and husband who were in eight novels published between 1978-1992. Her first novel was the Toby Dyke story *Give a Corpse a Bad Name* published in 1940. Ferrars' entry on Wikipedia is worth a look if only to see the great titles she came up with.

Erle Stanley Gardner (1889-1970) wrote something like 400 short stories for the pulp magazines between 1921 and 1932, creating a number of popular series characters. But his best-known creation is lawyer-sleuth Perry Mason, who made his first appearance in *The Case of the Velvet Claws*(1933). Having been a successful lawyer himself, Gardner was concerned – in real life and in his stories – with preventing miscarriages of justice, dealing with those falsely accused or wrongly convicted. An amazingly prolific writer – he dictated stories which were transcribed by several secretaries – Gardner wrote another 500 stories and articles after 1932 as well as around 150 books. There were 86 Perry Mason novels in total. In 1939 he created the pseudonym A. A. Fair so that he could publish more, creating the 29-book series featuring Bertha Cool and Donald Lam. Perry Mason appeared in eight films during the 1930s and a radio series during the 1940s, but Raymond Burr's portrayal of him on television is probably best-remembered – there were nine seasons from 1957-1966 and six television movies between 1985 and Burr's death in 1993. The Perry Mason stories usually climax with a dramatic courtroom scene which stands in for the traditional 'drawing room' gathering.

Georgette Heyer (1902-1974) wrote historical novels and regency romances as well as mysteries, publishing fifty-six novels and a collection of short stories. Her first 'thriller' *Footsteps in the Dark* was published in 1932, but she regarded her third *Death in the Stocks* (1935, vt. *Merely Murder*) as the first proper crime novel. It featured CID Sergeant Stanley Hemmingway and Superintendent Hannasyde. The author's husband was a barrister and would work out the plots for the mysteries, labelling characters 'A' and 'B' etc., and Heyer would then create the characters and flesh out the plot. Both

plots and characters have been criticised for being stereotypical, but she has been praised for her dry wit.

Michael Innes (1906-1994) – pseudonym of John Innes
Mackintosh (J. I. M.) Stewart. Sir John Appleby is a Scotland
Yard Detective Inspector, appearing first in *Death at the Pres-
ident's Lodging* (1936, vt. *Seven Suspects*) and in thirty-eight
books in total, the last published in 1986. His stories often
feature country house or academic settings, but he sometimes
experimented with more unusual locations – *Appleby on
Ararat* (1941) maroons his characters on a Pacific Island.

Ronald A. Knox (1888-1957) wrote six detective novels and
three collections of short stories, including five novels and a
short story featuring Miles Bredon, a private investigator employed by the Indescribable Insurance Company. He is perhaps better known today for his 'Decalogue' – ten rules which
mystery writers ought to abide by, that he first set down as
part of his introduction to *Best Detective Stories of the Year
1928* (1929). In January 1926 he was responsible for a radio
hoax broadcast by the BBC pretending to be a live report
about a revolution sweeping across London: Orson Welles has
credited this with inspiring his *War of the Worlds* radio broadcast.

Ngaio Marsh (1895-1982) wrote thirty-two novels featuring
Inspector Roderick Alleyn, the first being *A Man Lay Dead*
(1934). Alleyn has aristocratic family connections and a love
of Shakespeare, but he is a professional detective and not an
amateur sleuth. Her stories are often set in English country
houses or the world of the theatre, but his wife being a por-
trait painter also takes the detective into other spheres and
countries. Four of Marsh's novels are set in her native New
Zealand.

Gladys Mitchell (1901-1983) created Mrs. Beatrice Adela
Lestrange Bradley, an elderly psychoanalyst who consults for
the Home Office. Mitchell wrote sixty-six novels featuring the
character, the first being *Speedy Death* (1929) and the last being published in 1984. Described as being a "little, thin, black-
eyed, witch-like being" with a "saurian smile," Mrs. Bradley
appeared in younger and more glamorous form when she was

portrayed by Diana Rigg in five adaptations broadcast on the BBC 1998-2000.

Stuart Palmer (1905-1968). His first novel, *The Penguin Pool Murder* (1931), introduced Miss Hildegarde Withers, a spinster schoolteacher usually accompanied by her apricot poodle Talleyrand. She appeared in fourteen novels and more than two dozen stories during the author's lifetime. *The Penguin Pool Murder* was filmed by RKO in 1932. There were six movies featuring Miss Withers during the 1930s, plus *A Very Missing Person* (1972) based on a posthumously completed novel. During the 1950s a sitcom pilot for the *Amazing Miss Withers* was filmed featuring Agnes Moorehead.

Ellery Queen, pseudonym of Frederic Dannay (1905-1982) and Manfred B. Lee (1905-1971), who used the same name for the hero of their stories. Ellery Queen appeared in a series of short stories and novels beginning 1929 and continuing until 1971. He first appeared in the novel *The Roman Hat Mystery* (1929), written for a contest in *McClure's Magazine*. In 1945, Dannay and Lee founded their own publication, *Ellery Queen's Mystery Magazine,* which has continued to the present day. Queen is a writer who assists the investigations of his father, Inspector Richard Queen of the New York Police Department. Recurring locations include the fictional New England village of Wrightsville.

Arthur B. Reeve (1880-1936). His sleuth Professor Craig Kennedy appeared in a short story in the 1912 anthology *The Silent Bullet* and his last case was *The Stars Scream Murder* (1936). Reeve, a chemistry professor who also studied law, put emphasis on the science of crime solving. According to *The Oxford Companion to Crime and Mystery Writing,* Kennedy "... depends more on lie detectors, ballistics, voiceprints, and wiretapping to solve crimes than observation and deduction." There were eighty-two Craig Kennedy stories in total, collected in twelve volumes. As well as writing fiction and for a newspaper, Reeve also wrote screenplays and film serials from 1914-20, but remained on the East coast when film production migrated to Hollywood. He was co-writer of the script for *The Master Mystery* (1919) movie which starred Harry Houdini.

Mary Roberts Rinehart (1876-1958). Her best-known mystery novels are her first two, *The Circular Staircase* (1908) and *The Man in the Lower Ten* (1909) and she continued to write them into the late 1940s. She also wrote about Hilda Adams, a nurse hired by the police to work undercover during their trickier investigations. Rinehart has a reputation for writing 'had-I-but-known' fiction, in which a young woman looks back, wiser as a result of her experiences. The cliché 'the butler did it' is believed to have originated from one of her novels. *The Circular Staircase* was made into a silent movie in 1915 and filmed again for television in 1956 for the *Climax!* series. Rinehart also adapted the story into a play titled *The Bat* which was first performed in 1920. The play, about a costumed super-crook, was filmed three times – 1926, 1930 as *The Bat Whispers,* and 1959 starring Vincent Price and Agnes Moorhead – and is said by Bob Kane to have been one of the inspirations for *Batman.* A reading of *The Bat* released by RCA Victor in 1933 was a forerunner of the audiobook.

John Rhode (1884-1965) – pseudonym of Cecil John Charles Street, who wrote 144 mystery novels in total. Amateur detective and mathematician Dr. Lancelot Priestley appeared in seventy novels and in short stories, and often operates in the mode of an armchair detective, deducing the solution of a mystery from the evidence presented to him. Priestley first appeared in *The Paddington Mystery* (1925) and his last case was published in 1961. Rhode has a reputation for creating ingenious methods for killing off his victims.

Dorothy L. Sayers (1893-1957). Lord Peter Wimsey – Peter Death Bredon Wimsey, second son of the fifteenth Duke of Denver – first appeared in *Whose Body?* (1923) and featured in ten further novels and twenty-one short stories. Wimsey and his manservant Bunter have something in common with P. G. Wodehouse's Bertie Wooster and Jeeves, but Sayers' true inspirations are Sherlock Holmes and E. C. Bentley's Philip Trent. Sayers also edited the anthology *Great Stories of Detection, Mystery and Horror* (1928-1934, vt. *The Omnibus of Crime*), and her introduction to the first volume is one of the classic accounts of the genre.

Georges Simenon (1903-1989) wrote seventy-five novels and twenty-eight short stories about Paris detective Inspector Jules Maigret. The first, *Pietr-le-Letton* (*The Strange Case of Peter the Lett*) was published in 1931 and the final volume in 1972. Maigret's investigations rely on his understanding of human psychology rather than the discovery of clues and logical deduction.

Rex Stout (1886-1975). Nero Wolfe is perhaps the greatest of the great detectives in that he was said to weight 'one-seventh of a ton' – 320 pounds or 146 kilos, or thereabouts. He first appeared in *Fer-de-Lance* (1935) and in thirty-three novels and thirty-nine novellas. He employs his own chef and gardener – to help tend to his collection of 10,000 rare orchids – and he almost never leaves his New York apartment. He is assisted in his investigations by Archie Goodwin, who does all the legwork, bringing back information, witnesses and clues that Wolfe then examines in his role as an armchair detective. The combination of Nero Wolfe and the cynical first-person narration of Archie Goodwin allowed the author to combine the best elements of the classic detective story – including having all the characters summoned for the 'drawing room scene' – with the more active elements of the hard-boiled school that became popular in the 1930s. Nero Wolfe's adventures were continued by Robert Goldsborough after Rex Stout's death.

Josephine Tey (1896-1952) – pseudonym of Elizabeth Mackintosh. Author of eight mystery novels including *The Daughter of Time* (1951) in which a bedridden detective investigates the murders of the Princes in the Tower by Richard III, and which was voted the greatest mystery novel of all time by the Crime Writers' Association in 1990. Her first mystery, *The Man in the Queue* (1929, vt. *Killer in the Crowd*), concerns the defence of a wrongly accused man and introduces Inspector Alan Grant. *A Shilling for Candles* (1936) was filmed by Alfred Hitchcock as *Young and Innocent* in 1937. *The Franchise Affair* (1948) is a locked room mystery without a murder, filmed in 1950; and *Brat Farrar* (1949, vt. *Come and Kill Me*), a stand-alone mystery about an imposter, was filmed by Hammer in 1963 as *Paranoiac* but Tey receives no on-screen credit, with the screenplay being based only loosely on the original novel.

S. S. Van Dine (1887-1939) – pseudonym of Willard Huntington Wright and creator of the detective Philo Vance. He set out to create a series of novels set in Manhattan, with a detective to rival Sherlock Holmes, and with the emphasis more on the psychological makeup of the murder than on the interpretation of physical clues. *The Benson Murder Case* (1926) was the first of ten novels published up to 1939. More than a million copies of Philo Vance novels are reported to have been sold by 1930, but the author's popularity waned when reader interest was taken by the more hard-boiled style of detective fiction.

Patricia Wentworth (1878-1961) – pseudonym of Dora Amy Elles. Thirty-two of the author's seventy-one novels feature Miss Maud Silver, a spinster sleuth who relies on logic more than intuition to solve mysteries. Miss Silver's first case was in *Grey Mask* (1928) and her final one was published in 1961.

Bibliography

Note: Novels and short stories quoted in the text are not included in the list below.

Aamodt, Agnar and Enric Plaza, 'Case-Based Reasoning: Foundational Issues, Methodological Variations, and System Approaches,' in: *Artificial Intelligence Communications,* (IOS Press), Vol.&:1, p.29-59, 1994.

Adey, Robert, *Locked Room Murders and Other Impossible Crimes: A Comprehensive Bibliography.* Minneapolis: Crossover Press, 1991. 'Locked Room Murders - 20 Solutions' a list taken from this volume can be found at: http://jot101.com/2014/01/locked-room-murders-20-solutions/

Aisenberg, Nadya, *A Common Spring: Crime Novel and Classic.* Bowling Green: Bowling Green University Popular Press, 1979.

Arnold, Frederick, 'Watsons,' in: Winn (ed.) *Murder Ink.*

Ascari, Maurizio, *A Counter-History of Crime Fiction: Supernatural, Gothic, Sensational.* Basingstoke: Palgrave Macmillan, 2007.

Auden, W. H., 'The Guilty Vicarage,' in: *Harper's Magazine,* May 1948. Reprinted in: *The Dyer's Hand and Other Essays,* 1962.

Bargainnier, Earl F., *The Gentle Art of Murder: The Detective Fiction of Agatha Christie.* Ohio: Bowling Green University Popular Press, 1980.

Barzun, Jacques, 'Detection and the Literary Art,' in: Nevins (ed.) *The Mystery Writer's Art.*

Bean, Gordon, 'Maybe You Better Not Lock the Door,' in: Winn (ed.), *Murder Ink.*

Beldoch, Michael, 'Sensitivity to Expression of Emotional Meaning in Three Modes of Communication,' in: J. R. Davitz (ed.), *The Communication of Emotional Meaning*, McGraw-Hill, 1964.

Barnard, Robert, *A Talent to Deceive: An Appreciation of Agatha Christie.* London: William Collins Sons & Co., 1980.

Burack, A.S. (ed.), *Writing Detective and Mystery Fiction.* Boston: The Writer, Inc., 1945.

Cawelti, John G., *Adventure, Mystery, and Romance: Formula Stories as Art and Popular Culture.* Chicago: University of Chicago Press, 1976.

Champigny, Robert, *What Will Have Happened: A Philosophical and Technical Essay on Mystery Stories.* Bloomington: Indiana University Press, 1977.

Chesterton, G. K., 'A Defence of Detective Stories,' in: *The Defendant,* 1901.

Christie, Agatha, *Agatha Christie: An Autobiography.* London: Collins, 1977.

Cohn, Jan, *Improbable Fiction: The Life of Mary Roberts Rinehart.* Pittsburgh: University of Pittsburgh Press, 2006

Cook, Cathy (comp.), *The Agatha Christie Miscellany.* Stroud: The History Press, 2013.

Cook, Michael, *Narratives of Enclosure in Detective Fiction.* London: Palgrave Macmillan, 2011.

Crofts, Freeman Willis, 'The Writing of a Detective Novel,' in: *The Author's Handbook*, 1935.

De Quincey, Thomas, *On Murder, Considered as One of the Fine Arts,* (1827)

Dexter, Colin, 'Crosswords and Whodunits: A Correlation Between Addicts?' in: Winn (ed.), *Murder Ink.*

Douthwaite, John, 'The Social Function of the Detective Fiction of the Golden Age' at:
http://publifarum.farum.it/ezine_articles.php?art_id=263

Eliot, T. S., 'Wilkie Collins and Dickens,' in: *Times Literary Supplement,* August 1927, p.1. Reprinted in Eliot, *Selected Essays, 1917-1932* and as the introduction to *The Moonstone*, Oxford University Press (World Classics), 1928.

Freeman, R. Austin, 'The Art of the Detective Story,' in: Haycraft (ed.), *The Art of the Mystery Story: a Collection of Critical Essays,* 1946. Originally published May 1924.

Frey, James N., *How to Write a Damn Good Mystery.* New York: St. Martin's Press, 2004.

Goleman, Daniel, 'What Makes a Leader?' in: *On Emotional Intelligence* (HBR's 10 Must Reads). Boston: Harvard Business Review, 2015.

Goleman, Daniel, *Working with Emotional Intelligence.* London: Bloomsbury, 2009.

Grant-Adamson, Lesley, *Writing Crime Fiction.* Teach Yourself / Hodder & Stoughton Ltd., 2003.

Grella, George, 'The Formal Detective Novel,' in: Winks (ed.), *Detective Fiction*.

Harvard Business Review, *On Emotional Intelligence* (HBR's 10 Must Reads). Boston: Harvard Business Review, 2015.

Haycraft, Howard (ed.)., *The Art of the Mystery Story: a Collection of Critical Essays*, edited and with a commentary by Howard Haycraft. New York: Carroll & Graf Publishers, Inc., 1992. © 1946, 1974.

Haycraft, Howard, *Murder for Pleasure: The Life and Times of the Detective Story*. London: Davies, 1942.

Heilbrum, Carolyn G., 'The New Female Detective,' in: *Yale Journal of Law & Feminism*, Vol.14, Issue 3, 2002.

Herbert, Rosemary (ed.), *The Oxford Companion to Crime & Mystery Writing*. Oxford: Oxford University Press, 1999.

Hill, Reginald, 'A Pre-History,' in: H. R. F. Keating (ed.), *Whodunit? : A Guide to Crime, Suspense and Spy Fiction*. London: Windward (W.H. Smith & Son Ltd.), 1982.

Horsley, Lee, *Twentieth-Century Crime Fiction*. Oxford: Oxford University Press, 2005.

Johnson, Roger and Jean Upton (comp.), *The Sherlock Holmes Miscellany*. Stroud: The History Press, 2013.

Keating, H.R.F., *The Bedside Companion to Crime*. London: Michael O'Mara Books Limited, 1989.

Keating, H.R.F., *Whodunit? : A Guide to Crime, Suspense and Spy Fiction*. London: Windward (W.H. Smith & Son Ltd.), 1982.

Keating, H.R.F., *Writing Crime Fiction* (2nd ed.). London: A & C Black, 1994.

Knox, Ronald A., 'Detective Story Decalogue,' as the preface in: Ronald A. Knox and Henry Harrington (eds.), *The Best Detective Stories of the Year 1928*. London: Faber, 1929. Reprinted in Haycraft (ed.) *Murder for Pleasure*.

Leacock, Stephen, 'Murder at $2.50 a Crime,' in: Haycraft (ed.)*The Art of the Mystery Story*.

Lowndes, Robert A. W., 'The Contributions of Edgar Allan Poe,' in: Nevins (ed.), *The Mystery Writer's Art*.

Maddocks, J. and T. Sparrow, *The Individual and Team Effectiveness Questionnaires*, 2000. Diagram at: www.jcaglobal.com/products/emotional-intelligence/emotional-intelligence-profile/

Mahler, Matthew J., 'Whodunit: A Guide to the Obvious,' in: Winn (ed.) *Murder Ink*.

Mandel, Ernest, 'A Marxist Interpretation of the Crime Story,' in: Winks (ed.), *Detective Fiction.*

Maugham, W. Somerset, 'The Decline and Fall of the Detective Story,' in: *The Vagrant Mood. Six Essays.* London: William Heinemann, 1952.

Mernit, Billy, *Writing the Romantic Comedy: From 'Cute Meet' to 'Joyous Defeat': How to Write Screenplays that Sell.* New York: Harper Collins, 1990.

Murch, A. E., *The Development of the Detective Novel.* London: Peter Owen, 1968.

Murdock, Maureen, *The Heroine's Journey.* Boston: Shambala Publications Inc., 1990.

Nevins, Francis M., Jr., (ed.), *The Mystery Writer's Art.* Bowling Green, Ohio: Bowling Green University Popular Press, 1970.

Norville, Barbara, *Writing the Modern Mystery.* Cincinnati, Ohio: Writer's Digest Books, 1986.

Ousby, Ian, *The Crime and Mystery Book: A Reader's Companion.* London: Thames and Hudson, 1997.

Panek, Leroy Lad, *An Introduction to the Detective Story.* Ohio: Bowling Green University Popular Press, 1987.

Parker, Robert B., 'Marxism and the Mystery,' in: Winn (ed.), *Murder Ink.*

Pearson, Carol and Katherine Pope, *The Female Hero in American and British Literature.* New York: R. R. Bowker Co., 1981.

Peirce, Charles Sanders (1903) *Harvard Lectures on Pragmatism, Collected Papers* (Vol. 5, paragraphs 188-189)

Priestman, Martin (ed.), *The Cambridge Companion to Crime Fiction.* Cambridge: Cambridge University Press, 2003.

Queen, Ellery, 'Introduction' in: Vickers, Roy, *The Department of Dead Ends.* London: Bello (Pan Macmillan), 2012.

Radway, Janice A., *Reading the Romance: Women, Patriarchy, and Popular Literature.* Chapel Hill: The University of North Carolina Press, 1984.

Rinehart, Mary Roberts, *My Story.* Farrar & Rinehart Inc., 1931.

Rinehart, Mary Roberts, 'Thoughts...' in: *Ladies' Home Journal,* May 1931.

Rodell, Marie F., *Mystery Fiction: Theory and Technique.* London: Hammond, Hammond & Company, 1954.

Routley, Eric, *The Puritan Pleasures of the Detective Story: A Personal Monograph.* London: Victor Gollancz, 1972.

Sayers, Dorothy L., 'Introduction,' in: *The Omnibus of Crime*. New York: Payson and Clarke Ltd, 1929. Reprinted in Winks (ed.), *Detective Fiction* and Haycraft (ed.) *The Art of the Mystery Story*.

Scott, Sutherland, *Blood in Their Ink: The March of the Modern Mystery Novel*. London: Stanley Paul and Co Ltd., 1953.

Smith, Sydney, *Mostly Murder*. London: Harrap & Co.Ltd., 1959.

Symons, Julian, *Bloody Murder: From the Detective Story to the Crime Novel: A History*. London: Macmillan, 1992.

Tapply, William G., *The Elements of Mystery Fiction: Writing the Modern Whodunit* (2nd ed.). Scottsdale, Arizona: Poisoned Pen Press, 1995.

Thomson, H. Douglas, *Masters of Mystery: A Study of the Detective Story*. New York: Dover Publications, 1978.

TomCat (a.k.a Last Century Detective), 'My Favourite Locked Room Mysteries I: The Novels,' 2012 at: http://moonlight-detective.blogspot.co.uk/2012/03/my-favorite-locked-room-mysteries-i.html

Van Dine, S. S., 'Twenty Rules for Writing Detective Stories,' in: Haycraft (ed.), *The Art of the Mystery Story*.

Waugh, Hillary, *Hillary Waugh's Guide to Mysteries and Mystery Writing*. Cincinnati, Ohio: Writer's Digest Books, 1986.

Wells, Carolyn, *The Technique of the Mystery Story*. Springfield, Mass.: The Home Correspondence School, 1913/1929.

Wheat, Carolyn, *How to Write Killer Fiction: The Funhouse of Mystery and The Roller Coaster of Suspense*. Santa Barbara, Calif.: Perseverance Press, 2003.

Winks, Robin W. (ed.), *Detective Fiction: a Collection of Critical Essays*. Woodstock, Vermont: A Foul Play Press Book / The Countryman Press, 1988.

Winn, Dillys (ed.) *Murder Ink: The Mystery Reader's Companion*. New York: Workman Publishing, 1977.

Wynn, Douglas, *The Crime Writer's Handbook*. London: Allison & Busby, 2000.

Yates, Donald A., 'The Locked Room,' in: *Michigan Alumnus Quarterly Review*, Volume 63, Number 18, Spring 1957. Reprinted in: Nevins (ed.), *The Mystery Writer's Art*.

Acknowledgments

Sir Arthur Conan Doyle's Sherlock Holmes stories were the first detective stories I read: I worked my way through the whole 'canon' when I was eleven years old and I've been re-reading them ever since.

I came to Dame Agatha Christie's novels much later: as a teenager, I had been alienated by their 'snobbishness' and by the oddness of Hercule Poirot. Joan Hickson's portrayal of Miss Marple and David Suchet's Poirot made me give them a second chance, and I'm glad they did.

John G. Cawelti's book *Adventure, Mystery, and Romance* helped me to understand how and why 'formula' fiction really worked, and because of that, I was finally able to learn how to plot a novel.

Earl F. Bargainnier's *The Gentle Art of Murder* provided detailed insights into how Agatha Christie's novels worked, and this helped me put together my own versions of the murder mystery 'formula.'

Two 'how to' books about writing the traditional murder mystery proved invaluable: the copy of Carolyn Wells' *The Technique of the Mystery Story* I have is dated 1929, but there are references to it having been originally published in 1913. Marie F. Rodell's *Mystery Fiction: Theory and Technique* was first published in 1943 and revised in 1952.

INDEX

There is no secret formula for plot — but there is a pattern that has proved satisfying to readers and movie-goers for years. Once you have an understanding of this underlying structure you can apply it to a novel or screenplay in any genre.

In *Plot Basics* you'll see:

- How to break down your plot into four quarters and decide what must happen in each — applying the 'rule of three' to give a strong through-line with rising action and suspense.
- How to divide these into eight sequences that enable you to tell your story with maximum dramatic effect — including six major turning points plus a midpoint and a climax.
- What individual story elements belong in each of the eight sequences and how to develop them.

You can use the eight sequences method to plot a story from scratch. Apply it to edit the first draft of a novel or screenplay you already have. Or use it to take apart a story you've started but which isn't working. When you know what needs to go where in a story, you can get on with the fun part of writing and create something for readers or movie-goers to enjoy — safe in the knowledge that your plot works.

Available Now in Paperback and eBook

"... a gentle parody of the classic whodunit mystery novel and a note-perfect example of how it should be done. Highly recommended!"

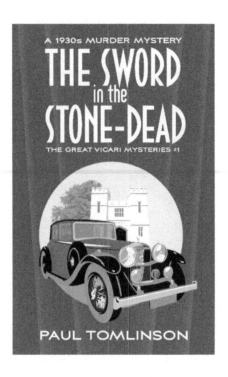

A retired stage magician and a chauffeur with a shady past team up to investigate when a King Arthur-themed party in a Victorian castle climaxes with a scream, a splash, and a body in the pond. Can they reveal whodunit, or will Excalibur again be drawn from a stone-cold corpse?

Available Now in Paperback and eBook

About the Author

Paul Tomlinson is the author of novels in the mystery, crime, science fiction, and fantasy genres. He has also published articles and author interviews in print magazines and online.

Contact him via his website at **www.paultomlinson.org** or on Facebook **@PaulTomlinson.org**

Books by Paul Tomlinson

Fiction:
The Great Vicari Mysteries series:
The Sword in the Stone-Dead
Murder by Magic
The Missing Magician

The Thurlambria series:
Slayer of Dragons
Fortune's Fool
Dead of Night

Robot Wrecker
Who Killed Big Dick?

Non-Fiction:
Harry Harrison: An Annotated Bibliography
Plot Basics: Plot Your Novel or Screenplay in Eight Sequences

Made in United States
North Haven, CT
09 January 2022

14486605R00143